I0199982

The Bhagavad Gita Reference Guide

A Handbook for All Spiritual Seekers

Compiled and with an Introduction

by

Rudra Shivananda

Alight Publications

2022

The Bhagavad Gita Reference Guide

By Rudra Shivananda
First Edition Published in April 2022

Alight Publications
PO Box 277
Live Oak, CA 95953
http://www.alightbooks.com

Hardcover ISBN: 978-1-931833-58-5

Printed in the United States of America

To All Sincere Seekers
Setting forth on the Path
Thirsting for knowledge

Table of Contents

Preface

I had not read the Bhagavad Gita when growing up or even during my first twenty years of spiritual journey because it was my assumption that it would only be of interest to someone who was on the devotional path of Lord Krishna. Of course, being brought up in an Indian family, I had a passing acquaintance with the story and characters of the Mahabharata, the monumental epic from which the Gita is taken.

Around 1989, I embarked on the spiritual path of Kriya Yoga, an ancient spiritual practice, re-introduced around 1860 to the spiritual world of Northern India. The renowned representative of Kriya Yoga in the West was Paramhansa Yogananda, the author of the well-known classic *Autobiography of a Yoga*.

One of the guidelines laid down by Yogananda's teacher Shri Yukteswar and his teacher, Lahiri Mahasaya, was that a Kriya practitioner should take time each day to read a few passages from the Gita. Of course, you will find that all three of these Yogis have written commentaries on the Gita.

A few years after I began my study of the Gita, I was visiting my favorite bookstore in Berkeley, Serendipity Bookstore, when the owner Peter Howard, asked me whether I was interested in a first edition copy of the Indian classic called the Bhagavad Gita. Peter and I had often discussed a wide variety of topics during my past visits which were primarily concerned with Science Fiction and Fantasy First Editions. However, I had also purchased some very old spiritual books from him. From that day onwards, I began my collection of the large numbers of English translations of the Gita. It has been a fascinating journey.

The impulse for this little book came from the frequent requests of friends and students to tell them what the BG is all about and recommend a translation to them. It became a ritual for me to explain about the many different translations and commentaries and their differences. Unfortunately, not everyone wanted to hear the long version and just wanted a copy that they can read.

The purpose of this text is to provide a short reference guide to those who want to know something about the Gita and may decide to actually read a translation and/or commentary. This is not meant to be a complete analysis, or an exhaustive bibliography, nor a scholarly work. I've included here references to the Western and Indian perspectives of the Gita and its English translations. It seemed useful as a reference guide to include what some of the great Indian commentators have given as the summary or crucial understanding of the Gita. It is my hope that it will be helpful to curious as well ardent spiritual seekers.

A cursory search at Amazon, yielded many old texts that have been reprinted with new covers. The first book was a reprint of Edwin Arnold's 1885 translation. There are also new works coming out all the time and it's not possible for me to claim that I have included all of them in the bibliography.

Introduction

The Bhagavad Gita, what is it?

To its admirers, the Bhagavad Gita is one of the world's most important books – a great resource for all of humanity.

Since 1785, when it was translated into English, the Gita has been a powerful influence in the West. The impact has been mostly indirectly through the Western philosophers, poets and other literati. The New England Transcendentalists—a loose group of nineteenth-century Americans who were an important school of thinkers and writers that in some respects anticipated later Theosophical thought—read the first English translation of the Gita. Henry David Thoreau, one of that group, wrote about reading the Gita on the shore of Walden Pond, and its philosophy inspired his famous essay, "On Civil Disobedience," about how to cope with societal injustice. Much later, when Mohandas Gandhi was a young man and a law student in England, he was introduced to the Gita by the Theosophists, after which he read Thoreau's essay, which in turn inspired his policy of *satyagraha* or passive resistance. In turn, Martin Luther King was inspired by Gandhi's policy to create his own program of nonviolence. The Gita has echoed back and forth across the globe between India and America, instigating thought and action on many aspects of contemporary society.

In India, the Gita is now considered the major guidebook to the spiritual life in the "Hindu tradition" or more aptly, Sanatana Dharma. It functioned to unify the diverse views of a plurality of yogic, religious and philosophical traditions. The irony is that this has been actualized only since the publication of the first English translation. Prior to 1785, the Gita, although considered one of the three pillars of Vedanta and as well as a key text of the Krishna Bhakti movement, was not well-known among the common people. It was through the Theosophical influence and then the Indian Nationalist movement that the Gita came to the forefront.

The Bhagavad Gita can be translated as 'The Song of God'. It is a very small part of the greatest and longest epic ever written—the Mahabharata, which recounts the story of a great civil war in Northern India. Epics typically show the values and defining characteristics of a people. The Mahabharata is in that way the quintessential story of India. But it is also the story of all human beings, a universal epic, for it deals with fundamental human motives, frustrations, quandaries, and joys. The Gita is around 700 verses that is from Book 6 (Bhishma Parva) of the Mahabharata.

Spiritually, the Gita is about moksha, or liberation from karma. There is also a religious dimension as well as teachings on moral and ethical conduct. The conceptual framework is a basic theme in the Mahabharata—*dharma* or the way we should act because of who and what we are. In particular, the Gita is about a moral quandary in which the hero in this civil war faces fundamental questions about the right way to live. The poem operates on two levels—historical and archetypal. It is a history of an actual battle fought near modern Delhi at a turning point in human history. But it is also an archetypal myth about the struggle that each one of us experiences within ourselves. This archetypal nature is amplified by the Kriya Yoga tradition, wherein all the characters in the epic represent human emotional and mental traits.

The dual level of the poem is made clear in the opening two words of the poem: "Dharmakshetre, Kurukshetre," which mean "On the field of dharma, on the Field of the Kurus." The Kurus were the ruling family of India at the time of the poem, and Kurukshetra is an actual geographical location, a field, near modern Delhi where the ancient civil war was fought. So, the second word of the poem tells us that we are dealing with a particular place and time, thousands of years ago, in the heroic age of India.

However, the first word of the poem tells us that we are dealing with a timeless reality. *Dharma* (a central word in the poem) means, among other things, the essential nature of a thing or person. And so the poem is about the “field” or subject matter of what is essentially real in life. In reading the Gita, we cannot ignore its historical setting, on the Field of the Kurus,but what is most important is that its message is relevant across time and space to multiple cultures.

The story centers on Prince Arjuna, the middle of five sons of the royal house (called Pandavas after their father Pandu). Their father has died, leaving them as wards of their uncle, who himself has a hundred sons. Arjuna’s cousins (called Kauravas— descendants of the ancient king Kuru), under the leadership of the eldest, the wicked Duryodhana, have plotted to cheat Arjuna and his brothers out of their legitimate inheritance and even to murder them.

Arjuna, who belongs to the *kshatriya* or warrior caste, is called upon by his duty in life to fight against evil and for the right. He therefore is required by his social duties to defend his brothers’ legitimate claim to their kingdom against their usurping cousins. On the eve of the battle, however, Arjuna experiences a crisis of conscience. On the one hand, he knows that his duty as a kshatriya warrior compels him to defend his brothers’ rights; on the other hand, however, his duty to his family requires that he harm none of them, whatever they may be or have done. And those he will be fighting include his cousins, his grandfather, and even his teacher, with whom the relationship bond is even stronger than with blood relatives.

Arjuna sees the terrible price to be paid for killing members of his own family. He sees no good coming from the battle and only evil from his own part in it. He therefore calls upon his friend and charioteer, Shri Krishna, for advice. Krishna is a cousin of Arjuna’s and a childhood friend, but he is not merely human. He is a divine incarnation—god made flesh. The Bhagavad Gita, which means“The Lord’s Song,” is Krishna’s answer to Arjuna’s cry for help.

Let us examine the moral and ethical dimension of the Gita. From this perspective, the archetypal meaning of the poem is that within each of us a battle rages between selfish impulses that ignore the claims of justice and mercy and a realization that ultimately, we are all connected in a unity that embraces all humanity and the whole world. Arjuna is the conscious mind, which must make the choice of how we will live. The wicked cousins are our ego impulses to self-centeredness and greed. Krishna is the divine spark within us, our higher Self, which is always available to rein in the horses of our feelings and thoughts and to guide us in the battle of life, if we will only seek that help.

Arjuna's moral quandary is a threefold one. Generalized to the common human situation, its three aspects can be formulated as follows

- How can we act freely and unconditionally?
- How can we have confidence in the power of goodness to make all things right?
- How do we choose between unclear alternatives to resolve the dilemmas we face?

The message that Krishna, our higher Self, gives to Arjuna, our conscious mind, is a threefold one. First, in all our actions, we must be motivated to do what is truly right, not what seems comfortable or convenient. That will give us the skill in action that we need and for which Karma Yoga (coming to wholeness by right action) is the answer.

Second, if we act out of that motive and with a realization that a divine plan orders all things in the world, the results of our actions will be good. That will give us the vision of Reality that we need and for which Bhakti Yoga (coming to wholeness by devotion and surrender) is the answer.

Third, we can know what we should do—what is truly a right action for us—only if we first know ourselves—who we, in truth, are. We are not the selfish desires of the wicked cousins. We are not the confused and uncertain mind of Arjuna. As Arjuna discovers at the end of the poem, we are, in fact, ourselves Krishna, the divine spark, the higher Self. That gives us the knowledge that we need to choose between unclear alternatives and for which Jnana Yoga (coming to wholeness by direct insight into the nature of things) is the answer.

The Gita is a song sung in the midst of a battle. This seems preposterous from the historical point of view but makes sense from the archetypal point of view. We are all engaged in a continuous war between our higher nature and our lower selves. The song of peace and harmony in the midst of life's confusion is a timeless assurance that we each have within us, the answers to all our questions and confusions. We need only call upon that inner power to discover who we are, what we can trust, and how we should act.

There are hundreds if not thousands of translations of the Gita in many languages. For the serious student, it is good to use several translations at the same time—to compare how they express the ideas of the Gita. In a later section, there will be a comparison of a few verses from some of the major English translations for you to check out. There is an old Italian proverb: *Traduttore, traditore* "The translator is a traitor." The play on words works better in Italian than in English, but the point of the proverb is that it is impossible to translate exactly the meanings, nuances, and associations of one language into another. So, in reading translations from another language, we are helped by using several different ones for the same text. Different translations will focus on different aspects of the same words and so help to convey a better-rounded understanding of the original.

If you like a literary translation, then Sir Edwin Arnold's poem, *The Song Celestial*, or Swami Prabhavananda and Christopher Isherwood's very readable translation, *The Song of God*, are always available in print. However, be aware that they are much freer versions, often not corresponding verse by verse with the original, but attempting to capture the general sense rather than the particular meanings. A very useful scholarly version is Winthrop Sargent's edition, *The Bhagavad Gita* which gives an interlinear translation and word-by-word gloss of the Sanskrit (in both Devanagari and transliteration) and has a helpful introduction. A translation by Annie Besant is noteworthy because of its theosophical foundation. For those interested in the commentaries, the one from Yogananda is very detailed and spiritually inclined.

Why is the Gita important?

Adi Shankaracharya

From a clear knowledge of the Bhagavad Gita all the goals of human existence become fulfilled. Bhagavad Gita is the manifest quintessence of all the teachings of the Vedic script

Mahatma Gandhi

When doubts haunt me, when disappointments stare me in the face, and I see not one ray of hope on the horizon, I turn to Bhagavad-Gita and find a verse to comfort me; and I immediately begin to smile in the midst of overwhelming sorrow. Those who meditate on the Gita will derive fresh joy and new meanings from it every day

Swami Vivekananda

Swami Vivekananda often said that the Bhagavad Gita was one of his two most favorite books (another one was "The Imitation of Christ"). In 1888-1893 when Vivekananda was travelling all over India as a wandering monk, he kept only two books with him — Gita and Imitation of Christ.

Pandit Jawaharlal Nehru

The Bhagavad-Gita deals essentially with the spiritual foundation of human existence. It is a call of action to meet the obligations and duties of life; yet keeping in view the spiritual nature and grander purpose of the universe

Sri Aurobindo

The Bhagavad-Gita is a true scripture of the human race a living creation rather than a book, with a new message for every age and a new meaning for every civilization.

Ralph Waldo Emerson

I owed a magnificent day to the Bhagavad-Gita. It was the first of books; it was as if an empire spoke to us, nothing small or unworthy, but large, serene, consistent, the voice of an old intelligence which in another age and climate had pondered and thus disposed of the same questions which exercise us.

Sri Ramakrishna

Seek that Divine Knowledge by knowing which nothing remains to be known! For such a person knowledge and ignorance has only one meaning: Have you knowledge of God? If yes, you a Jnani! If not, you are ignorant. As said in the Gita, chapter XIII/11, knowledge of Self, observing everywhere the object of true Knowledge i.e. God, all this is declared to be true Knowledge (wisdom); what is contrary to this is ignorance.

Carl Jung

The idea that man is like unto an inverted tree seems to have been current in by gone ages. The link with Vedic conceptions is provided by Plato in his Timaeus in which it states…" behold we are not an earthly but a heavenly plant." This correlation can be discerned by what Krishna expresses in chapter 15 of Bhagavad-Gita.

Henry David Thoreau

In the morning I bathe my intellect in the stupendous and cosmogonal philosophy of the Bhagavad-gita, in comparison with which our modern world and its literature seem puny and trivial.

Herman Hesse

The marvel of the Bhagavad-Gita is its truly beautiful revelation of life's wisdom which enables philosophy to blossom into religion.

Bal Gangadhar Tilak

The geeta was preached in preparatory lesson for living wordly life with an eye to release nirvana. My last prayer to everyone, therefore, is that, one should not fail to thoroughly understand this ancient science of worldly life as early as possible.

Annie beasant

It is meant to lift the aspirant from lower level of renunciation, where objects are renounced, to the loftier heights, where desires are dead, and where the yogi dwells in calm and in ceaseless contemplation while his body and mind are actively employed in duties that fell to his lot.

S Radhakrishnan
The message of the Gita is universal in its scope

Key Concepts discussed in the Gita

Dharma
In the Gita, dharma is both 'virtuous conduct' as well as 'the duties prescribed for the individual's social class or varna.'

There is a linkage between dharma and karma because a person's present dharma is a result of his or her past karma and is actually a part of one's nature.

In Chapter 2, verses 31-6, Lord Krishna tells Arjuna that he must fulfill the dharma of his warrior class, the kshatriyas, to fight against injustice.

In the early chapters where karma yoga is discussed, it is in relation to the performing of one's duty or dharma without desire for personal gain.

In Chapter 18, verses 41-6, the dharma of each varna is given and then linked to bhakti, devotion to God.

Karma
The law of cause and effect applying to all human thoughts, speech and actions through countless live times is a fundamental tenet of the Sanatana Dharma. It is karma that forces rebirth, but in Chapter 4, Lord Krishna explains that actions performed without selfish desire are akarma, that is without karmic repercussions, while inactions

can produce karma if motivated by desire.

In chapter 14, Lord Krishna teaches that karma is conditioned by the three gunas or universal primary characteristics. The Gunas are sattva, rajas and tamas.

In chapter 18, the first 20 verses reinforce the concept that renunciation of the selfish desire that motivates an action is more important that the renunciation of the action itself. Only this higher type of renunciation can liberate one from the cycle of birth and death.

Moksha

In Chapter 6, Dhyana Yoga, the yoga of meditation, is presented as a spiritual practice that leads to liberation from rebirth, that is moksha. Further, in chapters 7-12, we are shown that moksha can be bestowed as a gift of grace from the Lord to his devotees – refer 7.14, 11.55, 12.6-7, and 18.66. Although there is no description of moksha, it is clear that the Lord is in that state and that it is a joyful state and free of suffering.

The Three Gunas

A key element of Samkhya philosophy is that matter is pervaded by three fundamental qualities called the Gunas. There are sattva guna, rajas guna, and tamas guna. In chapter 14, there is extensive analysis of how the lives of living beings are influenced and shaped by them. This is further expanded in Chapter 17 and 18.18-40 to apply to various categories of human life, such as food, charity, austerity, knowledge, action and pleasure. In 14.25-26, the Lord makes clear that to reach the highest goal, one must transcend and be free from these three gunas.

Bhakti and the nature of God

The first six chapters of the Gita gives us the methods whereby a

person can by one's individual effort transform oneself and achieve higher realization, through karma and dhyana yogas.
However, the Lord also grants moksha as shown in 7.14, 10.11, 12.6-7, and 18.66
.

In chapter 7, 9 and the opening verses of chapter 10, there are discussions about the nature of God, culminating in the vision granted to Arjuna in chapter 11.

Ethical conduct and Characteristics of the Realized ones

Although the Gita is not a law book and doesn't give a list of do's and don'ts, in chapter 13.7-11, there is description of those qualities displayed by a person who possesses knowledge and presumably what one should aspire to.

In chapter 16, there are lists of the qualities of gods and demons.

Yoga

The Gita uses the term for all the paths that can lead to liberation. If we restrict ourselves to the current understanding of Classical or Patanjali Yoga, then in Chapters 6 and 8, the Lord gives instructions on meditation and inward contemplation, for the purpose of attaining the realization of the atman. This is the goal of the Upanishads and leads to transcendence of suffering.

Western Perspective of the Gita and its Translations

During my study of the English translations of the Gita, it became apparent that there were massive undercurrents of language, philosophy, history, religion and culture that needed to be analyzed to understand a particular translator's version of the Gita.

The following texts were invaluable for my understanding of these multifarious translations:

1. Gerald Larson's influential paper, "The Bhagavad Gita as cross-cultural process" in the 1975 issue of the Journal of American Academy of Religion.
2. Eric Sharpe's 1985 book, "The Universal Gita" published by Open Court.
3. Georg Feuerstein's 1983 book, "An Introduction to the Bhagavad Gita" published by Quest Books.
4. A more recent book (2015) that filled in a few historical gaps and is an easy read is that by Richard Davis, "The Bhagavad Gita – A Biography" published by Princeton University Press.

We begin our examination of the Western perspective with a few topics which have engrossed scholars of the Gita.

The Date of the Gita

The difficulty to ascertain a date for its composition is due to the fact that the Mahabharata war that frames it, is traditionally set to around 3000 BCE. Another factor is that a tool for dating texts based on the language in its written copies cannot be accurate because all sacred texts in India followed an oral tradition. What can be determined is the approximate date that a text was committed to writing, an event that was triggered by the Greek invasion of Northern India at the time of Alexander.

A scholar and translator of the Gita, RC Zaehner has neatly summed up this issue, "As with almost every major religious text from India, no firm date can be assigned to the Gita. It seems certain, however, that it was written later than the 'classical' Upanishads with the possible exception of the Maitri and that it is post-Buddhistic. One would probably not be going far wrong if one dated it at some time between the fifth and second centuries BC"

Is the Gita really a part of the Mahabharata?

Perhaps due to its independent importance, Western experts have indulged in various theories and conspiracies involving the Gita's composition and its placement in the epic Mahabharata. These usually follow the line that the followers of Vaisnavism adapted an originally Samkhya treatise or an Upanishad to their theistic philosophy and inserted it into the epic. There is even a theory that it is a subversive anti-vedic text masquerading as an orthodox composition.

However, the evidence is strong that the Gita was always a part of the epic because there are numerous references to it scattered throughout the large work. Also, it has been demonstrated that there is sufficient similarity in the use of words, language and thought between the two compositions.

Is the Gita a single composition?

Unable to reconcile the apparently diverse themes in the Gita with Western notions of a unified philosophical work, there have been efforts such as by R Garbe (1909) to separate out the layers presumably by different authors over a period of time and recover its original essence. In the Original Gita (1939), Rudolf Otto reduced the Gita by one-third in order to achieve his goal. He identified eight different treatises and a large number of interpolations using his training as a biblical scholar.

Franklin Edgerton (a renowned Sanskrit scholar) called out Otto's attempt, "...constantly, though no doubt unconsciously, distorts the text to make it seem favorable to his theories." As Edgerton further points out, Otto had a poor grasp of the Sanskrit language and "manhandled the language."

Why is the Gita inconsistent and contradictory in its philosophy?

We will discuss this further in the section concerning the Indian perspective. Here it suffices to provide a number of theories posited by Western scholars:

1. The Gita is a poem and is not a systematic treatise in philosophy. A composition in verse should not be judged in the same rigorous manner.
2. The apparent inconsistencies are due to the differences in the current usage of many Sanskrit terms from their meanings at the time of the composition.
3. It is not a philosophical work but a practical work that leads us through the correct choices to difficult moral and ethical issues. The author uses one argument after another in order to get the points across.

The Impact of the Gita on Western Consciousness and history

Both Sharpe and Davis have traced the impact of the Gita. They've shown how the concepts presented with the Gita has been introduced into the Western mind first indirectly through poets, and philosophers and later directly through religious leaders and Yoga sects.

Sharpe in particular traced the impact on the romantics and transcendentalists of the eighteenth and nineteenth centuries both in Europe and in the United States. Some of them may have had only a casual acquaintance while others delved deeper and were greatly influenced. However, it was not until the counter-culture movement of the 1960's that the variety of Indian religious or yogic leaders brought the message of the Gita directly to the people.

The indirect impact can be shown with T.S. Eliot, a noble prize-winning poet, who, although a devout Christian, was attracted by the nishkama karma (selfless work or action) expounded by Lord Krishna. Although there is much that was intertwined with his famous 'The Wasteland', it is in his 'Four Quartets' especially in the section called 'The Dry Salvages' that we find reference to Lord Krishna when talking about time:

I sometimes wonder if that is what Krishna meant –
Among other things – or one way of putting the same thing:
That at the future is a faded song,
a Royal Rose or a lavender spray
Of wistful regret for those who are not yet here to regret,
Pressed between yellow leave of a book
that has never been opened.

Later, Eliot refers to a central theme of the Gita, that of selfless actions:

'At the moment which is not of action or inaction
You can receive this: "on whatever sphere of being
The mind of a man may be intent
At the time of death" – that is the one axtion
(And the time of death is every moment)
Which shall fructify the lives of others:
And do not think of the fruit of action.
Fare foreward
O voyagers, O seamen.
You who come to port, and you whose bodies
Will suffer the trial and judgement of the sea,
Or whatever even, this is your real destination.'
So Krishna, as when he admonished Arjuna
On the field of battle,

Not fare well,
But fare forward, voyagers.

Why someone from a Western culture should study the Gita

There is no need for this question for those who are already on a path aligned with Indian traditions, such as those for seeking moksha from Yoga or those bhakti traditions of Vaishnavism. The Gita is considered an important text for yogic studies.

The Gita is recommended for those who are interested in the Eastern philosophies as well as comparative religious studies. It can also be useful for those looking for a recipe to live a moral life in trying conditions.

Translation bias is unavoidable

Professor Larsen has rightly pointed out that it would not be possible to "accurately" translate an ancient text written in an archaic language for a different culture. Accurately in this case to mean reflecting what the original writer intended for his or her audience of that time. The following are the type of decisions and biases that a translator has to compromise with:

1. A literal versus literary version: Professor Edgerton decided to preserve the linguistic characteristics of the original verses in his translation while Sir Edwin Arnold decided to provide his audience with a poetic style in keeping with the English language. The former is difficult to read but is perhaps a more accurate translation while the latter is a much more pleasant read but may be misleading in some verses, glossing over difficult concepts.

2. A bias towards the intended audience: some translations are made for students of Sanskrit or students in religious faculties, while others are written for the casual reader. Yet others may be intended for devotees of a particular religious or spiritual organization or sect.
3. There is an interpretive continuum: the translator has to decide whether the text should be translated according to what we now think it was meant at the time period of the composition or should it be translated in accordance with what it means now in the current cultural environment.
4. There are also biases based on the motivation and personal inclination of the translator: a theologian desiring to write a polemic against Hinduism would be motivated to degrade the translation while a devotee of Lord Krishna will skew his or her translation towards the supremacy of devotional versus karma and knowledge yogas.

A Continuum of translations and commentaries

There have been scholarly, poetical and philosophical British translations, followed by scholarly French and German translations. Only in recent times, has there been American translations – Edgerton (1944), Deutsch (1968), Stamford (1970), Bolle (1979) and Van Buitten (1980).

It is interesting to preview the English translations that have been made by those from an Indian tradition, before we examine the Indian Perspective on the Gita. The Western scholars have divided the Indian translations from their perspective of usefulness:

1. Western style scholarly treatments – Telang (1882), Belvalkar (1943) and Radhakrishnan (1948)
2. Traditional Indian commentaries from the Vedanta traditions – Shankara, Ramanuja, Madhava
3. From Yogic Masters – Sivananda, Yogananda, Maharishi Mahesh Yogi, Bhaktivedanta
4. Nationalist and Political – Tilak, Aurobindo, Ghandi

Indian Perspective of the Gita

The Gita is one of the most revered, read, studied, recited and quoted spiritual books in India. For many, it is a handbook to live and die by, a guide to achieve liberation from suffering. For some, it is an exposition of Vedanta, the most advanced Indian philosophical system. For others, it is a book of highest devotion to their personal God Vishnu. Yet others see a summary of the three main yogic paths for Self-Realization within the Gita, perhaps even, an integration or synthesis of yogic paths.

Traditionally, the three most important commentators of the Gita, are the three great teachers of Vedanta. The earliest is by Shankaracharya (circa 700 CE), the exponent of Advaita Vedanta – the pure non-dualist school. The second is by Ramanujacharya (1077 -1157 CE), the exponent of the Vishishtadvaita (qualified non-dualism) school of Vedanta. Finally, the third is by Madhavacharya (1238 – 1317 CE), the exponent of Dvaita (dualism) Vedanta.

For the purpose of understanding their different commentaries of the same text, it is sufficient to have an overview of the some of the main differences between these three different schools of Vedanta. We can examine what they teach about the nature and relationships of God, individual souls and the material universe.

For Shankaracharya, the ultimate reality is that of Nirguna Brahman, the self-existent Divine without attributes. All else is illusionary. The individual souls or jiva and the universe, prakriti are both maya and have no absolute existence. They are resolved back to Brahman. The liberation of the soul is the realization of the sole reality, and the soul bubble dissolves back into the ocean of existence. The method of realization is primarily Jnana Yoga – that of knowledge.

In the case of Ramanujacharya, the ultimate reality is that of Vishnu. The universe and souls are a play of the Lord. There are grades of salvation depending on the devotion of the soul, from being in the same world, being next to the Lord, or even merged with the Lord.

The distinguishing quality from Advaita, is that the merged soul still retains a separate identity (memory and experience from its many lifetimes).

There is total separation between the world, the souls and the Lord as far as Madhavacharya is concerned. In Dvaita, the Lord created the world and the souls. The world is real and so are the individual souls. Depending on the faith through devotion of the souls, the commensurate grace from the Lord descends and saves the soul. The Lord is Vishnu, who incarnated as Krishna and gave us the Gita.

A very detailed analysis of the commentaries from the above three schools is given in the book called, **The Hindu Gita by Arvind Sharma**, published by Open Court in 1986. Professor Sharma provided several possible solutions from the Indian tradition for the enigma that had troubled the Western perspective of the Gita, namely the apparent contradictions within the text. He has given examples of how interpretation of Indian scriptures follows a multivalent tradition, that is it is open to multiple interpretations depending on the readers experience, bias and school of learning. He has distinguished the univalent bias of Western philosophy from the multivalent Indian scriptures.

Examples of multivalent readings can be found in the interpretations of the Vedas as cited by Yaska (circa 500 BCE). For the Gita itself, Shankaracharya gave three interpretations of the same verse (chapter XVIII:41) in his commentary. We can also look within the text to find several optional paths to salvation in chapter XIII: 24-25.

In the following sections are a number of works that are valuable references for all students of the Gita.

A Comparison of the main translations of the Gita

Following are the different translations of verses 3:14-16 from the Gita. These verses were suggested for comparison by Professor Larson, together with verses 4:24 and 8:1-5 because they are considered difficult and ambiguous for translators. The following are given in no specific order and does not reflect a preference for one over another. Edwin Arnold's very readable version is not compared because it is by far the most popular and widely read. The right version is dependent on the readers background, need and expectation.

(1)

The Bhagavad-Gita A New Translation
Georg Feurstein with Brenda Feurstein
Shambhala Publications 2011
509 pages
Includes Introduction, Sanskrit Text, Translation, Word for Word translation, Index
Category: scholarly with a yogic bias

3:14 – 3:16
From food, beings come-into-being. Food is produced from rain. From sacrifice, the rain comes-into-being. Sacrifice is born from [ritual] action.
Know that [all] action arises from the world-ground. The world-ground is born from the Imperishable. Therefore the omnipresent world-ground is ever established in sacrifice.
Thus, he who does not turn the rotating wheel [of action as sacrifice] lives a wicked life, in vain, [attached to] sensual delight, O son-of-Partha [Arjuna].

4:24
The world-ground is the offering. The world-ground is the oblation offered by the world-ground's fire. The world-ground verily, is to be reached by him through concentration [upon] action, [which is of the nature of] the world-ground.

8:1-5
Arjuna said:
What is the world-ground (brahman)? What is the basis-of-self? What is action, O Purushotttama? And what is proclaimed [to be] the elemental-basis? What is [that which] is said [to be] the divine basis.
Who is here in the body [as] the sacrificial-basis, and how, O Madhusudana? And how are You to be known at the time of going-forth by [those who are of] restrained self?
The Blessed Lord said:

The Imperishable is the supreme Brahman. The own-being (svahhava) is called the basis-of-self. The creativity originating the state-of-existence of beings is designated as action.
The elemental-basis is the perishable state-of-existence, and the divine-basis is Spirit. I am the sacrificial-basis here in the body, O best of body-wearers.
And he who in the last hour, having released the body [while] remembering Me alone, goes forth – he goes to My state-of-existence; there is no doubt of this.

(2)

Bhagavad Gita
The Beloved Lord's Secret Love Song
Graham M. Schweig
Harper Collins 2007
363 Pages
Includes Introduction, English Transliteration and Index
Category: A free-form poetic translation for General reader

3:14 – 3:16
From foodstuffs
beings come into being;
from rain
foodstuffs manifest;
From sacrifice
rain comes into being;
sacrifices arises
from action.

Understand that action arises
from Brahman, the Vedas;
this Brahman arises originally
from the Imperishable.
Therefore eternal Brahman,

which pervades everything,
is established in sacrifice.

Thus the [sacrificial] cycle
has been set into motion;
one who does not
keep it turning in this world,
Whose life is impure,
who delights in the senses –
such a person lives in vain,
O Partha.

(3)

The Bhagavad Gita
A Walkthrough for Westerners
Jack Hawley
New World Library 2001
191 plus xxvi pages
Category: A liberal non-literal non-direct translation [the author studied a number of previous English translations as the basis for his interpretation] with index; dedicated to Sri Sathya Baba

3:14
The very cycle of life emanates from the subtle effects of sacrifice as here defined. Let me explain the cycle: all living creatures are nourished and sustained by food; food is nourished and sustained by rain; rain, the water of life, emanates from nature, called down from heaven, freely given (sacrificed) for the eventual benefit of humanity. All of life, Arjuna, is therefore born of, nourished, and sustained by selfless action, by sacrifice.

(4)

The Gita
A New Translation of Hindu Sacred Scripture
Irina N. Gajjar
Emerald Ink Publishing [2000]
Axios Press [2007]
318 pages plus xvii
Original translation from Sanskrit with Introduction
Category: written by a scholar for the general reader who is a Hindu or interested in Hinduism

3:14-16
People grow from food.
Food comes from rain.
Rain comes from prayers
and prayers are actions,
Actions come from the Vedas
and the Vedas come from God.
So action comes from God.
Arjun, life must follow this wheel
which turns and causes being born,
growing and dying.
Otherwise, life has no meaning.

4:24
A puja is a ceremony for God.
Its a sacrifice.
The puja is Brahma.
The fire which is part of the puja is Brahma.
The person who performs the puja is Brahma.

(5)

The Bhagavad Gita
Winthrop Sargeant
SUNY (Sate University of New York Press) [1994]
739 pages plus xxi
A translation from Sanskrit with Sanskrit text plus transliteration.
Category: tends toward scholarly

3:14-16

Beings exist from food.
Food is brought into being by rain,
Rain from sacrifice,
And sacrifice is brought into being by action.

Know that ritual action originates in Brahman (the Vedas)
And Brahman arises from the Imperishable;
Therefore the all-pervading Brahman
Is eternally established in sacrifice.

He who does, here on earth,
Turn the wheel thus set in motion,
Lives, Arjuna,
Maliciously, full of sense delights, and in vain.

4:24

Brahman is the offering, Brahman is the oblation
Poured out by Brahman into the fire of Brahman,
Brahman is to be attained by him
Who always sees Brahman in action.

8:3

The Blessed Lord spoke: Brahman is the supreme imperishable;
And the Adhyatma is said to be the
inherent nature of the individual, Which orginates the being of
creatures; Action is known as the creative power (of the individual,
which causes him to be reborn in this or that conditon of being)

(6)

The Bhagavad Gita and Its Message
Sri Aurobindo [1938]
Sri Aurobindo Ashram Trust [1995]
Lotus Light Publication
306 pages plus xix
With text, translation and Commentary
Category: Yogic and Mystic

3:14-16
From food creatures come into being, from rain is the birth of food, from sacrifice comes into being the rain, sacrifice is born of work; work know to be born from Brahman, Brahman is born of the Immutable; therefore is the all-pervading Brahman established in the sacrifice.

He who follows not here the wheel thus set in movement, evil is his being, sensual is his delight, in vain, O Partha, that man lives.

4:24
Brahman is the giving, Brahman is the offering, by Brahman it is offered into the Brahman fire, Brahman is that which to be attained by samadhi in Brahman-action.

8:3
The Blessed Lord said: The Akshara is the supreme Brahman; svabhava is called the adhyatman; karma is the name given to the creative movement, visarga which brings into existence all beings amd their subjective and objective states.

(7)

The Bhagavadgita
A New Translation
Kees Bolle
University of California Press [1979]
318 pages
Contains a Part 2 after the text translation with a very lucid and pointed essay of the author's reason to do a new translation and a comparison of previous translation. Instead of a normal index it has very useful Sanskrit concordance as well as an English guide to the concordance.
Category: Scholarly

3:14-16
From food, creatures arise.
Rain produces food.
Sacrifice brings rain.
Cultic work is the root of sacrifice.

Cultic work comes from the Divine,
the Divine from the one supreme, subtle sound.
Hence the Divine, although omnipresent,
is ever established in the sacrifice.

Whoever does not turn with the wheel
thus set in motion –
That man lives in vain, Son of Prtha.
He is of evil intent, engrossed in the senses.

(8)

The Bhagavad Gita
Ramananda Prasad
American Gita Society [1988][1996][1999]
345 pages
Sanskrit, transliteration and Commentary;
includes glossary and index
Category: Yogic, Kriya Yoga, general reader

3:14-15

The living beings are born from food grains, grains are produced by rain, rain comes (as a favor from Devas) if duty (Karma) is performed as selfless service (Seva, Yajna). Duty is prescribed in the Vedas. The Vedas come from Brahma (Eternal Being). Thus the all-pervading Brahma is ever present in Seva.

The word Brahma is a designation of the creator aspect of Eternal Being (Brahma, Brahman), and the word Brahmana refers to an intellectual class (caste) in India.

3:16
The One who does not help to keep the wheel of creation in motion by sacrificial duty (Seva), and who rejoices in sense pleasure, that sinful person lives in vain, O Arjuna.

(9)

The Yoga of the Bhagavat Gita
Krishna Prem
Watkins [1938]
220 pages
An illuminating explanation of the text by spiritual Master with an Introduction, Appendix and Glossary.
Category: Yogic, Bhakti

3:14-16
Having dealt with the practical importance of action, Sri Krishna next goes on to show its moral and cosmic significance. In a few rapid words He sketches the yajna chakra, the great Cycle of Sacrifice that forms the manifested Cosmos, and shows how action is rooted in the Imperishable.

Note: *It should not be supposed that verses 14 and 15 are are archaic "rain-making magic." "Food" signifies the gross material world of which forms are built and "rain" the forces of desire which brings those forms into being. The sacrifice is the sacrificial self-limitation by which the many issue from the One..*

4:24
Let it, however, once become clear that the manifestation is also an aspect of the Supreme Brahman and it will be evident that there must be a way of action which does not bind the Soul. And this is the realization that now begins to dawn in the heart of the disciple. He sees, though as yet but with his mind, for there is still a long and weary road to be traversed before the vision will permeate his whole being, that the action, the actor and the act are all so many manifestations of the stainless Eternal, and that if all action be but offered as a sacrifice in the consuming fire of that Brahman there can be no bondage; for the root-cause of the bondage, the ignorance which a dualism and a multiplicity where there in truth but One, is now removed.

(10)

Tat Tvam Asi
The Universal Message in the Bhagavadgita
In two volumes
P.V. Nath
Motilal Banarsidass [1998]
Volume 1: 435 pages plus xli
Sanskrit, transliteration, translation and commentary

3:14-15
From food, beings are born. Food is produced from rain. Rain comes from sacrifice. Sacrifice is born of action.
Know that action arise from the Vedas. The Vedas are born from the Imperishable Brahman. Therefore that the Supreme Being is established in in yajna.

Commentary:
What is yajna? It is a dedicated act towards purification of oneself. [...]
The sages gave ideas of pure thoughts and pure living to the subsequent generations. They have given us the sacred, Vedas, which are our ancient treasure. [...]

3:16
The man who does not follow the cycle thus set revolving, is a sinner, rejoicing in the senses. He lives in vain, O Partha.

Commentary:
This verse is meant to emphasize that one should do good deeds. It is like saying, "you go to jail for stealing", repeatedly in different ways.
The entire universal is surviving on the principle of this cycle of Brahman-Vedas-Karma-Yajna-Brahman. It is our duty to see that the cycle is revolving constantly. [...]

(11)

The Bhagavad-Gita
RC Zaehner
JM Dent & Sons and EP Dutton & Co [1966]
Oxford University Press [1969] [1973]
Introduction, Transliteration, Translation, Commentary, Appendix, Index
Category: Scholarly

3:14-16
From food do [all] contingent beings derive and food derives from rain; rain derives from sacrifice and sacrifice from works.
From Brahman work arises, know this, and Brahman is born from the imperishable; therefore is Brahman, penetrating everywhere, forever based on sacrifice.

So was the wheel in motion set: and whoso here fails his turning [with the turning of the wheel], living an evil life, the senses his pleasure-ground, lives out his life in vain.

8:3
The Blessed Lord said:
The Imperishable is the highest Brahman; it is called 'inherent nature' in so far as it appertains to (an individual) self, -- as the creative force known as 'works' which gives rise to the (separate) natures of contingent beings.

(12)

Yogesvari Srimad Bhagavad Gita
Yogic Commentary by Shailendra Sharma
[2012]
Category: Yogic, Kriya Yoga

3:14-15
All creatures are created by food, food is created by yajna and yajna happens through karma.
May it be known that karma originates from Brahma; Brahma is created from the Imperishable (Aksara). All-pervading Brahma is ever present in yajna.

Yogis who could awaken the immense dormant consciousness of their mind could understand that the immense consciousness of the mind is a manifestation of the omnipresent imperishable Supreme Being, the Time – that never passes away, the Time which is immutable and is yet manifested in the immensity of the mind. This body supports the mind and everything is experienced through medium of the body.

Food supports the body, which is created by the rains that result from the association of the earth and the sun.

(13)

The Bhagavad Gita
Interpretations of Lahiri Mahasaya
Translated from Bengali by Swami Satyeswarananda Giri
The Sanskrit Classics [1991]
Category: Yogic, Kriya Yoga

3:14-16
All beings come from the Self. The grain is produced from the rain, the clouds from oblation or sacrifice, oblation from the action (Karma or Kriya). So, the Self is in all. The Self is from Akshara

[Eternity]. Therefore the Self is in all oblations (Jajna, or Karmas, that is, Kriyas).

[These verses point out a cycle of manifestation, everything evolving from the Self dissolving in the Self or Source. All the beings, grain or food, rain, oblation or Kriyas are different states of vibrations, of the Self during manifestation.]

Such is the cycle: the life of one who is not there and performs all actions for the senses is in vain.

(14)

The Bhagavad Gita
Interpretations of Sriyukteswar
Translated from Bengali by Swami Satyeswarananda Giri
The Sanskrit Classics [1991]
328 pages
Category: Yogic, Kriya Yoga

3:14
Poetic Rendition:
All jivas, beings, are evolved from food; production of food depends on rain; rain is produced from sacrifice; sacrifice is rooted in the prescribed actions, jagya.

Elaborate Interpretations:
Food like nectar is defined as that which is an enjoyable state, Tranquility. All the bhutas, elements of the body, are nourished from it [Tranquility].
This nectar, dharmamegha, is produced from sahasrar, the thousands petals; and the lotus of thousand petals blooms completely by the practice of jagya.
The jagya is performed by the practice of Kriyas received from the Guru.

(15)

Srimad-Bhagavad-Gita
The Revelation of the Supreme Self
Swami Premananda [1949, 1971]
Self-Revelation Church
231 pages with Introduction
Category: Yogic, Kriya Yoga

3:14-15
All phenomena are born of the gross. The gross comes from the subtle. The subtle is caused by the essence of action. The essence of action results from action. Action is produced by vibration. Vibration emanates from the Imperishable. Therefore the eternal Reality is all-pervading and ever present in the action.

The Self is pure-consciousness. At Sahasraram it is reflected in its purest form. At Visuddha it produces the cosmic vibration. While at Anahata it becomes the desire. At Manipur it is the active force. At Sadhisthan it generates the consciousness of the subtle elements. At Muladhar it creates the thought of gross elements. Out of the thought of gross elements is actuated all form-consciousness. Thus the Self is all-pervading and ever present in all states of consciousness.

(16)

Bhagavad Gita
A New Translation
Stephen Mitchell [2000]
Harmony Books (Random House)
Category: Literary

3:14
Beings arise from food;
food arises from rain;

rain arises from worship;
worship, from ritual action;
ritual action, from God;
God, from deathless Self.
Thus, the all-present God
requires the worship of men.

(17)

God Talks With Arjuna
The Bhagavad Gita
Royal Science of God-Realization
Paramahansa Yogananda
Self-Realization Fellowship [1995,1999]
2 Volumes; 1174 pages; Introduction, illustrations and Addenda
Category: Yogic, Kriya Yoga

3:14-15
From food, creatures spring forth; from rain, food is begotten. From Yajna (the sacrificial cosmic fire), rain issues forth; the cosmic fire (cosmic light) is born of karma (divine vibratory action).

Know this divine vibratory activity to have come into being from Brahma (God's Creative Consciousness); and this Creative Consciousness to derive from the Imperishable (the Everlasting Spirit). Therefore, God's Creative Consciousness (Brahma), which is all-pervading, is inherently and inseparably present in Yajna (the cosmic fire or light, which turn is the essence of all the components of vibratory creation).

Pages 367-370: detailed exposition of these two verses
"*The following is the second paragraph from page 367:*
These stanzas describe the entire law of creation: the outward evolution of creation from Spirit into Cosmic Vibration, and the condensation of vibration as light into an and the universe in casual, astral and physical forms"

(18)

The Eternal Way
The inner meaning of the Bhagavad Gita
Roy Eugene Davis
CSA Press [1996]
317 pages; Introduction; Addendum with glossary

Type: Translation and Commentary
Category: Spiritual Tradition – Kriya Yoga

3:14-15

Beings exist because of food [nourishment]; food is produced by rain; rain is produced by sacrifice; and sacrifice is produced by work [actions].

Know that the principle of causation [karma] originates in the Field of God, and the Field of God emanates from the Imperishable [the Field of Absolute Pure Consciousness]. Therefore, the all-pervading Reality is present in sacrificial actions.

A commentary of 3 paragraphs:
God is present in all offerings to support evolution. [last line of second paragraph]

(19)

The Bhagavad Gita
Swami Sivananda
Divine Life Society [10th Edition 1995]
576 pages; Introduction, Appendix with Sanskrit index

Type: Translation [with Sanskrit] and Commentary
Category: Spiritual Tradition – Yoga

3:14

From food come forth beings; from rain food is produced; from sacrifice arises rain and sacrifice is born of action.

Here Yajna means "Apurva" or the subtle principle or the unseen form which a sacrifice assumes between the time of its performance and the time when its fruits manifest themselves.

(20)

Abhinavagupta's Commentary on the Bhagavad Gita
Translated from Sanskrit with introduction and notes
by Boris Marjanovic
Indica Books (2nd edition in 2004)
Type: Translation with Sanskrit and plus commentary
Category: Spiritual Tradition – Kashmiri Shaivism

3:14 - 3:16
All creatures come ino existence from annam; annam comes from parjanya; parjanya comes from yajna and yajna is born of action (karman)
Know that action comes from the Brahman. The Brahman springs from the imperishable (aksharam). Therefore, the all-pervading

Brahman is ever established in yajna.
[...one page of explanation fo the terms used...]
He who does not here on earth follow the wheel thus revolving, whose life is sinful, who lives for the gratification fo the senses, he lives in vain, O Partha.

4:24
Brahman is the act of offering. Brahman is the oblation poured by Brahman into the fire that is Brahman. To Brahman alone he must go who is fixed in Brahman through action.

[...a page of commentary follows this verse..]

(21)

The Bhagaval Gita as it is by A.C Bhaktivedanta Swami.
With introduction, translation, and authorized purport
by A.C. Bhaktivedanta Swami.
London: Collier-Macmillan, [1968]. 318 p.; 21 cm. (Collier Books)
Category: Spiritual, Bhakti, Krishna Consciousness

4.24
A person who is fully absorbed in Krsna Consciousness is sure to attain the spiritual kingdom through his full contribution to spiritual activities, for the consummation is absolute and the things are offered are also of the same spiritual nature.

(22)

The Bhagavad-gita; translated and interpreted
by Franklin Edgerton
Cambridge, Mass.: Harvard University Press [1944]
London: H. Milford, Oxford University Press
2 volumes [Harvard Oriental series]
Category: Extreme Scholarly

4.24
The (sacrificial) presentation is Brahman; Brahman is the oblation; In the (sacrificial) fire of Brahman it is poured by Brahman; Just to Brahman must he go, Being concentrated upon the (sacrificial) action that is Brahman.

(23)

Bhagavad-gita, the song of God.
Translated by Swami Prabhavananda
and Christopher Isherwood, with an introduction by Aldous Huxley
Hollywood: The Marcel Rodd [1944].
Category: Vedantic, English Literary, General reader

4.24
Brahman is the ritual,
Brahman is the offering,
Brahman is he who offers
To the fire that is Brahman.
If a man sees Brahman in every action,
He will find Brahman.

(24)

The Bhagavadgita. With an introductory essay, Sanskrit text, English translation and notes
by Sarvepalli Radhakrishnan.
London: George allen & Unwin.[1947] 388 p.

Category: General reader, Vedanta,

4:24
For him the act of offering is God, the oblation is God. By God is it offered into the fire of God, God is that which is to be attained by him who realizes God in his works.

(25)

The Bhagavadgita in the Mahabharata: the text and translation
by J.A.B. Van Buitenen.
Chicago: University of Chicago Press. [1979] ;
Includes bibliographical references

Category: cross-boundary – good for general reader and yet does not sacrifice critical scholarship

4.24
Brahman is the offering, brahman is the oblation that is poured into the brahman fire by brahman; he who thus contemplates the act as nothing but brahman must reach brahman.

8:3
The Lord said: The supreme Brahman is the imperishable. The individual self is called nature. And the outpouring that brings about the origination of the being of the creatures is called act. The "elemental" is transitory being; the spirit is the 'divine', and I myself am the "sacrificial" here in this body.

Figure 1
Useful Reference Books for the study of Bhagavad Gita

Figure 2
Books for Translation Comparison : 1-5

Figure 3
Books for Translation Comparison : 6-10

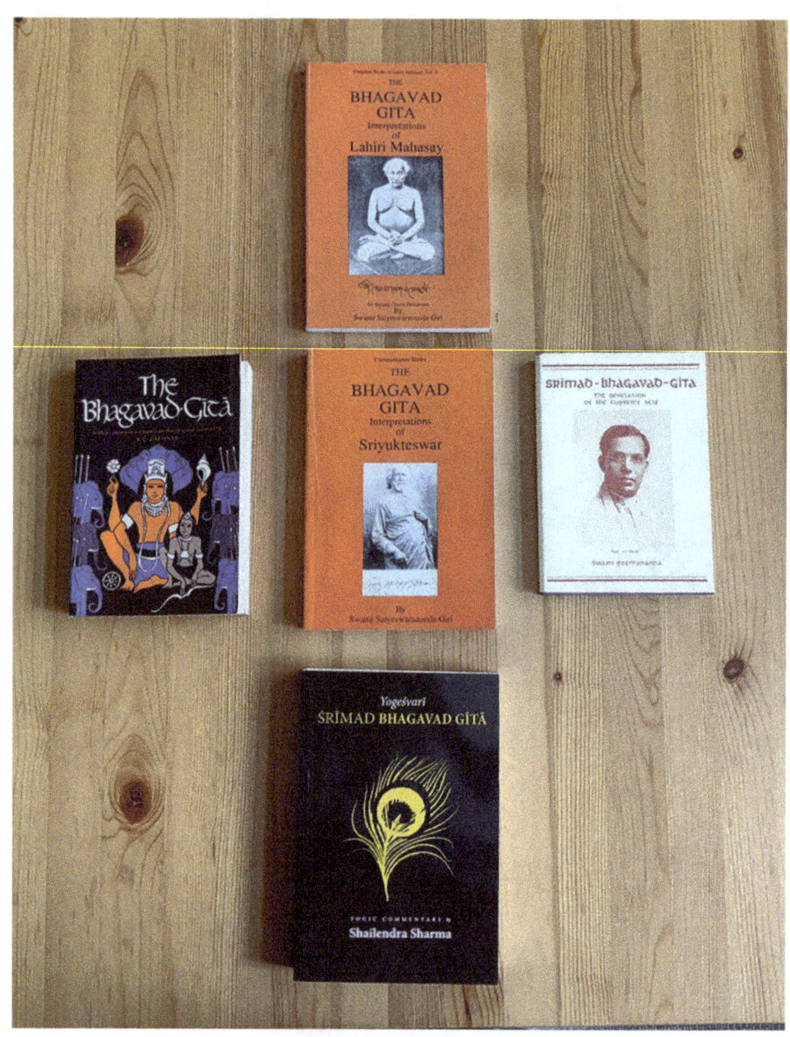

Figure 4
Books for Translaton Comparison : 11-15

Figure 5
Books for Translation Comparison : 16-20

Figure 6
Books for Translation Comparison : 20-25

The following material is considered to be useful to students of the Bhagavad Gita:

The Gita Dhyanam - chanted before the study of the Gita

The Gita Mahatmya - chanted after the study of the Gita

The Gita Chalisa - forty verses from the Gita that can be chanted as a short-hand for the whole of the Gita

The Gitartha Samgraha by Yamunacharya - a concise summary of the Gita from the perspective of the Vishishadvaita School of Indian Philosophy

The Summary of the Gita by Abhinavagupta that gives the Gita from the perspective of Kashmiri Shaivism

The Ten Key verses from the Advaita Darshana or Non-Dual school of philosophy (suggested by a contemporary member)

Gita Dhyanam

Om paarthaaya pratibodhitaam bhagavataa naaraayanenaswayam,
Vyaasena grathitaam puraanamuninaa madhye mahaabhaaratam;
Advaitaamritavarshineem bhagavateem ashtaadashaa dhyaayineem,
Amba twaam anusandadhaami bhagavadgeete bhavadweshineem

Om. O Bhagavad Gita, with which Partha was illuminated by Lord Narayana Himself, and which was composed within the Mahanharata by the ancient sage, Vyasa, O Divine Mother, the destroyer of rebirth, the showerer of nectar of Advaita, and consisting of eighteen discourses – upon Thee, O gita, O affectionate Mother, I meditate.

Namostu te Vyaasa vishaalabuddhe phullaaravindraayatapatranetra;
Yena twayaa bhaaratatailapoornah prajwaalito jnaanamayah pradeepah.

Salutations unto thee, O Vyasa, of broad intellect and with eyes like the petals of a full-blown lotus, by whom the lamp of knowledge, filled with the oil of the Mahabharata, has been lit.

Prapannapaarijaataaya totravetraikapaanaye;
Jnaanamudraaya krishnaaya geetaamritaduhe namah.

Salutations to Lord Krishna, the Parijata or the Kalpataru or the bestower of all desires for those who take refuge in Him, the holder of the whip in one hand, the holder of the symbol of divine knowledge and the milker of the divine nectar of Bhagavad Gita.

Sarvopanishado gaavo doghdhaa gopaalanandanah;
Partho vatsah sudheer bhoktaa dugdham geetaamritam mahat.

All the Upanishads are the cows; the milker is Krishna; the cowherd boy, Partha (Arjuna), is the calf; men of purified intellect are the drinkers; the milk is the great nectar of the Gita.

Vasudevasutam devam kamsachaanooramardanam;
Devakeeparamaanandam krishnam vande jagadgurum.

I salute Sri Krishna, the world-teacher, son of Vasudeva, the destroyer of Kansa and Chanura, the supreme bliss of Devaki.

Bheeshmadronatataa jayadrathajalaa gaandhaaraneelotpalaa;
Shalyagraahavatee kripena vahanee karnena velaakulaa;
Ashwatthaama-vikarna-ghora-makaraa duryodhanaavartinee;
Sotteernaa khalu paandavai rananadee kaivartakah keshavah.

With Kesava as the helmsman, verily was crossed by the Pandavas the battle-river, who's banks were Bhishma and Drona, whose waters was Jayadratha, whose blue lotus was the King of Gandhara, whose crocodile was Salya, whose current was Kripa, whose billow are Karna, whose terrible alligators were Vikarna and Asvatthama, whose whirlpools was Duryodhana.

Paaraasharya vachah sarojamamalam geetaarthagandhotkatam;
Naanaakhyaanakakesaram harikathaa sambodhanaabhoditam;
Loke sajjana shatpdairaharahah papeeyamaanam mudaa;
Bhooyadbhaaratapankajam kalimala pradhwamsinah shreyase.

May this lotus of the Mahabharata, born in the lake of the words of Vyasa, sweet with the fragrance of the meaning of the Gita, with many stories as its stamens, fully opened by the discourse of Hari, the destroyer of the sins of Kali, and drunk joyously by the bees of good men in the world, become day by day the bestowal of good.

Mookam karoti vaachaalam pangum langhayate girim;
Yatkripaa tamaham vande paramaanandamaadhavam.

I salute the Madhava, the source of supreme bliss, whose grace makes the dumb eloquent and the cripple cross mountains.

Yam brahma varunedrarudramarutah stuwanti divyaih stavaih;
Vedaih saangapadakramopanishadair gaayanti yam saamagaah,
Dhyaanaavasthitatadgatena manasaa pashyanti yam yogino,
Yasyaantam na viduh suraasuraganaa devaaya tasmai namah.

Salutations to that God whom Brahma, Indra, Varuna, Rudra and the Maruts praise with divine hymns, of whom the Sama-chanters sing by the Vedas and their Angas (in the Pada and Krama methods), and by the Upanishads; whom the Yogis see with their minds absorbed in Him through meditation, and whose ends the hosts of Devas and Asuras know not.

Gita Mahatmya (by Adi Shankaracharya)

gita shastram idam punyam yah pathet prayatat puman

vishnoh padam avapnoti bhaya sokadi varjitah

When a person reads, recites or studies with proper attention this auspicious Shastra, Bhagavad gita, he will attain the feet of Sri Vishnu and will become free from fear, worries and all other problems.

gitadhyayana-silasya pranayama parasya cha

naiva santi hi papani purva janma krtani cha

By meditating on Bhagavad gita with full attention and controlling one's life energy, one will become free from sin and from the reactions of the wrong actions performed during previous lifetimes.

malanir mochanam pumsam jala-snanam dine dine

sakrid gitambhasi snanam samsara-mala nasanam

One can become free from contamination by taking bath with water every day, but if one takes bath even once only in the sacred waters of Mother Gita, all the impurities of samsara are destroyed.

gita sugita kartavya kim anyah shastra vistaraih

ya svayam padmanabhasya mukha-padmad vinihsrita

The wonderful song called Bhagavad Gita has been spoken by the lotus mouth of the Lord Padmanabha himself. What other shastras do we need to seek then?

bharatamrita sarvasam vishnor vaktrad-vinihsritam

gita-gangodakam pitva punar janma na vidyate

One who drinks the sacred waters of the Ganga and the Gita, the nectar of the Mahabharata, spoken directly by Sri Vishnu, will not have to take another birth in the material world.

sarvopanishado gavo dogdha gopala-nandanah

partho vatsah sudhir bhokta dugdham gitamritam mahat

Comparing all the Upanishads as a cow, Krishna the son of the cowherd chief is the milkman, Arjuna the son of Pritha is the calf, and the intelligent people will enjoy the great nectar of Bhagavad gita as the milk

ekam shastram devaki-putra gitam eko devo devaki putra eva

eko mantras tasya namani yani karmapy ekam tasya devasya seva

Let there be one shastra only: the Gita of Krishna the son of Devaki. Let there be one God only: Krishna the son of Devaki. Let there be one mantra only: his holy names. Let there be one work only: service to that God.

Gita Chalisa

[by the American/International Gita Society]

The following is a compilation of 40 most important verses from the Bhagavadgita, which sum up its philosophy and important concepts.

King inquired: Sanjaya, please tell me, in detail, what did my people and the Pandavas do in the battlefield before the war started? (1.01)

Sanjaya said: O King, Lord Krishna spoke these words to Arjuna whose eyes were tearful and downcast, and who was overwhelmed with compassion and despair. (2.01)

Lord Krishna said: You grieve for those who are not worthy of grief, and yet speak words of wisdom. The wise grieves neither for the living nor for the dead. (2.11)

Just as the soul acquires a childhood body, a youth body, and an old age body during this life; similarly, the soul acquires another body after death. This should not delude the wise. (2.13)

Just as a person puts on new garments after discarding the old ones; similarly, the living entity or the individual soul acquires new bodies after casting away the old bodies. (2.22)

Treating pleasure and pain, gain and loss, and victory and defeat alike, engage yourself in your duty. By doing your duty this way you will not incur sin. (2.38)

You have control over doing your respective duty only, but no control or claim over the results. The fruits of work should not be your motive, and you should never be inactive. (2.47)

A Karma-yogi or the selfless person becomes free from both vice and virtue in this life itself. Therefore, strive for selfless service. Working to the best of one's abilities without becoming selfishly attached to the fruits of work is called Karma-yoga or Seva. (2.50)

Because the mind, when controlled by the roving senses, steals away the intellect as a storm takes away a boat on the sea from its destination ¾ the spiritual shore of peace and happiness. (2.67)

The forces of Nature do all works. But due to delusion of ignorance people assume themselves to be the doer. (3.27)

Thus, knowing the Self to be superior to the intellect, and controlling the mind by the intellect that is purified by spiritual practices, one must kill this mighty enemy, lust, O Arjuna. (3.43)

Whenever there is a decline of Dharma Righteousness) and a predominance of Adharma Unrighteousness), O Arjuna, then I manifest Myself. I appear from time to time for protecting the good, for transforming the wicked, and for establishing world order Dharma). (4.07-08)

I created the four divisions of human society based on aptitude and vocation. Though I am the author of this system of the division of labor, one should know that I do nothing directly and I am eternal. (4.13)

The one who sees inaction in action, and action in inaction, is a wise person. Such a person is a yogi and has accomplished everything. (4.18)

Spirit shall be realized by the one who considers everything as a manifestation or an act of the Spirit. (4.24)

Verily, there is no purifier in this world like the true knowledge of the Supreme Being. One discovers this knowledge within, naturally, in course of time when one's mind is cleansed of selfishness by Karma-yoga. (4.38)

But, true renunciation, O Arjuna, is difficult to attain without Karma-yoga. A sage equipped with Karma-yoga quickly attains Nirvana. (5.06)

One who does all work as an offering to God — abandoning selfish attachment to the results — remains untouched by Karmic reaction or sin as a lotus leaf never gets wet by water. (5.10)

Those who perceive Me in everything and behold everything in Me, are not separated from Me, and I am not separated from them. (6.30)

Four types of virtuous ones worship or seek Me, O Arjuna. They are: The distressed, the seeker of Self-knowledge, the seeker of wealth, and the enlightened one who has experienced the Supreme. (7.16)

After many births the enlightened one resorts to Me by realizing that everything is, indeed, My or Supreme Being's) manifestation. Such a great soul is very rare. (7.19)

The ignorant ones — unable to understand My immutable, incomparable, incomprehensible, and transcendental form — assume that I, the Supreme Being, am formless and take forms or incarnate. (7.24)

Remembering whatever object one leaves the body at the end of life, one attains that object. Thought of whatever object prevails during one's lifetime, one remembers only that object at the end of life and achieves it. (8.06)

Therefore, always remember Me and do your duty. You shall certainly attain Me if your mind and intellect are ever focused on Me. (8.07)

I am easily attainable, O Arjuna, by that ever-steadfast devotee who always thinks of Me and whose mind does not go elsewhere. (8.14)

I personally take care of both spiritual and material welfare of those ever-steadfast devotees who always remember and adore Me with single-minded contemplation. (9.22)

Whosoever offers Me a leaf, a flower, a fruit, or water with devotion; I accept and eat the offering of devotion by the pure-hearted. (9.26)

Engage your mind in always thinking of Me, be devoted to Me, worship Me, and bow down to Me. Thus, uniting yourself with Me by setting Me as the supreme goal and the sole refuge, you shall certainly come to Me. (9.34)

I am the origin of all. Everything emanates from Me. The wise ones who understand this adore Me with love and devotion. (10.08)

The one who does all works for Me, and to whom I am the supreme goal; who is my devotee, who has no attachment, and is free from enmity towards any being; attains Me, O Arjuna. (11.55)

Therefore, focus your mind on Me, and let your intellect dwell upon Me alone through meditation and contemplation. Thereafter you shall certainly attain Me. (12.08)

The one who sees the same eternal Supreme Lord dwelling as Spirit equally within all mortal beings truly sees. (13.27)

The one who offers service to Me with love and unswerving devotion transcends three modes of material Nature, and becomes fit for Nirvana, or salvation. (14.26)

I am seated in the inner psyche of all beings. The memory, Self-knowledge, and the removal of doubts and wrong notions about God come from Me. I am verily that which is to be known by the study of all the Vedas. I am, indeed, the author as well as the student of the Vedas. (15.15)

Lust, anger, and greed are the three gates of hell leading to the downfall or bondage) of the individual. Therefore, one must learn to give up these three. (16.21)

Speech that is non-offensive, truthful, pleasant, beneficial, and is used for the regular study of scriptures is called the austerity of word. (17.15)

By devotion one truly understands what and who I am in essence. Having known Me in essence, one immediately merges with Me. (18.55)

The Supreme Lord — as the controller abiding in the inner psyche of all beings — causes them to work out their Karma like a puppet of Karma created by the free will) mounted on a machine. (18.61)

Set aside all meritorious deeds and religious rituals, and just surrender completely to My will with firm faith and loving devotion. I shall liberate you from all sins, the bonds of Karma. Do not grieve. (18.66)

The one who shall propagate this supreme secret philosophy or the transcendental knowledge of the Gita) amongst My devotees, shall be performing the highest devotional service to Me, and shall certainly come to Me. No other person shall do a more pleasing service to Me, and no one on the earth shall be more dear to Me. (18.68-69)

Wherever there will be both Krishna, the Lord of yoga, or Dharma in the form of the scriptures, and Arjuna with the weapons of duty and protection; there will be everlasting prosperity, victory, happiness, and morality. This is my conviction. (18.78)

"May the Lord bless all with Goodness, Prosperity, and Peace."

Sri Yamunacharya was a senior comtemporary of Ramanujacharya (1077 -1157 CE), the foremost exponent of the Vishishtadvaita (qualified non-dualism) school of Vedanta - essentially being one with God but still somehow separate from the Being of God.

Many Western translators consider his synopsis of the Gita to be "closest to the intent of the author of the Gita". This may also be due to the closeness of the Vishishtadvaita philosophy to that of the major forms of Christian mysticism, which try to embrace non-duality with a personal God - being one with the body of Christ but not one with the Trintiy.

The Gitartha – Samgraha of Sri Yamunacharya

1) In the scripture known as the Bhagavad Gita, Narayana, the Supreme Brahman, is declared. He is attainable by Bhakti alone, which is to be brought about by the observance of one's own Dharma, acquisition of knowledge and renunciation of attachment.

2) In the first six chapters, the performance of desireless Karma and Jnana, with the practice of Yoga in view, is enjoined for the realization of the self.

3) In the middle six chapters, Bhakti Yoga, which can be brought by Karma and Jnana is treated for the attainment of the exact knowledge of Bhagavan, the Supreme Being, as He is.

4) In the last six chapters, which expands on what has gone before, is treated matter (Pradhana)in the primordial condition, matter in its evolved state, the self (Purusa), and Isvara the Ruler of all. Also, the disciplines relating to work, to knowledge and to devotion are again dealt with by way of supplementing and completing what has been taught earlier.

5) The treatise was initiated for the sake of Arjuna, who was overtaken by misplaced love and compassion and also perplexity as to what was Dharma and what Adharma, and who took refuge in Sri Krishna.

6) The knowledge of Sankhya and Yoga, which comprehend in their scope the eternal self and disinterested activity respectively, leading to the state of steady wisdom, is taught in the second chapter for removing Arjuna's delusion.

7) In the third chapter is taught the need for the performance of works without attachment to any fruits other than the pleasure of the Lord and for the protection of the world, ascribing the agency to the

Gunas or placing it in the Lord of all.

8) In the fourth chapter the following matters are treated: His nature is explained incidentally. Next it is taught that Karma Yoga has an aspect other than action, i.e., knowledge - aspect. The varieties of Karma Yoga and the eminence of knowledge in it, are emphasized.

9) In the fifth chapter are set forth the ease and quick efficiency of Karma Yoga, some of its elements and the mode of knowledge of Brahman, i.e., the individual self.

10) In the sixth chapter are taught the practice of Yoga (concentration and meditation), the fourfold divisions of (successful) Yogins, the means to success in Yoga, and the supremacy of Yoga concerning Himself.

11) In the seventh chapter is taught the exact knowledge of Himself, His concealment by the Prakriti, the surrender to Him as the means to overcome this, observations on various types of devotees and the superiority of the man of wisdom among these devotees.

12) In the eighth chapter are discussed the distinctions of what are to be understood and acquired by each of the three classes of devotees - those who are after prosperity, after the true nature of the self and after the feet of the Lord.

13) In the ninth chapter are treated His own eminence, His undiminished supremacy as the Divine even when He assumes embodiments as Incarnations, the excellence of Mahatmas or devotees who seek God alone, and the discipline of Bhakti of devotion to God.

14) In the tenth chapter are described in detail the infinite auspicious attributes of the Lord and His absolute control over everything, to generate and develop Bhakti or devotion to God in the minds of aspirants.

15) In the eleventh chapter, Arjuna receives the divine vision which gives immediate vision of God and it is stated that bhakti is the only means for knowing and attaining him in this way.

16) In the twelve chapter, it is stated that the Lord has a vast love for his devotees and bhakti is superior. Also given are the means to practice bhakti, directions for meditating on the self and modes of spiritual practice.

17) In the thirteenth chapter, the nature of the body, method of self-realization, the nature of the self, the cause of bondage, and the differentiation between body and self are described.

18) In the fourteenth chapter, the gunas as agents of action, cause of bondage and how to eliminate their influence are described. Also, described are the three ends of heaven, abiding in the self and existence within the Lord can be attained.

19) In the fifteenth chapter, the Supreme Lord is declared to be different from the self both in its state of union with matter and in its liberated state, because He pervades, sustains and rules over the individual souls and the world.

20) In the sixteenth chapter is first described the differences between the natures of devas and asuras in order to establish the proper conduct to be pursued by submission to the shastras.

21) In the seventeenth chapter, the following topics are discussed: rejection of paths not recommended by the shastras, the injunctions of the shastras in accordance with the gunas, and the characteristics of the three words, ‘om’, ‘tat’, and ‘sat’.

22) The final chapter describes the mental state necessary for allowing that the Lord is the real controller, the necessity of developing the sattvic nature, the spiritual end gained by fulfilling one’s duties, and the bhakti yoga.

23) Karma Yoga means 'to practice austerity, pilgrimage, charity, yajna and other such acts.' Jnana Yoga means 'to control the mind and then to abide within the purified self.'

24) Bhakti Yoga means 'to practice meditation and other forms of worship with the undeviating love for the Supreme Being.' These three yogas are interconnected.

25) There are required, and occasional duties connected to all three yogas, as they are means of worshipping the Supreme Lord. All three grant vision of the self, but bhakti can be practiced before such vision by means of japa, bhajan, pilgrimage, etc. even with only superficial love of God.

26) One attains supreme devotion and thereby reaches God's domain when ignorance is removed, and one perceives the self as subservient to Him. There is vaidhi (regulated) bhakti, para (higher) bhakti, and finally parama (supreme) bhakti.

27) Bhakti Yoga can grant prosperity and sovereignty if one desires them. If one desires to attain the self, all three yogas are effective in the attainment of kaivalya (separation from matter).

28) The understanding that God is the highest end is common to all three types of yogin, but if one overlooks the other two aspires only for the Lord, one will attain him completely.

29) The jnanin is one who is devoted exclusively to the Lord and whose whole existence depends upon him. Contact with God is his only joy and separation his only grief. His thoughts are always only focused on God.

30) When one finds pleasure only in thinking, meditating, speaking, worshipping and praising the Lord, then the senses, intellect, mind and vital energies all become concentrated upon him.

31) To please the Lord, without any other motive, one should give

up dependence on anything but him and abandon any fear that this means one will be incomplete.

32) Such a person finds pleasure only in undeviating service to God. He then attains to His domain. This Gita Shastra is meant for such a devotee. This is a summary of its meaning.

Summary of the Gita by Abhinavagupta

(1)

A wise person, who was compelled into the troubling union between knowledge and ignorance, should, having analyzed and rejected both, enter the state free from thought.

(2)

The most amazing, indeed, is the movement of the mind. Through (the process of) giving up one object it jumps to other ones, taking thus recourse to (new) objects that are again to be given up.

(3)

One who approaches one's wealth, wife or even one's body with a sense of difference from his real nature, what kind of harm could be done to such a person by the changing nature of his mind?

(4)

Whichever act, preceded by the desire inherent in the sense organs, one might perform, this act will make gods in the form of sense organs fulfilled and in return they will bless people with auspicious results.

(5)

He who perceives all creatures as being equal is fit for liberation, even if he is ignorant in the matters of worldly affairs.

(6)

Only by attaining God's name everything is achieved, just as rice grains blossom when the rainy season comes.

(7)

Pure devotion is the wish-fulfilling tree by means of which one may fulfill hopes proper to be desired by the *sadhaka.*

(8)

When the Lord is known to be present in all the *tattvas*, then for a yogin there is no place either externally or internally where *Paramesvara* is not present.

(9)

That all merciful *Parasakti,* which blesses all living beings, blossoms and expands in that unitary consciousness called *Brahman',* therefore, one should strive to attain that highest reality.

(10)

Whatever might be the object of one's experience and whatever might form the content of one's desire, one should while persistently dissolving all of that, meditate on the *Brahman,* which is the highest peace.

(11)

Having the realization of the oneness of consciousness, which is manifested as pure, pure-cum-impure and impure, a meditator possessing a balanced mind observes the three states of consciousness with equilibrium

(12)

The yogin absorbed in God and taken by the bliss of that absorption spontaneously experiences the reality of the *Brahman* in all states and conditions of life.

(13)

The difference between *Purusa* and *Prakrti* exists only for those who are confused, but those who are perfect realize the entire universe as the pure *atman.*

(14)

A yogin, who has become free from error caused by *ahamkara,* as a result of the nectar of blooming devotion, such a yogin although living in the midst of the three *gunas* is beyond their influence.

(15)

The sage who has transcended the great delusion caused by the notion of duality and who has realized his consciousness as being pervaded by the *Brahman,* that wise man even while performing worldly activities should permanently remain absorbed in the highest reality.

(16)

At the time of indecision one should not use one's own mind to decide the course of action, but rather should rely on the *sastras* whose purpose is to increase knowledge.

(17)

He, Siva alone assumes the form of different instruments; his *sakti,* which is free from all attributes, is action. In this way, to those who possess knowledge, all actions, such as charity, austerity or sacrifice, culminate in *moksa.*

(18)

Whatever action might be performed by a yogin — who has freed his mind dominated by the three *gunas,* which are of the nature of knowledge, confusion and inertia, and who has attained Visnu, who is beyond thought, through the beauty of the realization of his own self — that action is performed effortlessly because he is engaged only in such activities of the sense organs, which arise in him on their own. To such a yogin Siva is everything.

Ten Key Verses of BG for Advaita

(1)

The Blessed Lord said:
You grief for those who call for no grief; at the same time, you utter words of wisdom. The wise grief neither for the dead nor for the living.
(BG 2.11)

(2)

O Arjuna! How can a man who knows It as the imperishable, the eternal, the unborn, the undecaying, cause anyone to be slain? Whom can he slay?
BG 2.21

(3)

The Blessed Lord said:
When one wholly discards desires of the heart and becomes exclusively content with the Self, one is called a sage of stable wisdom. O Arjuna!
BG 2.55

(4)

The entire world has been pervaded by Me in my Unmanifest form. All beings dwell in Me but I dwell not in them.
BG 9.4

(5)

The Blessed Lord said:
O sinless one! Two kinds of disciplines in this world were set forth by Me in times of yore – for the Samkhyas the discipline of knowledge, and for the Yogins, that of works.
BG 3.3

(6)

To work alone you have the right and never to the fruits (of works). Don't be impelled by the fruits of works; (at the same time) don't be

tempted to withdraw from works.
BG 2.47

(7)

Through the performance of his works as worship man wins perfection – worshipping Him from whom all beings have proceeded and by whom all this has been pervaded.
BG 18.46

(8)

Indeed, renunciation, might-armed! is hard to win without Karma Yoga. With Yoga, the silent sage attains Brahman without much delay.
BG 5.6

(9)

Mentally renouncing all works, and self-controlled, the embodied being happily sits in the nine-gated city, neither working nor causing others to work.
BG 5.13

(10)

Giving up all Dharma (acts of righteousness), seek refuge in Me alone; I shall liberate you from all sins; grief not.
BG 18.66

The Bhagavad Gita
Translation by
Swami Swarupananda
[1909]

In the tradition of Advaita Vedanata

Chapter One
The Grief of Arjuna

Dhritarashtra said:
1) Tell me, O Sanjaya! Assembled on Kurukshetra, the center of religious activity, desirous to fight, what indeed did my people and the Pandavas do?

Sanjaya said:
2) But then King Duryodhana, having seen the Pandava forces in battle array, approached his teacher Drona and spoke these words:
3) "Behold, O Teacher! this mighty army of the sons of Pandu, arrayed by the son of Drupada, your gifted pupil.
4-6) "Here [are] heroes, mighty archers, the equals in battle of Bhima and Arjuna–the great warriors Yuyudhana, Virata, Drupada; the valiant Dhrishtaketu, Chekitana, and the king of Kashi; the best of men, Purujit, Kuntibhoja, and Shaibya; the powerful Yudhamanyu, and the brave Uttamaujas, the son of Subhadra and the sons of Draupadi–all of whom are lords of great chariots.
7) "Hear also, O best of the twice-born! the names of those who [are] distinguished amongst ourselves, the leaders of my army. These I relate [to you] for your information.
8) "Yourself and Bhishma and Karna and Kripa, the victorious in war. Ashvatthama and Vikarna and Jayadratha, the son of Somadatta.
9) "And many other heroes also, well-skilled in fight, and armed with many kinds of weapons, are here, determined to lay down their lives for my sake.
10) "This our army defended by Bhishma [is] impossible to be counted, but that army of theirs, defended by Bhima [is] easy to number.
11) "[Now] do, being stationed in your proper places in the divisions of the army, support Bhishma alone."
12) That powerful, oldest of the Kurus, Bhishma the grandsire, in order to cheer Duryodhana, now sounded aloud a lion-roar and blew his conch.
13) Then following Bhishma, conchs and kettle-drums, tabors,

trumpets, and cowhorns blared forth suddenly from the Kaurava side, and the noise was tremendous.
14) Then, also, Madhava and Pandava, stations in their magnificent Chariot yoked with white horses, blew their divine conchs with a furious noise.
15) Hrishikesha blew the Panchajanya, Dhananjaya, the Devadatta,and Vrikodara, the doer of terrific deeds, his large conch Paundra.
16) King Yudhishthira, son of Kunti, blew the conch named Anantavijaya, and Nakula and Sahadeva, their Sughosha and Manipushpaka.
17) The expert bowman, king of Kashi, and the great warrior Shikhandi, Dhristadyumna, and Virata, and the unconquered Satyaki;
18) O Lord of Earth! Drupada and the sons of Draupadi, and the mighty-armed son of Subhadra, all, also blew each his own conch.
19) And the terrific noise resounding throughout heaven and earth rent the hearts of Dhritarashtra's party.
20) Then, O Lord of Earth, seeing Dhritarashtra's party standing marshalled and the shooting about to begin, the Pandava, whose ensign was the monkey, raising his bow, said the following words to Krishna:

Arjuna said:
21-22) Place my chariot, O Achyuta! between the two armies that I may see those who stand here prepared for war. On this eve of battle [let me know] with whom I have to fight.
23) For I desire to observe those who are assembled here for fight, wishing to please the evil-minded Duryodhana by taking his side on this battle-field.

Sanjaya said:
24-25) O Bharata, commanded thus by Gudakesha, Hrishikesha drove that grandest of chariots to a place between the two hosts, facing Bhishma, Drona, and all the rulers of the earth, and then spoke thus, "Behold, O Partha, all the Kurus gathered together!"
26) Then saw Partha stationed there in both the armies, grandfathers, fathers- in-law, and uncles, brothers and cousins, his own and their sons and grandsons, and comrades, teachers, and other friends

as well.
27) Then, he, the son of Kunti, seeing all those kinsmen stationed in their ranks, spoke thus sorrowfully, filled with deep compassion.

Arjuna said:
28-29) Seeing, O Krishna, these my kinsmen gathered here eager for fight, my limbs fail me, and my mouth is parched up. I shiver all over, and my hair stands on end. The bow Gandiva slips from my hand, and my skin burns.
30) Neither, O Keshava, can I stand upright. My mind is in a whirl. And I see adverse omens.
31) Neither, O Krishna, do I see any good in killing these my own people in battle. I desire neither victory nor empire, nor yet pleasure.
32-34) Of what avail is dominion to us, of what avail are pleasures and even life, if these, O Govinda! for whose sake it is desired that empire, enjoyment, and pleasure should be ours, themselves stand here in battle, having renouncedlife and wealth–teachers, uncles, sons, and also grandfathers, maternal uncles, fathers-in-law, grand sons, brothers-in-law, besides other kinsmen.
35) Even tough these were to kill me, O slayer of Madhu, I could not wish to kill them–not even for the sake of dominion over the three worlds, how much less for the sake of the earth!
36) What pleasure indeed could be ours, O Janardana, from killing these sons of Dhritarashtra? Sin only could take hold of us by the slaying of these felons.
37) Therefore we ought not to kill our kindred, the sons of Dhritarashtra. For how could we, O Madhava, gain happiness by the slaying of our own kinsmen?
38-39) Though these, with understanding overpowered by greed, see no evil due to decay of families, and no sin in hostility to friends, why should we O Janaradana, who see clearly the evil due to the decay of families, not turn away from this sin?
40) On the decay of a family the immemorial religious rites of that family die out. On the destruction of spirituality, impiety further overwhelms the whole of the family.
41) On the prevalence of impiety, O Krishna, the women of the family become corrupt; and women being corrupted, there arises, O

Varshneya, intermingling of castes.
42) Admixture of castes, indeed is for the hell of the family and the destroyers of the family; their ancestors fall, deprived of the offerings of rice-ball and water.
43) By these misdeeds of the destroyers of the family, bringing about confusion of castes, are the immemorial religious rites of the caste and the family destroyed.
44) We have heard, O Janardana, that dwelling in hell is inevitable for those men in whose families religious practices have been destroyed.
45) Alas, we are involved in a great sin, in that we are prepared to slay our kinsmen, out of greed for the pleasures of a kingdom!
46) Verily, if the sons of Dhritarashtra, weapons in hand, were to slay me, unresisting and unarmed, in the battle, that would be better for me.

Sanjaya said:
47) Speaking thus in the midst of the battle-field, Arjuna, casting away his bow and arrows, sank down on the seat of his chariot, with his mind distressed with sorrow.

Chapter Two
The Way of Knowledge

Sanjaya said:
1) To him who was thus overwhelmed with pity and sorrowing, and whose eyes were dimmed with tears, Madhusudana spoke these words.

The Blessed Lord said:
2) In such a crisis, whence comes upon you, O Arjuna, this dejection, un- Arya-like, disgraceful, and contrary to the attainment of heaven?
3) Yield not to unmanliness, O son of Pritha! Ill does it become you. Cast off this mean faintheartedness and arise, O scorcher of your enemies!

Arjuna said:
4) But how can I, in battle, O slayer of Madhu, fight with arrows against Bhishma and Drona, who are rather worthy to be worshipped, O destroyer of foes!
5) Surely it would be better even to eat the bread of beggary in this life than to slay these great-souled masters. But if I kill them, even in this world, all my enjoyment of wealth and desires will be stained with blood.
6) And indeed I can scarcely tell which will be better, that we should conquer them, or that they should conquer us. The very sons of Dhritarashtra–after slaying whom we should not care to live–stand facing us.
7) With my nature overpowered by weak commiseration, with a mind in confusion about duty, I supplicate You. Say decided what is good for me. I am Your disciple. Instruct me who have taken refuge in You.
8) I do not see anything to remove this sorrow which blasts my senses, even were I to obtain unrivalled and flourishing dominion over the earth, and mastery over the gods.

Sanjaya said:

9) Having spoken thus to the Lord of the senses, Gudakesha, the scorcher of foes, said to Govinda, "I shall not fight," and became silent.
10) To him who was sorrowing in the midst of the two armies, Hrishikesha, as if smiling, O descendant of Bharata, spoke these words.

The Blessed Lord said:
11) You have been mourning for them who should not be mourned for. Yet you speak words of wisdom. The [truly] wise grieve neither for the living nor for the dead.
12) It is not that I have never existed, nor you, nor these kings. Nor is it that we shall cease to exist in the future.
13) As are childhood, youth, and old age, in this body, to the embodied soul, so also is the attaining of another body. Calm souls are not deluded thereat.
14) Notions of heat and cold, of pain and pleasure, are born, O son of Kunti, only of the contact of the senses with their objects. They have a beginning and an end. They are impermanent in their nature. Bear them patiently, O descendant of Bharata.
15) That calm man who is the same in pain and pleasure, whom these cannot disturb, alone is able, O great amongst men, to attain to immortality.
16) The unreal never is. The real never is not. Men possessed of the knowledge of the Truth fully know both these.
17) That by which all this is pervaded–That know for certain to be indestructible. None has the power to destroy this Immutable.
18) Of this indwelling self–the ever-changeless, the indestructible, the illimitable–these bodies are said to have an end. Fight, therefore, O descendant of Bharata.
19) He who takes the self to be the slayer, and he who takes it to be the slain, neither of these knows. It does not slay, nor is it slain.
20) This is never born, nor does it die. It is not that, not having been, it again comes into being. [Or according to another view: It is not that having been, it again ceases to be.] This is unborn, eternal, changeless, ever-itself. It is not killed when the body is killed.
21) He that knows this to be indestructible, changeless, without

birth, and immutable, how is he, O son of Pritha, to slay or cause another to slay?

22) Even as a man casts off worn-out clothes, and puts on others which are new, so the embodied casts off worn-out bodies, and enters into others which are new.

23) This [self], weapons cut not; this, fire burns not; this, water wets not; and this, wind dries not.

24) This self cannot be cut, nor burnt, nor wetted, nor dried. Changeless, all-pervading, unmoving, immovable, the self is eternal.

25) This [self] is said to be unmanifested, unthinkable, and unchangeable. Therefore, knowing this to be such, you ought not to mourn.

26) But if you should take this to have constant birth and death, even in that case, O mighty-armed, you ought not to mourn for this.

27) Of that which is born, death is certain; of that which is dead, birth is certain. Over the unavoidable, therefore, you ought not to grieve.

28) All beings are unmanifested in their beginning, O Bharata, manifested in their middle state, and unmanifested again in their end. What is there then to grieve about?

29) Some look upon the self as marvelous. Others speak of it as wonderful. Others again hear of it as a wonder. And still others, though hearing, do not understand it at all.

30) This, the indweller in the bodies of all, is ever indestructible, O descendant of Bharata. Therefore you ought not to mourn for any creature.

31) Looking at your own dharma, also, you ought not to waver, for there is nothing higher for a kshatriya than a righteous war.

32) Fortunate certainly are the kshatriyas, O son of Pritha, who are called to fight in such a battle that comes unsought as an open gate to heaven.

33) But if you refuse to engage in this righteous warfare, then forfeiting your own dharma and honor, you shall incur sin.

34) The world also will ever hold you in reprobation. To the honored, disrepute is surely worse than death.

35) The great chariot-warriors will believe that you have withdrawn from the battle through fear. And you will be lightly esteemed by them who have thought much of you.

36) your enemies also, cavilling at your great prowess, will say of you things that are not to be uttered. What could be more intolerable than this?

37) Dying you gain heaven; conquering you enjoy the earth. Therefore, O son of Kunti, arise, resolved to fight

38) Having made pain and pleasure, gain and loss, conquest and defeat, the same, engage then in battle. So shall you incur no sin.

39) The wisdom of self-realization has been declared unto you. Hearken now to the wisdom of yoga, endued with which, O son of Pritha, you shall break through the bonds of karma.

40) In this, there is no waste of the unfinished attempt, nor is there production of contrary results. Even very little of this dharma protects from the great terror.

41) In this, O scion of Kuru, there is but a single one-pointed determination. The purposes of the undecided are innumerable and many-branching.

42-44) O Partha, no set determination is formed in the minds of those that are deeply attached to pleasure and power, and whose discrimination is stolen away by the flowery words of the unwise, who are full of desires and look upon heaven as their highest goal and who, taking pleasure in the panegyric words of the Vedas, declare that there is nothing else. Their flowery words are exuberant with various specific rites as the means to pleasure and power and are the causes of [new] births as the result of their works [performed with desire].

45) The Vedas deal with the three gunas. Be free, O Arjuna, from the triad of the gunas, free from the pairs of opposites, ever-balanced, free from [the thought of] getting and keeping, and established in the self.

46) To the Brahmin who has known the self, all the Vedas are of so much use as a reservoir is, when there is a flood everywhere.

47) Your right is to work only; but never to the fruits thereof. Be not the producer of the fruits of [your] actions; neither let your attachment be towards inaction.

48) Being steadfast in yoga, O Dhananjaya, perform actions, abandoning attachment, remaining unconcerned as regards success and failure. This evenness of mind [in regard to success and failure] is known as yoga.

49) Word [with desire] is verily far inferior to that performed with the mind undisturbed by thoughts of results. O Dhananjaya, seek refuge in this evenness of mind. Wretched are they who act for results.

50) Endued with this evenness of mind, one frees oneself in this life, alike from vice and virtue. Devote yourself, therefore, to this yoga. Yoga is the very dexterity of work.

51) The wise, possessed of this evenness of mind, abandoning the fruits of their actions, freed for ever from the fetters of birth, go to that state which is beyond all evil.

52) When your intellect crosses beyond the taint of illusion, then shall you attain to indifference, regarding things heard and things yet to be heard.

53) When your intellect, tossed about by the conflict of opinions, has become immovable and firmly established in the self, then you shall attain self-realization.

Arjuna said:

54) What, O Keshava, is the description of the man of steady wisdom, merged in samadhi? How [on the other hand] does the man of steady wisdom speak, how sit, how walk?

The Blessed Lord said:

55) When a man completely casts away, O Partha, all the desires of the mind, satisfied in the self alone by the self, then is he said to be one of steady wisdom.

56) He whose mind is not shaken by adversity, who does not hanker after happiness, who has become free from affection, fear, and wrath, is indeed the muni of steady wisdom.

57) He who is everywhere unattached, not pleased at receiving good, nor vexed at evil, his wisdom is fixed.

58) When also, like the tortoise withdrawing its limbs, he can completely withdraw the senses from their objects, then his wisdom

becomes steady.

59) Objects fall away from the abstinent man, leaving the longing behind. But his longing also ceases, who see the Supreme.

60) The turbulent senses, O son of Kunti, do violently snatch away the mind of even a wise man, striving after perfection.

61) The steadfast, having controlled them all, sits focussed on Me as the Supreme. His wisdom is steady, whose senses are under control.

62) Thinking of objects, attachment to them is formed in a man. From attachment longing, and from longing anger grows.

63) From anger comes delusion, and from delusion loss of memory. From loss of memory comes the ruin of discrimination, and from the ruin of discrimination he perishes.

64) But the self-controlled man, moving among objects with senses under restraint, and free from attraction and aversion, attains to tranquillity.

65) In tranquillity, all sorrow is destroyed. For the intellect of him, who is tranquil-minded, is soon established in firmness.

66) No knowledge [of the self] has the unsteady. Nor has he meditation. To the unmeditative there is no peace. And how can one without peace have happiness?

67) For, the mind, which follows in the wake of the wandering senses, carries away his discrimination, as a wind [carries away from its course] a boat on the waters.

68) Therefore, O mighty-armed, his knowledge is steady, whose senses are completely restrained from their objects.

69) That which is night to all beings, in that the self-controlled man wakes. This in which all being wake, is night to the self-seeing muni.

70) As into the ocean–brimful, and still–flow the waters, even so the muni into whom enter all desires, he, and not the desirer of desires, attains to peace.

71) That man who lives devoid of longing, abandoning all desires, without the sense of "I" and "mine," he attains to peace.

72) This is to have one's being in Brahma, O son of Pritha. None, attaining to this, becomes deluded. Being established therein, even at the end of life, a man attains to oneness with Brahman.

Chapter Three
The Way of Action

Arjuna said:
1) If, O Janardana, according to You, knowledge is superior to action, why then, O Keshava, do You engage me in this terrible action?
2) With these seemingly conflicting words You are, as it were, bewildering my understanding. Tell me that one thing for certain by which I can attain to the highest.

The Blessed Lord said:
3) In the beginning [of creation], O sinless one, the twofold path of devotion was given by Me to this world: the path of knowledge for the meditating, the path of work for the active.
4) By non-performance of work none reaches worklessness; by merely giving up action no one attains to perfection.
5) Verily none can ever rest for even an instant without performing action; for all are made to act, helplessly indeed, by the gunas, born of Prakriti.
6) He who, restraining the organs of action, sit revolving in the mind thought regarding objects of sense, he, of deluded understanding, is called a hypocrite.
7) But, O Arjuna, he who, controlling by the senses by the mind, unattached, directs his organs of action to the path of work, excels.
8) Do you perform obligatory action; for action is superior to inaction; and even the bare maintenance of your body would not be possible if you are inactive.
9) The world is bound by actions other than those performed for the sake of yajna; do you, therefore, O son of Kunti, perform action for yajna alone, devoid of attachment.
10) The Prajapati, having in the beginning created mankind together with yajna, said, "By this shall you multiply: this shall be the milk cow of your desire."
11) "Cherish the devas with this, and may those devas cherish you: thus cherishing one another, you shall gain the highest good.

12) "The devas, cherished by yajna, will give you desired-for-objects." So, he who enjoys objects given by the devas without offering [in return] to them, is verily a thief.

13) The good, eating the remnants of yajna, are freed from all sins: but those who cook food [only] for themselves, those sinful ones eat sin.

14) From food come forth beings: from rain food is produced: from yajna arises rain; and yajna is born of karma.

15) Know karma to have risen from the Veda, and the Veda from the Imperishable. Therefore the all-pervading Veda is ever centered in yajna.

16) He who here follows not the wheel thus set revolving, living in sin, and satisfied in the senses, O son of Pritha–he lives in vain.

17) But the man who is devoted to the self, and is satisfied with the self, and content in the self alone, has no obligatory duty.

18) He has no object in this world [to gain] by doing [an action], nor [does he incur any loss] by non-performance of action–nor has he [need of] depending on any being for any object.

19) Therefore, do you always perform actions which are obligatory, without attachment; by performing action without attachment, one attains to the highest.

20) Verily by action alone, Janaka and others attained perfection; also, simply with the view for the guidance of men, you should perform action.

21) Whatsoever the superior person does, that is followed by others. What he demonstrates by action, that people follow.

22) I have, O son of Pritha, no duty, nothing that I have not gained; and nothing that I have to gain in the three worlds; yet, I continue in action.

23) If ever I did not continue in work without relaxation, O son of Pritha, men would, in every way, follow in My wake.

24) If I did not do work, these worlds would perish. I should be the cause of the admixture [of races], and I should ruin these beings.

25) As do the unwise, attached to work, act, so should the wise act, O descendant of Bharata, [but] without attachment, desirous of the guidance of the world.

26) One should not unsettle the understanding of the ignorant,

attached to action; the wise one, [himself] steadily acting, should engage [the ignorant] in all work.

27) The gunas of Prakriti perform all action. With the understanding deluded by egoism, man thinks, “I am the doer.”

28) But one, with true insight into the domains of guna and karma, knowing that gunas as senses merely rest on gunas as objects, does not become attached.

29) Men of perfect knowledge should not unsettle [the understanding of] people of dull wit and imperfect knowledge, who deluded by the gunas of Prakriti attach [themselves] to the functions of the gunas.

30) Renouncing all actions to Me, with mind centered on the self, getting rid of hope and selfishness, fight–free from [mental] fever.

31) Those men who constantly practice this teaching of Mine, full of shraddha and without cavilling, they too are freed from work.

32) But those who decrying this teaching of Mine do not practice [it], deluded in all knowledge, and devoid of discrimination, know them to be ruined.

33) Even a wise man acts in accordance with his own nature; beings follow nature: what can restraint to?

34) Attachment and aversion of the senses for their respective objects are natural: let none come under their sway: they are his foes.

35) Better is one’s own dharma, [though] imperfect, than the dharma of another well-performed. Better is death in one’s own dharma: the dharma of another is fraught with fear.

Arjuna said:

36) But impelled by what does man commit sin, though against his wishes, O Varshneya, constrained as it were by force?

The Blessed Lord said:

37) it is desire–it is anger, born of the Rajo-guna: of great craving, and of great sin; know this as the foe here [in this world].

38) As fire is enveloped by smoke, as a mirror by dust, as an embryo by the secundine, so is it covered by that.

39) Knowledge is covered by this, the constant foe of the wise, O son of Kunti, the unappeasable fire of desire.

40) The senses, the mind, and the intellect are said to be its abode: through these, it deludes the embodied by veiling his wisdom.

41) Therefore, O Bull of the Bharata race, controlling the senses at the outset, kill it–the sinful,the destroyer of knowledge and realization.

42) The senses are said to be superior [to the body]; the mind is superior to the senses; the intellect is superior to the mind; and that which is superior to the intellect is he [the atman].

43) Thus, knowing Him who is superior to the intellect, and restraining the self by the self, destroy, O mighty-armed, that enemy, the unseizable foe, desire.

Chapter Four
The Way of Renunciation of Action in Knowledge

The Blessed Lord said:
1) I told this imperishable yoga to Vivasvat; Vivasvat told it to Manu; [and] Manu told it to Ikshvaku:
2) Thus handed down in regular succession, the royal sages knew it. This yoga, by long lapse of time, declined in this world, O scorcher of foes.
3) I have this day told you that same ancient yoga, [for] you are My devotee, and My friend, and this secret is profound indeed.

Arjuna said:
4) Later was Your birth, and that if Vivasvat prior; how then should I understand that You told this in the beginning?

The Blessed Lord said:
5) Many are the births that have been passed by Me and you, O Arjuna. I know them all, while you know not, O scorcher of foes.
6) Though I am unborn, of changeless nature and Lord of beings, yet subjugating My Prakriti, I come into being by My own Maya.
7) Whenever, O descendant of Bharata, there is decline of dharma, and rise of Adharma, then I body Myself forth.
8) For the protection of the good, for the destruction of the wicked, and for the establishment of dharma, I come into being.
9) He who thus knows, in true light, My divine birth and action, leaving the body, is not born again: he attains to Me, O Arjuna.
10) Freed from attachment, fear, and anger, absorbed in Me, taking refuge in Me, purified by the fire of knowledge, many have attained My Being.
11) In whatever way men worship Me, in the same way do I fulfil their desires; [it is] My path, O son of Pritha, [that] men tread, in all ways.
12) Longing for success in action, in this world, [men] worship the gods. Because success, resulting from action, is quickly attained in the human world.

13) The fourfold caste was created by Me, by the differentiation of guna and karma. Though I am the author thereof, know Me to be the non-doer, and changeless.

14) Actions do not taint Me, nor have I any thirst for the result of action. He who knows Me thus is not fettered by action.

15) Knowing thus, the ancient seekers after freedom also performed action. Do you, therefore, perform action, as did the ancients in olden times.

16) Even sages are bewildered as to what is action and what is inaction. I shall, therefore, tell you what action is, by knowing which you will be freed from evil.

17) For verily, [the true nature] even of action [enjoined by the shastras] should be known, as also [that] of forbidden action, and of inaction: the nature of karma is impenetrable.

18) He who sees inaction in action, and action in inaction is intelligent among men, he is a yogi and a doer of all action.

19) Whose undertakings are all devoid of plan and desire for results, and whose actions are burnt by the fire of knowledge, him the sages call wise.

20) Forsaking the clinging to fruits of action, ever satisfied, depending on nothing, though engaged in action, he does not do anything.

21) Without hope, the body and mind controlled, and all possessions relinquished, he does not suffer any evil consequences, by doing mere bodily action.

22) Content with what comes to him without effort, unaffected by the pairs of opposites, free from envy, even-minded in success and failure, though acting, he is not bound.

23) Devoid of attachment, liberated, with mind centered in knowledge, performing work for yajna alone, his whole karma dissolves away.

24) The process is Brahman, the clarified butter is Brahman, offered by Brahman in the fire of Brahman; by seeing Brahman in action, he reaches Brahman alone.

25) Some yogis perform sacrifices to devas alone, while others offer the self as sacrifice by the self in the fire of Brahman alone.

26) Some again offer hearing and other senses as sacrifice in the

fire of control, while others offer sound and other sense-objects as sacrifice in the fire of the senses.

27) Some again offer all the actions of senses and the functions of the vital energy, as sacrifice in the fire of control in self, kindled by knowledge.

28) Others again offer wealth, austerity, and yoga, as sacrifice, while others, of self-restraint and rigid vows, offer study of the scriptures and knowledge, as sacrifice.

29) Yet some offer as sacrifice, the outgoing into the incoming breath, and the incoming into the outgoing, stopping the courses of the incoming and outgoing breaths, constantly practicing the regulation of the vital energy; while others yet of regulated food, offer in the pranas the functions thereof.

30-31) All of these are knowers of yajna, having their sins consumed by yajna, and eating of the nectar–the remnant of yajna–they go to the Eternal Brahman. [Even] this world is not for the non-performer of yajna, how then another, O best of the Kurus?

32) Various yajnas, like the above, are strewn in the storehouse of the Veda. Know them all to be born of action; and thus knowing, you shall be free.

33) Knowledge-sacrifice, O scorcher of foes, is superior to sacrifice [performed] with [material] objects. All action in its entirety, O Partha, attains its consummation in knowledge.

34) Know that, by prostrating yourself, by questions, and by service; the wise, those who have realized the Truth, will instruct you in that knowledge.

35) Knowing which, you shall not, O Pandava, again get deluded like this, and by which you shall see the whole of creation in [your] self and in Me.

36) Even if you are the most sinful among all the sinful, yet by the raft of knowledge alone you shall go across all sin.

37) As blazing fire reduces wood into ashes, so, O Arjuna, does the fire of knowledge reduce all karma to ashes.

38) Verily there exists nothing in this world purifying like knowledge. In good time, having reached perfection in yoga, one realizes that oneself in one's own heart.

39) The man with shraddha, the devoted, the master of one's

senses, attains [this] knowledge. Having attained knowledge one goes at once to the Supreme Peace.

40) The ignorant, the man without shraddha, the doubting self, goes to destruction. The doubting self has neither this world, nor the next, nor happiness.

41) With work renounced by yoga and doubts rent asunder by knowledge, O Dhananjaya, actions do not bind him who is poised in the self.

42) Therefore, cutting with the sword of knowledge, this doubt about the self, born of ignorance, residing in your heart, take refuge in yoga. Arise, O Bharata!

Chapter Five
The Way of Renunciation

Arjuna said:
1) Renunciation of action, O Krishna, you commend, and again, its performance. Which is the better one of these? Do You tell me decisively.

The Blessed Lord said:
2) Both renunciation and performance of action lead to freedom: of these, performance of action is superior to the renunciation of action.
3) He should be known a constant sannyasi, who neither likes nor dislikes: for, free from the pairs of opposites, O mighty-armed, he is easily set free from bondage.
4) Children, not the wise, speak of knowledge and performance of action as distinct. He who truly lives in one, gains the fruits of both.
5) The plane which is reached by the jnanis is also reached by the karma yogis. He who sees knowledge and performance of action as one alone sees.
6) Renunciation of action, O mighty-armed, is hard to attain to without performance of action; the man of meditation, purified by devotion to action, quickly goes to Brahman.
7) With the mind purified by devotion to performance of action, and the body conquered, and senses subdues, one who realizes one's self as the self in all beings, though acting, is not tainted.
8-9) The knower of Truth, [being] centered [in the self] should think, "I do nothing at all"–though seeing, hearing, touching, smelling, eating, going, sleeping, breathing, speaking, letting go, holding, opening, and closing the eyes–convinced that it is the senses that move among sense objects.
10) He who does actions forsaking attachment, resigning them to Brahman, is not soiled by evil, like unto a lotus leaf by water.
11) Devotees in the path of work perform action, only with body, mind, senses, and intellect, forsaking attachment, for the purification of the heart.

12) The well-poised, forsaking the fruit of action, attains peace, born of steadfastness; the unbalanced one, led by desire, is bound by being attached to the fruit (of action).

13) The subduer (of the senses), having renounced all actions by discrimination, rests happily in the city of the nine gates, neither acting, nor causing (others) to act.

14) Neither agency, nor actions does the Lord create for the world, nor (does he bring about) the union with the fruit of action. It is universal ignorance that does (it all).

15) The Omnipresent takes note of the merit or demerit of none. Knowledge is enveloped in ignorance, hence do beings get deluded.

16) But whose ignorance is destroyed by the knowledge of self– that knowledge of theirs, like the sun, reveals the Supreme (Brahman).

17) Those who have their intellect absorbed in That, whose self is That, whose steadfastness is in That, whose consummation is That, their impurities cleansed by knowledge, they attain to non-return (Moksha).

18) The knowers of the self look with an equal eye on a Brahmana endowed with learning and humility, a cow, an elephant, a dog, and a pariah.

19) (Relative) existence has been conquered by them, even in this world, whose mind rests in evenness, since Brahman is even and is without imperfection: therefore they indeed rest in Brahman.

20) Resting in Brahman, with intellect steady, and without delusion, the knower of Brahman neither rejoiceth on receiving what is pleasant, nor grieveth on receiving what is unpleasant.

21) With the heart unattached to external objects, he realizes the joy that is in the self. With the heart devoted to the meditation of Brahman, he attains undecaying happiness.

22) Since enjoyments that are contact-born are parents of misery alone, and with beginning and end, O son of Kunti, a wise man does not seek pleasure in them.

23) He who can withstand in this world, before the liberation from the body, the impulse arising from lust and anger, he is steadfast (in yoga), he is a happy man.

24) Whose happiness is within, whose relaxation is within,

whose light is within, that Yogi alone, becoming Brahman, gains absolute freedom.

25) With imperfections exhausted, doubts dispelled, senses controlled, engaged in the good of all beings, the Rishis obtain absolute freedom.

26) Released from lust and anger, the heart controlled, the self realized, absolute freedom is for such Sannyasins, both here and hereafter.

27-28) Shutting out external objects; steadying the eyes between the eyebrows; restricting the even currents of prana and apana inside the nostrils; the senses, mind, and intellect controlled; with Moksha as the supreme goal; freed from desire, fear, and anger: such a man of moderation is verily free for ever.

29) Knowing Me as the dispenser of yajnas and asceticisms, as the Great Lord of all worlds, as the friend of all beings, he attains Peace.

Chapter Six
The Way of Meditation

The Blessed Lord said:

1) He who performs his bounden duty without leaning to the fruit of action–he is a renouncer of action as well as of steadfast mind: not he who is without fire, nor he who is without action.

2) Know that to be devotion to action, which is called renunciation, O Pandava, for none becomes a devotee to action without forsaking Sankalpa.

3) For the man of meditation wishing to attain purification of heart leading to concentration, work is said to be the way: For him, when he has attained such (concentration), inaction is said to be the way.

4) Verily, when there is no attachment, either to sense-objects, or to actions, having renounced all Sankalpas, then is one said to have attained concentration.

5) A man should uplift himself by his own self, so let him not weaken this self. For this self is the friend of oneself, and this self is the enemy of oneself.

6) The self (the active part of our nature) is the friend of the self, for him who has conquered himself by this self. But to the unconquered self, this self is inimical, (and behaves) like (an external) foe.

7) To the self-controlled and serene, the Supreme Self is the object of constant realization, in cold and heat, pleasure and pain, as well as in honour and dishonour.

8) Whose heart is filled with satisfaction by wisdom and realization, and is changeless, whose senses are conquered, and to whom a lump of earth, stone, and gold are the same: that Yogi is called steadfast.

9) He attains excellence who looks with equal regard upon well-wishers, friends, foes, neutrals, arbiters, the hateful, the relatives, and upon the righteous and the unrighteous alike.

10) The yogi should constantly practise concentration of the heart, retiring into solitude, alone, with the mind and body subdued, and free from hope and possession.

11) Having established in a cleanly spot his seat, firm, neither too high nor too low, made of a cloth, a skin, and Kusha-grass, arranged in consecution.
12) There, seated on that seat, making the mind one-pointed and subduing the action of the imaging faculty and the senses, let him practise yoga for the purification of the heart.
13) Let him firmly hold his body, head, and neck erect and still, (with the eye-balls fixed, as if) gazing at the tip of his nose, and not looking around.
14) With the heart serene and fearless, firm in the vow of a Brahmachari, with the mind controlled, and ever thinking of Me, let his sit (in yoga) having Me as his supreme goal.
15) Thus always keeping the mind steadfast, the Yogi of subdued mind attains the peace residing in Me–the peace which culminates in Nirvana (Moksha).
16) (Success in) yoga is not for him who eats too much or too little–nor, O Arjuna, for him who sleeps too much or too little.
17) To him who is temperate in eating and recreation, in his effort for work, and in sleep and wakefulness, yoga becomes the destroyer of misery.
18) When the completely controlled mind rests serenely in the self alone, free from longing after all desires, then is one called steadfast (in the self).
19) "As a lamp in a spot sheltered from the wind does not flicker"–even such has been the simile used for a Yogi of subdued mind, practising concentration in the self.
20-23) When the mind, absolutely restrained by the practice of concentration, attains quietude, and when seeing the self by the self, one is satisfied in his own self; when he feels that infinite bliss–which is perceived by the (purified) intellect and which transcends the senses, and established wherein he never departs from his real state; and having obtained which, regards no other acquisition superior to that, and where established, he is not moved even by heavy sorrow; let that be known as the state, called by the name of yoga–a state of severance from the contact of pain. This yoga should be practised with perseverance, undisturbed by depression of heart.
24) Abandoning without reserve all desires born of Sankalpa, and completely restraining, by the mind alone, the whole group of

senses from their objects in all directions;
25) With the intellect set in patience, with the mind fastened on the self, let him attain quietude by degrees: let him not think of anything.
26) Through wahtever reason the restless, unsteady mind wanders away, let him, curbing it from that, bring it under the subjugation of the self alone.
27) Verily, the supreme bliss comes to that Yogi, of perfectly tranquil mind, with passions quieted, Brahman-become, and freed from taint.
28) The Yogi, freed from tain (of good and evil), constantly engaging the mind thus, with ease attains the infinite bliss of contact with Brahman.
29) With the heart concentrated by yoga, with the eye of evenness for all things, he beholds the self in all beings and all beings in the self.
30) He who sees Me in all things, and sees all things in Me, he never becomes separated from Me, nor do I become separated from him.
31) Hw who being established in unity, worships Me, who am dwelling in all beings, whatever his mode of life, that yogi abides in Me.
32) He who judges of pleasure or pain everywhere, by the same standard as he applies to himself, that Yogi, O Arjuna, is regarded as the highest.

Arjuna said:
33) This yoga which has been taught by You, O slayer of Madhu, as characterized by evenness, I do not see (the possibility of) its lasting endurance, owing to restlessness (of the mind.)
34) Verily, the mind, O Krishna, is restless, turbulent, strong, and unyielding; I regard it quite as hard to achieve its control, as that of the wind.

The Blessed Lord said:
35) Without doubt, O mighty-armed, the mind is restless, and difficult to control; but through practice and renunciation, O son of Kunti, it may be governed.

36) Yoga is hard to be attained by one of uncontrolled self: such is My conviction; but the self-controlled, striving by right means can obtain it.

Arjuna said:
37) Though possess of shraddha but unable to control himself, with the mind wandering away from yoga, what end does one, failing to gain perfection in yoga, meet, O Krishna?
38) Does he not, fallen from both, perish, without support, like a rent cloud, O mighty-armed, deluded in the path of Brahman?
39) This doubt of mine, O Krishna, you should completely dispel; for it is not possible for any but you to dispel this doubt.

The Blessed Lord said:
40) Verily, O son of Pritha, there is destruction for him, neither here nor hereafter for, the doer of good, O my son, never comes to grief.
41) Having attained to the worlds of the righteous, and dwelling there for everlasting years, one falled from yoga reincarnates in the home of the pure and the prosperous.
42) Or else he is born into a family of wise yogis only; verily, a birth such as that is very rare to obtain in this world.
43) There he is united with the intelligence acquired in his former body, and strives more than before, for perfection, O son of the Kurus.
44) By that previous practice alone, he is borne on in spite of himself. Even the enquirer after yoga rises superior to the performer of Vedic actions
45) The Yogi, striving assiduously, purified of taint, gradually gaining perfection through many births, then reaches the highest goal.
46) The Yogi is regarded as superior to those who practice asceticism, also to those who have obtained wisdom (through the shastras). He is also superior tothe performers of action (enjoined in the Vedas). Therefore, be a Yogi, O Arjuna!
47) And of all Yogis, he who with the inner self merged in Me, with shraddha devotes himself to Me, is considered by Me the most steadfast.

Chapter Seven
The Way of Knowledge With Realization

The Blessed Lord said:

1) With the mind intent on me, O son of Pritha, taking refuge in Me, and practicing yoga, how you shall without doubt know Me fully, that do you hear.

2) I shall tell you in full, of knowledge, speculative and practical, knowing which, nothing more here remains to be know.

3) One, perchance, in thousands of men, strives for perfection; and one perchance, among the blessed ones, striving thus, knows Me in reality.

4) Bhumi (earth, Ap (water), Anala (fire), Vayu (air), Kha (ether), intellect, and egoism: thus is My Prakriti divided eightfold.

5) This is the lower (Prakriti). But different from it, know, O mighty-armed, My higher Prakriti–the principle of self-consciousness, by which this universe is sustained.

6) Know that these (two Prakritis) are the womb of all beings, I am the origin and dissolution of the whole universe.

7) Beyond Me, O Dhananjaya, there is naught. All this is strung in Me, as a row of jewels on a thread.

8) I am the sapidity in water, O son of Kunti; I, the radiance in the moon and the sun; I am the Om in all the Vedas, sound in Akasha, and manhood in men.

9) I am the sweet fragrance in earth, and the brilliance in fire am I; the life in all beings, and the austerity am I in ascetics.

10) Know me, O son of Pritha, as the eternal seed of all beings. I am the intellect of the intelligent, and the heroism of the heroic.

11) Of the strong, I am the strength devoid of desire and attachment. I am, O bull among the Bharatas, desire in beings, unopposed to dharma.

12) And whatever states pertaining to sattwa, and those pertaining to rajas, and to tamas, know them to proceed from Me alone; still I am not in them, but they are in Me.

13) Deluded by these states, the modifications of the three gunas (of Prakriti), all this world does not know Me who is beyond them, and immutable.

14) Verily, this divine illusion of Mine, constituted of the gunas, is difficult to cross over; those who devote themselves to Me alone, cross over this illusion.

15) They do not devote themselves to Me–the evil-doers, the deluded, the lowest of men, deprived of discrimination by Maya, and following the way of the Asuras.

16) Four kinds of virtuous men worship Me, O Arjuna–the distressed, the seeker of knowledge, the seeker of enjoyment, and the wise, O bull among the Bharatas.

17) Of them, the wise man, ever-steadfast, (and fired) with devotion to the One, excels; for supremely dear am I to the wise, and he is dear to Me.

18) Noble indeed are they all, but the wise man I regard as My very self; for with the mind steadfast, he is established in Me alone, as the supreme goal.

19) At the end of many births, the man of wisdom takes refuge in Me, realizing that all this is Vasudeva (the innermost self). Very rare is that great soul.

20) Others, again, deprived of discrimination by this or that desire, following this or that rite, devote themselves to other gods, led by their own natures.

21) Whatsoever form any devotee seeks to worship with shraddha–the shraddha of his do I make unwavering.

22) Endued with that shraddha, he engages in the worship of that, and from it, gains his desires–these being verily dispensed by Me alone.

23) But the fruit (accruing) to these men of little understanding is limited. The worshippers of the devas go to the devas; My devotees too come to me.

24) The foolish regard Me, the unmanifested, as come into manifestation, not knowing My supreme state–immutable and transcendental.

25) Veiled by the illusion born of the congress of the gunas, I am not manifest to all. This deluded world knows Me not–the Unborn, the Immutable.

26) I know, O Arjuna, the beings of the whole past, and the present, and the future, but Me none knoweth.

27) By the delusion of the pairs of opposites, arising from desire and aversion, O descendant of Bharata, all beings fall into delusion at birth, O scorcher of foes.

28) Those men of virtuous deeds, whose sin has come to an end–they, freed from the delusion of the pairs of opposites, worship Me with firm resolve.

29) Those who strive for freedom from old age and death, taking refuge in Me–they know Brahman, the whole of Adhyatma, and karma in its entirety.

30) Those who know Me with the Adhibhuta, the Adhidaiva, and the Adhiyajna, (continue to) know Me even at the time of death, steadfast in mind.

Chapter Eight
The Way to the Imperishable Brahman

Arjuna said:
1) What is the Brahman, what is Adhyatma, what is karma, O best of Purushas? What is called Adhibhuta, and what Adhidaiva?
2) Who, and in what way, is Adhiyajna here in this body, O destroyer of Madhu? And how are You known at the time of death, by the self-controlled?

The Blessed Lord said:
3) The Imperishable is the Supreme Brahman. Its dwelling in each individual body is called Adhyatma; the offering in sacrifice which causes the genesis and support of beings, is called karma.
4) The perishable adjunct is the Adhibhuta, and the Indweller is the Adhidaivata; I alone am the Adhiyajna here in this body, O best of the embodied.
5) And he who at the time of death, meditating on Me alone, goes forth, leaving the body, attains My Being: there is no doubt about this.
6) Remembering whatever object, at the end, he leaves the body, that alone is reached by him, O son of Kunti, (because) of his constant thought of that object.
7) Therefore, at all times, constantly remember Me, and fight. With mind and intellect absorbed in Me, you shall doubtless come to Me.
8) With the mind not moving towards anything else, made steadfast by the method of habitual meditation, and dwelling on the Supreme, Resplendent Purusha, O son of Pritha, one goes to Him.
9-10) The Omniscient, the Ancient, the Overruler, minuter than an atom, the Sustainer of all, of form inconceivable, self-luminous like the sun, and beyond the darkness of Maya–he who meditates on Him thus, at the time of death, full of devotion, with the mind unmoving, and also by the power of yoga, fixing the whole prana betwixt the eyebrows, he goes to that Supreme, Resplendent Purusha.
11) What the knowers of the Veda speak of as Imperishable, what the self- controlled (Sannyasis), freed from attachment enter, and

to gain which goal they live the life of a Brahmachari, that I shall declare unto thee in brief.

12-13) Controlling all the senses, confining the mind in the heart, drawing the prana into the head, occupied in the practice of concentration, uttering the one-syllabled "Om"–the Brahman, and meditating on Me–he who so departs, leaving the body, attains the Supreme Goal.

14) I am easily attainable by that ever-steadfast Yogi who remembers Me constantly and daily, with a single mind, O son of Pritha.

15) Reaching the highest perfection and having attained Me, the great-souled ones are no more subject to rebirth–which is the home of pain, and ephemeral.

16) All the worlds, O Arjuna, including the realm of Brahma, are subject to return, but after attaining Me, O son of Kunti, there is no rebirth.

17) They who know (the true measure of) day and night, know the day of Brahma, which ends in a thousand Yugas, and the night which (also) ends in a thousand Yugas.

18) At the approach of (Brahma's) day, all manifestations proceed from the unmanifested state; at the approach of night, they merge verily into that alone, which is called the unmanifested.

19) The very same multitude of beings (that existed in the preceding day of Brahma), being born again and again, merge, in spite of themselves, O son of Pritha, (into the unmanifested), at the approach of night, and re-manifest at the approach of day.

20) But beyond this unmanifested, there is that other Unmanifested, Eternal Existence–That which is not destroyed at the destruction of all beings.

21) What has been called Unmanifested and Imperishable, has been described as the Goal Supreme. That is My highest state, having attained which, there is no return.

22) And that Supreme Purusha is attainable, O son of Pritha, by whole-souled devotion to Him alone, in Whom all beings dwell, and by Whom all this is pervaded.

23) Now I shall tell thee, O bull of the Bharatas, of the time (path) travelling in which, the Yogis return, (and again of that, tak-

ing which) they do not return.

24) Fire flame, daytime, the bright fortnight, the six months of the Northern passage of the sun–taking this path, the knowers of Brahman go to Brahman.

25) Smoke, night-time, the dark fortnight, the six months of the Southern passage of the sun–taking this path the Yogi, attaining the lunar light, returns.

26) Truly are these bright and dark paths of the world considered eternal: one leads to non-return; by the other, one returns.

27) No Yogi, O son of Pritha, is deluded after knowing these paths. Therefore, O Arjuna, be steadfast in yoga, at all times.

28) Whatever meritorious effect is declared (in the Scriptures) to accrue from (the study of) the Vedas, (the performance of) yajnas, (the practice of) austerities and gifts–above all this rises the Yogi, having known this, and attains to the primeval, supreme Abode.

Chapter Nine
The Way of the Kingly Knowledge and the Kingly Secret

The Blessed Lord said:

1) To thee, who dost not carp, verily shall I now declare this, the most profound knowledge, united with realization, having known which, you shall be free from evil (Samsara).

2) Of sciences, the highest; of profundities, the deepest; of purifiers, the supreme, is this; realizable by direct perception, endowed with (immense) merit, very easy to perform, and of an imperishable nature.

3) Persons without shraddha for this dharma, return, O scorcher of foes, without attaining Me, to the path of rebirth fraught with death.

4) All this world is pervaded by Me in My unmanifested form: all beings exist in Me, but I do not dwell in them.

5) Nor do beings exists in Me, (in reality), behold My divine yoga! Bringing forth and supporting the beings, My Self does not dwell in them.

6) As the mighty wind, moving always everywhere, rests ever in the Akasha, know that even so do all beings rest in Me.

7) At the end of a Kalpa, O son of Kunti, all beings go back to My Prakriti: at the beginning of (another) Kalpa, I send them forth again.

8) Animating My Prakriti, I project again and again this whole multitude of beings, helpless under the sway of Prakriti.

9) These acts do not bind Me, sitting as one neutral, unattached to them, O Dhananjaya.

10) By reason of My proximity, Prakriti produces all this, the moving and the unmoving; the world wheels round and round, O son of Kunti, because of this.

11) Unaware of My higher state, as the great Lord of being, fools disregard Me, dwelling in the human form.

12) Of vain hopes, of vain works, of vain knowledge, and senseless, they verily are possessed of the delusive nature of Rakshasas and Asuras.

13) But the great-souled ones, O son of Pritha, possessed of the Divine Prakriti, knowing Me to be the origin of beings and immutable, worship Me with a single mind.

14) Glorifying Me always and striving with firm resolve, bowing down to Me in devotion, always steadfast, they worship Me.

15) Others, too, sacrificing by the yajna of knowledge (I.e., seeing the self in all), worship Me the All-Formed, as one, as distinct, as manifold.

16) I am the Kratu, I the Yajna, I the Svadha, I the Aushadha, I the Mantra, I the Ajya, I the fire, and I the oblation.

17) I am the Father of this world–the Mother, the Sustainer, the Grandfather, the Purifier, the (one) thing to be known, (the syllable) Om, and also the Rik, Saman, and Yajus.

18) The Goal, the Supporter, the Lord, the Witness, the Abode, the Refuge, the Friend, the Origin, the Dissolution, the Substratum, the Storehouse, the Seed immutable.

19) (As the sun) I give heat; I withhold and send forth rain; I am immortality and also death; being and non-being am I, O Arjuna!

20) The knowers of the three Vedas, worshipping Me by yajna, drinking the Soma, and (thus) being purified from sin, pray for passage to heaven; reaching the holy world of the Lord of the devas, they enjoy in heaven the divine pleasures of the devas.

21) Having enjoyed the vast Svarga-world, they enter the mortal world, on the exhaustion of their merit: Thus, abiding by the injunctions of the three (Vedas), desiring desires, they (constantly) come and go.

22) Persons who, meditating on Me as non-separate, worship Me in all beings, to them thus ever zealously engaged, I carry what they lack and preserve what they already have.

23) Even those devotees, who endued with shraddha, worship other gods, they too worship Me alone, O son of Kunti, (but) by the wrong method

24) For I alone am the Enjoyer, and Lord of all yajnas; but because they do not know Me in reality, they return, (to the mortal world).

25) Votaries of the devas go to the devas' to the Pitris, go their votaries; to the Bhutas, go the Bhuta worshippers; My votaries too

come unto Me.

26) Whoever with devotion offers Me a leaf, a flower, a fruit, or water, that I accept–the devout gift of the pure-minded.

27) Whatever you do, whatever you eat, whatever you off in sacrifice, whatever you give away, whatever austerity ou practice, O son of Kunti, do that as an offering unto Me.

28) Thus shall you be freed from the bondages of actions, bearing good and evil results: with the heart steadfast in the yoga of renunciation, and liberated you shall come unto Me.

29) I am the same to all beings: to Me there is none hateful or dear. But those who worship Me with devotion, are in Me, and I too am in them.

30) If even a very wicked person worships Me, with devotion to none else, he should be regarded as good, for he has rightly resolved.

31) Soon does he become righteous, and attain eternal Peace, O son of Kunti; boldly can you proclaim, that My devotee is never destroyed.

32) For, taking refuge in Me, they also, O son of Pritha, who might be of inferior birth–women, Vaishyas, as well as Shudras–even they attain to the Supreme Goal.

33) What need to mention holy Brahmanas, and devoted Rajarshis! Having obtained this transient, joyless world, worship Me.

34) Fill your mind with Me, be My devotee, sacrifice unto Me, bow down to Me; thus having made your heart steadfast in Me, taking Me as the Supreme Goal, you shall come to Me.

Chapter Ten
Glimpses of the Divine Glory

The Blessed Lord said:

1) Again, O mighty-armed, listen to My supreme word, which I wishing your welfare, will tell thee who art delighted (to hear Me).

2) Neither the hosts of devas, nor the great Rishis, know My origin, for in every way I am the source of all the devas and the great Rishis.

3) He who knows Me, birthless and beginningless, the great Lord of worlds–he, among mortals, is undeluded, he is freed from all sins.

4-5) Intellect, knowledge, non-delusion, forbearance, truth, restraint of the external senses, calmness of heart, happiness, misery, birth, death, fear, as well as fearlessness, non-injury, evenness, contentment, austerity, benevolence, good name, (as well as) ill-fame–(these) different kinds of qualities of beings arise from Me alone.

6) The seven great Rishis as well as the four ancient manus, possessed of powers like Me (due to their thoughts being fixed on Me), were born of (My) mind; from them are these creatures in the world.

7) He who in reality knows these manifold manifestations of My being and (this) yoga power of Mine, becomes established in the unshakable yoga; there is no doubt about it.

8) I am the origin of all, from Me everything evolves–thus thinking, the wise worship Me with loving consciousness.

9) With their minds wholly in Me, with their senses absorbed in Me, enlightening one another, and always speaking of Me, they are satisfied and delighted.

10) To them, ever steadfast and serving Me with affection, I give that buddhi- yoga by which they come unto Me.

11) Out of mere compassion for them, I, abiding in their hearts, destroy the darkness (in them) born of ignorance, by the luminous lamp of knowledge.

Arjuna said:

12-13) The Supreme Brahman, the Supreme Abode, the Supreme

Purifier, are You. All the Rishis, the deva-Rishi Narada as well as Asita, Devala, and Vyasa have declared You as the Eternal, the self-luminous Purusha, the first Deva, Birthless, and All-pervading. So also you yourself say to me.

14) I regard all this that you say to me as true, O Keshava. Verily, O Bhagavan, neither the devas nor the Danavas know Your manifestation.

15) Verily, you yourself know yourself by yourself, O Supreme Purusha, O Source of being, O Lord of beings, O Deva of Devas, O Ruler of the World.

16) You should indeed speak, without reserve of Your divine attributes by which, filling all these worlds, you existest.

17) How shall I, O Yogi, meditate ever to know You? In what things, O Bhagavan, are you to be thought of by me?

18) Speak to me again in detail, O Janardana, of your yoga-powers and attributes; for I am never satiated in hearing the ambrosia (of Your speech).

The Blessed Lord said:

19) I shall speak to thee now, O best of the Kurus, of my divine attributes, according to their prominence; there is no end to the particulars of My manifestation.

20) I am the Self, O Gudakesha, existent in the heart of all beings; I am the beginning, the middle, and also the end of all beings.

21) Of the Adityas, I am Vishnu; of luminaries, the radiant Sun; of the winds, I am Marichi; of the asterisms, the Moon.

22) I am the Sama-Veda of the Vedas, and Vasava (Indra) of the gods; of the senses I am the mind and intelligence in living beings am I.

23) And of the Rudras I am Shankara; of the Yakshas and Rakshasas, the Lord of wealth (Kubera); of the Vasus I am Pavaka; and of mountains, Meru am I.

24) And of priests, O son of Pritha, know Me the chief, Brihaspati; of generals, I am Skanda; of bodies of water, I am the ocean.

25) Of the great Rishis I am Bhrigu; of words I am the one syllable "Om;" of yajnas I am the yajna of japa (silent repetition); of immovable things the Himalaya.

26) Of all trees (I am) the Ashvattha, and Narada of deva-Rishis; Chitraratha of Gandharvas am I, and the Muni Kapila of the perfected ones.

27) Know me among horses as Uchchaisshravas, Amrita-born; of lordly elephants Airavata, and of men the king.

28) Of weapons I am the thunderbolt, of cows I am Kamadhuk; I am the Kandarpa, the cause of offspring; of serpents I am Vasuki.

29) And Ananta of snakes I am, I am Varuna of water-beings; and Aryaman of Pitris I am, I am Yama of controllers.

30) And Prahlada am I of Diti's progeny, of measurers I am Time; and of beasts I am the lord of beasts [lion], and Garuda of birds.

31) Of purifiers I am the wind, Rama of warriors am I; of fishes I am the shark, of streams I am Jahnavi (the Ganga).

32) Of manifestations I am the beginning, the middle and also the end; of all knowledges I am the knowledge of the self, and Vada of disputants.

33) Of letters the letter A am I, and Dvandva of all compounds; I alone am the inexhaustible Time, I the Sustainer (by dispensing fruits of actions) All-formed.

34) An I am the all-seizing Death, and the prosperity of those who are to be prosperous; of the feminine qualities (I am) Fame, Prosperity (or beauty, Inspiration, Memory, Intelligence, Constancy and Forbearance.

35) Of Samas also I am the Brihat-Sama, of metres Gayatri am I; of months I am Margashirsha, of seasons the flowery season.

36) I am the gambling of the fraudulent, I am the power of the powerful; I am victory, I am effort, I am sattwa of the sattwic.

37) Of the Vrishnis I am Vasudeva; of the Pandavas, Dhananjaya; and also of the Munis I am Vyasa; of the sages, Ushanas the sage.

38) Of punishers I am the sceptre; of those who seek to conquer, I am statesmanship; and also of things secret I am silence, and the knowledge of knowers am I.

39) And whatsoever is the seed of all beings, that also am I, O Arjuna. There is no being, whether moving or unmoving, that can exist without Me.

40) There is no end of My divine attributes, O scorcher of foes; but this is a brief statement by Me of the particulars of My divine attributes.

41) Whatever being there is great, prosperous, or powerful, that know to be a product of a part of My splendour.

42) Or what avails thee to know all this diversity, O Arjuna? (Know this that) I exist, supporting this whole world by a portion of Myself.

Chapter Eleven
The Vision of the Universal Form

Arjuna said:
1) By the supremely profound words, on the discrimination of self, that have been spoken by You out of compassion towards me, this my delusion is gone.
2) Of You, O lotus-eyed, I have heard at length, of the origin and dissolution of beings, as also Your inexhaustible greatness.
3) So it is, O Supreme Lord,! as You have declared Yourself. (Still) I desire to see Your Ishvara-Form, O Supreme Purusha.
4) If, O Lord, You think me capable of seeing it, the, O Lord of Yogis, show me Your immutable Self.

The Blessed Lord said:
5) Behold, O son of Pritha, by hundreds and thousands, My different forms celestial, of various colours and shapes.
6) Behold the Adityas, the Vasus, the Rudras, the twin Ashvins, and the Maruts; behold, O descendant of Bharata, many wonders never seen before.
7) See now, O Gudakesha, in this My body, the whole universe centred in one–including the moving and the unmoving–and all else that you desirest to see.
8) But you cannot see me with these eyes of yours; I give thee supersensuous sight; behold My supreme yoga power.

Sanjaya said:
9) Having thus spoken, O King, Hari, the Great Lord of Yoga, showed unto the son of Pritha, His Supreme Ishvara-Form:
10) With numerous mouths and eyes, with numerous wondrous sights, with numerous celestial ornaments, with numerous celestial weapons uplifted;
11) Wearing celestial garlands and apparel, anointed with celestial-scented unguents, the All-wonderful Resplendent, Boundless, and All-formed.
12) If the splendour of a thousand suns were to rise up simultaneously in the sky, that would be like the splendour of that Mighty

Being.

13) There in the body of the God of gods, the son of Pandu then saw the whole universe resting in one, with its manifold divisions.

14) Then Dhananjaya, filled with wonder, with his hairs standing on end, bending down his head to the Deva in adoration, spoke with joined palms.

Arjuna said:

15) I see all the devas, O Deva, in Your body, and hosts of all grades of beings; Brahma, the Lord, seated on the lotus, and all the Rishis and celestial serpents.

16) I see You of boundless form on every side with manifold arms, stomachs, mouths, and eyes; neither the end nor the middle, nor also the beginning of You do I see, O Lord of the universe, O Universal Form.

17) I see You with diadem, club, and discus; a mass of radiance shining everywhere, very hard to look at, all around blazing like burning fire and sun, and immeasurable.

18) You are the Imperishable, the Supreme Being, the one thing to be known. You are the great Refuge of this universe; You are the undying Guardian of the Eternal dharma, You are the Ancient Purusha, I ween.

19) I see You without beginning, middle, or end, infinite in power, of manifold arms; the sun and the moon Your eyes, the burning fire Your mouth; heating the whole universe with Your radiance.

20) This space betwixt heaven and earth and all the quarters are filled by You alone; having seen this, Your marvelous and awful form, the three worlds are trembling with fear, O Great-souled One.

21) Verily, into You enter these hosts of devas; some extol You in fear with joined palms; "May it be well!" thus saying, bands of great Rishis and Siddhas praise You with splendid hymns.

22) The Rudras, Adityas, Vasus, Sadhyas, Vishva-devas, the two Ashvins, Maruts, Ushmapas, and hosts of Gandharvas, Yakshas, Asuras, and Siddhas–all these are looking at You, all quite astounded.

23) Having seen Your immeasurable Form–with many mouths and eyes, O mighty-armed, with many arms, thighs, and feet, with many stomachs, and fearful with many tusks–the worlds are terri-

fied, and so am I.

24) On seeing You touching the sky, shining in many a colour, with mouths wide open, with large fiery eyes, I am terrified at heart, and find no courage nor peace, O Vishnu.

25) Having seen Your mouths, fearful with tusks, (blazing) like Pralaya-fires, I know not the four quarters, nor do I find peace; have mercy, O Lord of the devas, O Abode of the universe.

26-27) All those sons of Dhritarashtra, with hosts of monarchs, Bhishma, Drona, and Sutaputra, with the warrior chiefs of ours, enter precipitately into Your mouth, terrible with tusks and fearful to behold. Some are found sticking in the interstices of Your teeth, with their heads crushed to powder.

28) Verily, as the many torrents of rivers flow towards the ocean, so do those heroes in the world of men enter Your fiercely flaming mouths.

29) As moths precipitately rush into a blazing fire only to perish, even so do these creatures also precipitately rush into Your mouths only to perish.

30) Swallowing all the worlds on every side with Your flaming mouths, You are licking Your lips. Your fierce rays, filling the whole world with radiance, are burning, O Vishnu!

31) Tell me who You are, fierce in form. Salutation to You, O Supreme Deva! have mercy. I desire to know You, O Primeval One. I know not indeed Your purpose.

The Blessed Lord said:

32) I am the mighty world-destroying Time, here made manifest for the purpose of infolding the world. Even without thee, none of the warriors arrayed in the hostile armies shall live.

33) Therefore arise and acquire fame. Conquer the enemies, and enjoy the unrivalled dominion. Verily by Myself have they been already slain; be merely an apparent cause, O Savyasachin (Arjuna).

34) Drona, Bhishma, Jayadratha, Karna as well as other brave warriors–these already killed by Me, do you kill. Be not distressed with fear; fight, and you shall conquer your enemies in battle.

Sanjaya said:

35) Having heard this speech of Keshava, the diademed one (Arjuna), with joined palms, trembling, prostrated himself, and again

addresssed Krishna in a choked voice, bowing down, overwhelmed with fear.

Arjuna said:
36) It is meet, O Hrishikesha, that the world is delighted and rejoices in Your praise, that rakshasas fly in fear to all quarters and all the hosts of Siddhas bow down to You in adoration.
37) And why should they not, O Great-souled One, bow to You, greater than, and the Primal Cause of even Brahma, O Infinite Being, O Lord of the devas, O Abode of the universe? You are the Imperishable, the Being and the non-Being, (as well as) That which is Beyond (them).
38) You are the Primal Deva, the Ancient Purusha; You are the Supreme Refuge of this universe, You are the Knower, and the One Thing to be known; You are the Supreme goal. By You is the universe pervaded, O boundless Form.
39) You are Vayu, Yama, Agni, Varuna, the Moon, Prajapati, and the Great- grandfather. Salutation, salutation to You, a thousand times, and again and again salutation, salutation to You!
40) Salutation to You before and behind, salutation to You on every side, O All! You, infinite in power and infinite in prowess, pervadest all; wherefore You are All.
41-42) Whatever I have presumptuously said from carelessness or love, addressing You as "O Krishna, O Yadava, O friend," regarding You merely as a friend, unconscious of this Your greatness–in whatever way I may have been disrespectful to You in fun, while walking, reposing, sitting, or at meals, when alone (with You), O Achyuta, or in company–I implore You, Immeasurable One, to forgive all this.
43) You are the Father of the world, moving and unmoving; the object of its worship; greater than the great. None there exists who is equal to You in the three worlds; who then can excel You, O You of power incomparable?
44) So prostrating my body in adoration, I crave Your forgiveness, Lord adorable! As a father forgiveth his son, friend a dear friend, a eloed one his love, even so should You forgive me, O Deva.
45) Overjoyed am I to have seen what I saw never before; yet my mind is distracted with terror. Show me, O Deva, only that form

of Yours. Have mercy, O Lord of Devas, O Abode of the universe.
46) Diademed, bearing a mace and a discus, You I desire to see as before. Assume that same four-armed Form, O You of thousand arms, of universal Form.

The Blessed Lord said:
47) Graciously have I shown to thee, O Arjuna, this Form supreme, by My own yoga power, this resplendent, primeval, infinite, universal Form of Mine, which hathnot been seen before by anyone else.
48) Neither by the study of the Veda and yajna, nor by gifts, nor by rituals, nor by severe austerities, am I in such Form seen, in the world of men, by any other than thee, O great hero of the Kurus.
49) Be not afraid nor bewildered, having beheld this Form of Mine, so terrific. With your fears dispelled and with gladdened heart, now see again this former Form of Mine.

Sanjaya said:
50) So Vasudeva, having thus spoken to Arjuna, showed again His own Form; and the Great-souled One, assuming His gently Form, pacified him who was terrified.

Arjuna said:
51) Having seen this Your gentle human Form, O Janardana, my thoughts are now composed, and I am restored to my nature.

The Blessed Lord said:
52) Very hard indeed it is to see this Form of Mine which you have hast seen. Even the devas ever long to behold this Form.
53) Neither by the Vedas, nor by austerity, nor by gifts, nor by sacrifice can I be seen as you have seen Me.
54) But by single-minded devotion I may in this form, be known, O Arjuna, and seen in reality, and also entered into O scorcher of foes.
55) He who does work for Me alone and has Me for his goal, is devoted to Me, is freed from attachment, and bears enmity towards no creature–he entereth into Me, O Pandava.

Chapter Twelve
The Way of Devotion

Arjuna said:
1) Those devotees who, ever-steadfast, thus worship You, and those also who worship the Imperishable, the Unmanifested–which of them are better versed in yoga?

The Blessed Lord said:
2) Those who, fixing their mind on Me, worship Me, ever-steadfast, and endowed with supreme shraddha, they in My opinion are the best versed in yoga.
3-4) But those also, who worship the Imperishable, the Indefinable, the Unmanifested, the Omnipresent, the Unthinkable, the Unchangeable, the Immovable, the Eternal–having subdued all the senses, even-minded everywhere, engaged in the welfare of all beings–verily they read only Myself.
5) Greater is their trouble whose minds are set on the Unmanifested; for the goal of the Unmanifested is very hard for the embodied to reach.
6-7) But those who worship Me, resigning all actions in Me, regarding me as the Supreme Goal, meditating on Me with single-minded yoga–to those whose mind is set on Me, verily, I become ere long, O son of Pritha, the Saviour out of the ocean of the mortal Samsara.
8) Fix your mind on Me only, place your intellect in Me: (then) you shall no doubt live in Me hereafter.
9) If you are unable to fix your mind steadily on Me, then by abhyasa-yoga do you seek to reach Me, O Dhananjaya.
10) If also you are unable to practice Abhyasa, be intent on doing actions for my sake. Even by doing actions for My sake, you shall attain perfection.
11) If you are unable to do even this, then taking refuge in Me, abandon the fruit of all action, being self-controlled.
12) Better indeed is knowledge than (blind) Abhyasa; meditation (with knowledge) is more esteemed than (mere) knowledge; than meditation the renunciation of the fruit of action; peace imme-

diately follows renunciation.

13-14) He who hates no creature, and is friendly and compassionate towards all, who is free from the feelings of "I" and "mine," even-minded in pain and pleasure, forbearing, ever content, steady in meditation, self-controlled, and possessed of firm conviction, with mind and intellect fixed on Me–he who is thus devoted to Me, is dear to Me.

15) He by whom the world is not agitated and who cannot be agitated by the world, who is freed from joy, envy, fear, and anxiety–he is dear to Me.

16) He who is free from dependence, who is pure, prompt, unconcerned, untroubled, renouncing every undertaking–he who is thus devoted to Me, is dear to Me.

17) He who neither rejoices, nor hates, nor grieves, nor desires, renouncing good and evil, full of devotion, he is dear to Me.

18-19) He who is the same to friend and foe, and also in honor and dishonor; who is the same in heat and cold, and in pleasure and pain; who is free from attachment; to whom censure and praise are equal; who is silent, contend with anything, homeless, steady-minded, full of devotion–that man is dear to Me.

20) And they who follow this Immortal Dharma, as described above, endued with shraddha, regarding Me as the Supreme Goal, and devoted–they are exceedingly dear to Me.

Chapter Thirteen
The Discrimination of the Kshetra and the Kshetrajna

Arjuna said:
Prakriti and Purusha, also the kshetra and the knower of the kshetra, knowledge, and that which ought to be known–these, O Keshava, I desire to learn.

The Blessed Lord said:
1) This body, O son of Kunti, is called kshetra, and he who knows it is called kshetrajna by those who know of them (kshetra and kshetrajna).
2) Me do you also know, O descendant of Bharata, to be kshetrajna in all kshetras. The knowledge of kshetra and kshetrajna is considered by Me to be the knowledge.
3) What the kshetra is, what is properties are, what its modifications are, what effects arise from what causes, and also who He is and what His powers are, that hear from Me in brief.
4) (This truth) has been sung by Rishis in many ways, in various distinctive chants, in passages indicative of Brahman, full of reasoning, and convincing.
5-6) The great Elements, Egoism, Intellect, as also the Unmanifested (Mula Prakriti), the ten senses and the one (mind), and the five objects of the senses; desire, hatred, pleasure, pain, the aggregate, intelligence, fortitude–the kshetra has been thus briefly described with its modifications.
7) Humility, unpretentiousness, non-injury, forbearance, uprightness, service to the teacher, purity, steadiness, self-control;
8) The renunciation of sense-objects, and also absence of egoism; reflection on the evils of birth, death, old age, sickness, and pain;
9) Non-attachment, non-identification of self with son, wife, home, and the rest, and constant even-mindedness in the occurrence of the desirable and the undesirable;
10) Unswerving devotion to Me by the yoga of non-separation, resort to sequestered places, distaste for the society of men;
11) Constant application to spiritual knowledge, understanding

of the end of true knowledge; this is declared to be knowledge, and what is opposed to it is ignorance.

12) I shall describe that which has to be known, knowing which one attains to immortality, the beginningless Supreme Brahman. It is called neither being nor non-being.

13) With hands and feet everywhere, with eyes, heads, and mouths everywhere, with ears everywhere in the universe–That exists pervading all.

14) Shining by the functions of all the senses, yet without the senses; Absolute, yet sustaining all; devoid of gunas, yet their experiencer.

15) Without and within (all) beings; the unmoving and also the moving; because of Its subtlety incomprehensible; It is far and near.

16) Impartible, yet It exists as if divided in beings: It is to be known as sustaining beings; and devouring, as well as generating (them).

17) The Light even of lights, It is said to be beyond darkness; Knowledge, and the One Thing to be known, the Goal of knowledge, dwelling in the hearts of all.

18) Thus kshetra, knowledge, and that which has to be known, have been briefly stated. Knowing this, My devotee is fitted for My state.

19) Know that Prakriti and Purusha are both beginningless; and know also that all modifications and gunas are born of Prakriti.

20) In the production of the body and the senses, Prakriti is said to be the cause; in the experience of pleasure and pain, Purusha is said to be the cause.

21) Purusha seated in Prakriti, experiences the gunas born of Prakriti; the reason of his birth in good and evil wombs is his attachment to the gunas.

22) And the Supreme Purusha in this body is also called the Looker-on, the Permitter, the Supporter, the Experiencer, the Great Lord, and the Highest Self.

23) He who thus knows the Purusha and Prakriti together with the gunas, whatever his life, is not born again.

24) Some by meditation behold the self in their own intelligence by the purified heart, others by the path of knowledge, others again

by karma-yoga.

25) Others again not knowing thus, worship as they have heard from others. Even these go beyond death, regarding what they have heard as the Supreme Refuge.

26) Whatever being is born, the moving or the unmoving, O bull of the Bharatas, know it to be from the union of kshetra and kshetrajna.

27) He sees, who sees the Supreme Lord, existing equally in all beings, deathless in the dying.

28) Since seeing the Lord equally existent everywhere, he injures not self by self, and so goes to the highest Goal.

29) He sees, who sees that all actions are done by Prakriti alone and that the self is actionless.

30) When he sees the separate existence of all being inherent in the One, and their expansion from That (One) alone, he then becomes Brahman.

31) Being without beginning and devoid of gunas, this Supreme Self, immutable, O son of Kunti, though existing in the body neither acts nor is affected.

32) As the all-pervading Akasha, because of its subtlety, is not tainted, so the self existent everywhere in the body is not tainted.

33) As the one sun illumines all this world, so does He who abides in the kshetra, O descendant of Bharata, illumine the whole kshetra.

34) They who thus with the eye of knowledge perceive the distinction between the kshetra and the kshetrajna, and also the emancipation from the Prakriti of beings, they go to the Supreme.

Chapter Fourteen
The Discrimination of the Three Gunas

The Blessed Lord said:

1) Again I shall tell you that supreme knowledge which is above all knowledge, having known which all the Munis have attained to high perfection after this life.

2) They who, having devoted themselves to this knowledge, have attained to My Being, are neither born at the time of creation, nor are they troubled at the time of dissolution.

3) My womb is the great Prakriti; in that I place the germ; from thence, O descendant of Bharata, is the birth of all beings.

4) Whatever forms are produced, O son of Kunti, in all the wombs, the great Prakriti is their womb, and I the seed-giving Father.

5) Sattwa, rajas, and tamas–these gunas, O mighty-armed, born of Prakriti, bind fast in the body the indestructible embodied one.

6) Of these sattwa, because of its stainlessness, luminous and free from evil, binds, O sinless one, by attachment to happiness, and by attachment to knowledge.

7) Know rajas to be of the nature of passion, giving rise to thirst and attachment; it binds fast, O son of Kunti, the embodied one, by attachment to action.

8) And know tamas to be born of ignorance, stupefying all embodied beings; it binds fast, O descendant of Bharata, by miscomprehension, indolence, and sleep.

9) Sattwa attaches to happiness, and rajas to action, O descendant of Bharata; while tamas, verily, shrouding discrimination, attaches to miscomprehension.

10) Sattwa arises, O descendant of Bharata, predominating over rajas and tamas; likewise rajas over sattwa and tamas; so, tamas over sattwa and rajas.

11) When through every sense in this body, the light of intelligence shines, then it should be known that sattwa is predominant.

12) Greed, activity, the undertaking of actions, unrest, longing–these arise when rajas is predominant, O bull of the Bharatas.

13) Darkness, inertness, miscomprehension, and delusion–these arise when tamas is predominant, O descendant of Kuru.
14) If the embodied one meets death when sattwa is predominant, then he attains to the spotless regions of the worshippers of the Highest.
15) Meeting death in rajas he is born among those attached to action; so dying in tamas, he is born in the wombs of the irrational.
16) The fruit of good action, they say, is Sattvika and pure; verily, the fruit of rajas is pain, and ignorance is the fruit of tamas.
17) From sattwa arises wisdom, and from rajas greed; miscomprehension, delusion and ignorance arise from tamas.
18) The sattwa-abiding go upwards; the rajasic dwell in the middle; and the tamasic, abiding in the function of the lowest guna, go downwards.
19) When the seer beholds no agent other than the gunas and knows That which is higher than the gunas, he attains to My being.
20) The embodied one having gone beyond these three gunas, out of which the body is evilved, is freed from birth, death, decay, and pain, and attains to immortality.

Arjuna said:
21) By what marks, O Lord, is he (known) who has gone beyond these three gunas? What is his conduct, and how does he pass beyond these three gunas?

The Blessed Lord said:
22) He who hates not the appearance of light (the effect of sattwa), activity (the effect of rajas), and delusion (the effect of tamas), (in his own mind), O Pandava, nor longs for them when absent;
23) He who, sitting like one unconcerned, is moved not by the gunas, who knowing that the gunas operate, is self-centered and swerves not;
24) Alike in pleasure and apin, self-abiding, regarding a clod of earth, a stone and gold alike; the same to agreeable and disagreeable, firm, the same in censure and praise;
25) The same in honor and disgrace, the same to friend and foe, relinquishing all undertakings–he is said to have gone beyond the

gunas.

26) And he who serves Me with unswerving devotion, he, going beyond the gunas, is fitted for becoming Brahman.

27) For I am the abode of Brahman, the Immortal and Immutable, of everlasting dharma and of Absolute Bliss.

Chapter Fifteen
The Way to the Supreme Spirit

The Blessed Lord said:
1) They speak of an eternal Ashvattha rooted above and branching below whose leaves are the Vedas; he who knows it, is a Veda-knower.
2) Below and above spread its branches, nourished by the gunas; sense-objects are its buds; and below in the world of man stretch forth the roots, originating action.
3-4) Its form is not here perceived as such, neither its end, nor its origin, nor its existence. Having cut asunder this firm-rooted Ashvattha with the strong axe of non-attachment–then that Goal is to be sought for, going whither they (the wise) do not return again. I seek refuge in that Primeval Purusha whence streamed forth the Eternal Activity.
5) Free from pride and delusion, with the evil of attachment conquered, ever dwelling in the self, with desires completely receded, liberated from the pairs of opposites known as pleasure and pain, the undeluded reach that Goal Eternal.
6) That the sun illumines not, nor the moon, nor fire; that is My Supreme Abode, going whither they return not.
7) An eternal portion of Myself having become a living soul in the world of life, draws (to itself) the (five) senses with mind for the sixth, abiding in Prakriti.
8) When the Lord obtains a body and when He leaves it, He takes these and goes, as the wind takes the scents from their seats (the flowers).
9) Presiding over the ear, the eye, the touch, the taste, and the smell, as also the mind, He experiences objects.
10) While transmigrating (from one body to another), or residing (in the same) or experiencing, or when united with the gunas–the deluded do not see Him; but those who have the eye of wisdom behold Him.
11) The Yogis striving (for perfection) behold Him dwelling in themselves; but the unrefined and unintelligent, even though striv-

ing, see Him not.

12) The light which residing in the sun illumines the whole world, that which is in the moon and in the fire–know that light to be Mine.

13) Entering the earth with My energy, I support all beings, and I nourish all the herbs, becoming the watery moon.

14) Abiding in the body of living beings as (the fire) Vaishvanara, I, associated with prana and apana, digest the fourfold food.

15) I am centered in the hearts of all; memory and perception as well as their loss come from Me. I am verily that which has to be known by all the Vedas, I indeed am the Author of the Vedanta, and the Knower of the Veda am I.

16) There are two Purushas in the world–the Perishable and the Imperishable. All beings are the Perishable, and the Kutastha is called Imperishable.

17) But (there is) another, the Supreme Purusha, called the Highest Self, the immutable Lord, who pervading the three worlds, sustains them.

18) As I transcend the Perishable and am above even the Imperishable, therefore am I in the world and in the Veda celebrated as Purushottama (the Highest Purusha).

19) He who, free from delusion, thus knows Me, the Highest Spirit, he knowing all, worships Me with all his heart, O descendant of Bharata.

20) Thus, O sinless one, has this most profound teaching been imparted by Me. Knowing this one attains the highest intelligence and will have accomplished all one's duties, O descendant of Bharata.

Chapter Sixteen
The Classification of the Divine and the Non- divine Attributes

The Blessed Lord said:

1) Fearlessness, purity of heart, steadfastness in knowledge and yoga; almsgiving, control of the senses, yajna, reading of the shastras, austerity, uprightness;

2) Non-injury, truth, absence of anger, renunciation, tranquillity, absence of calumny, compassion to beings, uncovetousness, gentleness, modesty, absence of fickleness;

3) Boldness, forgiveness, fortitude, purity, absence of hatred, absence of pride; these belong to one born for a divine state, O descendant of Bharata.

4) Ostentation, arrogance, and self-conceit, anger as also harshness and ignorance, belong to one who is born, O Partha, for an asuric state.

5) The divine state is deemed to make for liberation, the asuric for bondage; grieve not, O Pandava, you are born for a divine state.

6) There are two types of beings in this world, the divine and the asuric. The divine have been described at length; hear from Me, O Partha, of the asuric.

7) The persons of asuric nature know not what to do and what to refrain from; neither is purity found in them nor good conduct, nor truth.

8) They say, "The universe is without truth, without a (moral) basis, without a God, brought about by mutual union, with lust for its cause; what else?"

9) Holding this view, these ruined souls of small intellect and fierce deeds, rise as the enemies of the world for its destruction.

10) Filled with insatiable desires, full of hypocrisy, pride, and arrogance, holding evil ideas through delusion, they work with impure resolve.

11) Beset with immense cares ending only with death, regarding gratification of lust as the highest, and feeling sure that that is all;

12) Bound by a hundred ties of hope, given over to lust and

wrath, they strive to secure by unjust means hoards of wealth for sensual enjoyment.

13) "This today has been gained by me; this desire I shall obtain; this is mind, and this wealth also shall be mine in the future.

14) "That enemy has been slain by me, and others also shall I slay. I am the Lord, I enjoy, I am successful, powerful, and happy.

15) "I am rich and well-born. Who else is equal to me? I will sacrifice, I will give, I will rejoice." Thus deluded by ignorance,

16) Bewildered by many a fancy, covered by the meshes of delusion, addicted to the gratification of lust, they fall down into a foul hell.

17) Self-conceited, haughty, filled with the pride and intoxication of wealth, they perform sacrifices in name, out of ostentation, disregarding ordinance.

18) Possessed of egoism, power, insolence, lust, and wrath, these malignant people hate Me (the self within) in their own bodies and those of others.

19) These malicious and cruel evil-doers, most degraded of men, I hurl perpetually into the wombs of Asuras only, in these worlds.

20) Obtaining the asuric wombs, and deluded birth after birth, not attaining to Me, they thus fall, O son of Kunti, into a still lower condition.

21) Triple is this gate of hell, destructive of the self–lust, anger and greed; therefore one should forsake these three.

22) The man who has got beyond these three gates of darkness, O son of Kunti, practices what is good for himself, and thus goes to the Goal Supreme.

23) He who, setting aside the ordinance of the shastra, acts under the impulse of desire, attains not to perfection, nor happiness, nor the Goal Supreme.

24) So let the shastra be your authority in ascertaining what ought to be done and what ought not to be done. Having known what is said in the ordinance of the shastra, ou should act here.

Chapter Seventeen
The Enquiry into the Threefold Shraddha

Arjuna said:
1) Those who, setting aside the ordinance of the shastra, perform sacrifice with shraddha, what is their condition, O Krishna? (Is it) sattwa, rajas, or tamas?

The Blessed Lord said:
2) Threefold is the shraddha of the embodied, which is inherent in their nature–the satwic, rajasic, and the tamasic. Do you hear of it.
3) The shraddha of each is according to his natural disposition, O descendant of Bharata. The man consists of his shraddha; he verily is what his shraddha is.
4) Sattwic men worship the devas; rajasika, the yakshas and the rakshasa; the others–the tamasic men–the pretas and the hosts of bhutas.
5-6) Those men who practice severe austerities not enjoined by the shastras, given to ostentation and egoism, endowed with the power of lust and attachment, torture senseless as they are, all the organs in the body, and Me dwelling in the body within; know them to be of asuric resolve.
7) The food also which is liked by each of them is threefold, as also yajna, austerity, and almsgiving. Do you hear this, their distinction.
8) The foods which augment vitality, energy, strength, health, cheerfulness, and appetite, which are savory and oleaginous, substantial and agreeable, ae liked by the sattwic.
9) The foods that are bitter, sour, saline, excessively hot, pungent, dry, and burning, are liked by the rajasic, and are productive of pain, grief, and disease.
10) That which is stale, tasteless, stinking, cooked overnight, refuse, and impure, is the food liked by the tamasic.
11) That yajna is sattwic which is performed by men desiring no fruit, as enjoined by ordinance, with their mind fixed on the yajna only, for its own sake.
12) That which is performed, O best of the Bharatas, seeking for

fruit and for ostentation, know it to be a rajasic yajna.

13) The yajna performed without heed to ordinance, in which no food is distributed, which is devoid of mantras, gifts, and shraddha, is said to be tamasic.

14) Worship of the devas, the twice-born, the gurus, and the wise; purity, straightforwardness, continence, and non-injury are called the austerity of the body.

15) Speech which causes no vexation, and is true, as also agreeable and beneficial, and regular study of the Vedas–these are said to form the austerity of speech.

16) Serenity of mind, kindliness, silence, self-control, honesty of motive–this is called the mental austerity.

17) This threefold austerity practiced by steadfast men, with great Shraddha, desiring no fruit, is said to be sattwic.

18) That austerity which is practiced with the object of gaining welcome, honor, and worship, and with ostentation, is here said to be rajasic, unstable, and transitory.

19) That austerity which is practiced out of a foolish notion, with self-torture, or for the purpose of ruining another, is declared to be tamasic.

20) "To give is right"–gift given with this idea, to one who does no service in return, in a fit place and to a worthy person, that gift is held to be sattwic.

21) And what is given with a view to receiving in return, or looking for the fruit, or again reluctantly, that gift is held to be rajasic.

22) The gift that is given at the wrong place or time, to unworthy persons, without regard or with disdain, that is declared to be tamasic.

23) "Om, Tat, Sat": this has been declared to be the triple designation of Brahman. By that were made of old the Brahmanas, the Vedas, and the yajnas.

24) Therefore, uttering "Om" are the acts of sacrifice, gift, and austerity as enjoined in the ordinances, always begun by the followers of the Vedas.

25) Uttering "Tat," without aiming at fruits, are the various acts of yajna, austerity, and gift performed by the seekers of Moksha.

26) The word "Sat" is used in the sense of reality and of good-

ness; and so also, O Partha, the word "Sat" is used in the sense of an auspicious act.

27) Steadiness in yajna, austerity, and gift is also called "Sat": as also action in connection with these (or, action for the sake of the Lord) is called "Sat."

28) Whatever is sacrificed, given, or performed and whatever austerity is practiced without shraddha, it is called Asat, O Partha; it is naught here or hereafter.

Chapter Eighteen

The Way of Liberation in Renunciation

Arjuna said:

1) I desire to know severally, O mighty-armed, the truth of sannyasa, O Hrishikesha, as also of tyaga, O slayer of Keshi.

The Blessed Lord said:

2) The renunciation of kamya actions the sages understand as sannyasa: the wise declare the abandonment of the fruit of all works as tyaga.

3) Some philosophers declare that all actions should be relinquished as an evil, whilst others (say) that the work of yajna, gift, and austerity should not be relinquished.

4) Hear from Me the final truth about relinquishment, O best of the Bharatas. For relinquishment has been declared to be of three kinds, O tiger among men.

5) The work of yajna, gift, and austerity should not be relinquished, but it should indeed be performed; (for) yajna, gift, and austerity are purifying to the wise.

6) But even these works, O Partha, should be performed, leaving attachment and the fruits; such is My best and certain conviction.

7) But the renunciation of obligatory action is not proper. Abandonment of the same from delusion is declared to be tamasic.

8) He who from fear of bodily trouble relinquishes action, because it is painful, thus performing a rajasic relinquishment, he obtains not the fruit thereof.

9) When obligatory work is performed, O Arjuna, only because it ought to be done, leaving attachment and fruit, such relinquishment is regarded as sattwic.

10) The relinquisher endued with sattwa and a steady understanding and with his doubts dispelled, hates not a disagreeable work nor is attached to an agreeable one.

11) Actions cannot be entirely relinquished by an embodied being, but he who relinquishes the fruits of actions is called a relin-

quisher.

12) The threefold fruit of action–disagreeable, agreeable, and mixed–accrues to non-relinquishers after death, but never to relinquishers.

13) Learn from Me, O mighty-armed, these five causes for the accomplishment of all works as declared in the wisdom which is the end of all action;

14) The body, the agent, the various senses, the different functions of a manifold kind, and the presiding divinity, the fifth or these;

15) Whatever action a man performs by his body, speech, and mind–whether right or the reverse–these five are its causes.

16) Such being the case, he who through a non-purified understanding looks upon his self, the Absolute, as the agent–he of perverted mind sees not.

17) He who is free from the notion of egoism, whose intelligence is not affected (by good or evil), though he kills these people, he kills not, nor is bound (by the action).

18) Knowledge, the known and the knower form the threefold cause of action. The instrument, the object, and the agent are the threefold basis of action.

19) Knowledge, action and agent are declared in the Sankhya philosophy to be of three kinds only, from the distinction of gunas: hear them also duly.

20) That by which the one indestructible Substance is seen in all being, inseparate in the separated, know that knowledge to be sattwic.

21) But that knowledge which sees in all beings various entities of distinct kinds as different from one another, know that knowledge as rajasic

22) Whilst that which is confined to one single effect as if it were the whole, without reason, without foundation in truth, and trivial–that is declared to be tamasic.

23) An ordained action done without love or hatred by one not desirous of the fruit and free from attachment, is declared to be sattwic.

24) But the action which is performed desiring desires, or with self-conceit and with much effort, is declared to be rajasic.

25) That action is declared to be tamasic which is undertaken through delusion, without heed to the consequence, loss (of power and wealth), injury (to others), and (one's own) ability.

26) An agent who is free from attachment, non-egotistic, endued with fortitude and enthusiasm, and unaffected in success or failure, is called sattwic.

27) He who is passionate, desirous of the fruits of action, greedy, malignant, impure, easily elated or dejected, such an agent is called rajasic.

28) Unsteady, vulgar, arrogant, dishonest, malicious, indolent, desponding, and procrastinating, such an agent is called tamasic.

29) Hear the triple distinction of intellect and fortitude, according to the gunas, as I declare them exhaustively and severally, O Dhananjaya.

30) That which knows the paths of work and renunciation, right and wrong action, fear and fearlessness, bondage and liberation, that intellect, O Partha, is sattwic.

31) That which has a distorted apprehension of dharma and its opposite and also of right action and its opposite, that intellect, O Partha, is rajasic.

32) That which, enveloped in darkness, regards adharma as dharma and views all things in a perverted light, that intellect, O Partha, is tamasic.

33) The fortitude by which the functions of the mind, the prana, and the senses, O Partha, are regulated, that fortitude, unswerving through yoga, is sattwic.

34) But the fortitude by which one regulates (one's mind) to dharma, desire, and wealth, desirous of the fruit of each from attachment, that fortitude, O Partha, is rajasic.

35) That by which a stupid man does not give up sleep, fear, grief, despondency, and also overweening conceit, that fortitude, O Partha, is tamasic.

36) And now hear from Me, O bull of the Bharatas, of the threefold happiness that one learns to enjoy by habit, and by which one comes to the end of pain.

37) That which is like poison at first, but like nectar at the end; that happiness is declared to be sattwic, born of the translucence of

intellect due to self-realization.

38) That which arises from the contact of object with sense, at first like nectar, but at the end like poison, that happiness is declared to be rajasic.

39) That happiness which begins and results in self-delusion arising from sleep, indolence, and miscomprehension, that is declared to be tamasic.

40) There is no entity on earth, or again in heaven among the devas, that is devoid of these three gunas, born of Prakriti.

41) Of Brahmanas and kshatriyas and vaishyas, as also of shudras, O scorcher of foes, the duties are distributed according to the Gunas born of their own nature.

42) The control of the mind and the senses, austerity, purity, forbearance, and also uprightness, knowledge, realization, belief in a hereafter–these are the duties of the brahmanas, born of (their own) nature.

43) Prowess, boldness, fortitude, dexterity, and also not flying from battle, generosity and sovereignty are the duties of the kshatriyas, born of (their own) nature.

44) Agriculture, cattle-rearing, and trade are the duties of the Vaishyas, born of (their own) nature; and action consisting of service is the duty of the shudras, born of (their own) nature.

45) Devoted each to his own duty, man attains the highest perfection. How engaged in his own duty, he attains perfection, that hear.

46) From whom is the evolution of all beings, by whom all this is pervaded, worshipping Him with his own duty, a man attains perfection.

47) Better is one's own dharma, (though) imperfect than the dharma of another well-performed. He who does the duty ordained by his own nature incurs no evil.

48) One should not relinquish, O son of Kunti, the duty to which one is born, though it is attended with evil; for, all undertakings are enveloped by evil, as fire by smoke.

49) He who intellect is unattached everywhere, who has subdued his heart, whose desires have fled, he attains by renunciation to the supreme perfection, consisting of freedom from action.

50) Learn from Me in brief, O son of Kunti, how reaching such perfection, he attains to Brahman, that supreme consummation of knowledge.

51) Endued with a pure intellect; subduing the body and the senses with fortitude; relinquishing sound and such other sense-objects; abandoning attraction and hatred;

52) Resorting to a sequestered spot; eating but little; body, speech, and mind controlled; ever engaged in meditation and concentration; possessed of dispassion;

53) Forsaking egoism, power, pride, lust, wrath, and property; freed from the notion of "mine;" and tranquil–he is fit for becoming Brahman.

54) Brahman-become, tranquil-minded, he neither grieves nor desires; the same to all beings, he attains to supreme devotion unto Me.

55) By devotion he knows me in reality, what and who I am; then having known Me in reality, he forthwith enters into Me.

56) Even doing all actions always, taking refuge in Me–by My grace he attains to the eternal, immutable State.

57) Resigning mentally all deeds to Me, having Me as the highest goal, resorting to buddhi-yoga do you ever fix your mind on Me.

58) Fixing your mind on Me, you shall, by My grace, overcome all obstacles; but if from self-conceit you will not hear Me, you shall perish.

59) If, filled with self-conceit, you think, "I will not fight," vain is this your resolve; your prakriti will constrain you.

60) Fettered, O son of Kunti, by your own karma, born of your own nature, what you, from delusion, desire not to do, you shall have to do in spite of yourself.

61) The Lord, O Arjuna, dwells in the hearts of all beings, causing all beings, by His Maya, to revolve, (as if) mounted on a machine.

62) Take refuge in Him with all your heart, O Bharata; by His grace you shall attain supreme peace (and) the eternal abode.

63) Thus has wisdom, more profound than all profundities, been declared to you by Me; reflecting over it fully, act as you like.

64) Hear again My supreme word, the profoundest of all; be-

cause you are dearly beloved of Me, therefore, will I speak what is good to you.

65) Occupy your mind with Me, be devoted to Me, sacrifice to Me, bow down to Me. You shall reach Myself; truly do I promise unto you, (for) you are dear to Me.

66) Relinquishing all dharmas take refuge in Me alone; I will liberate you from all sins; grieve not.

67) This is never to be spoken by you to one who is devoid of austerities or devotion, nor to one who does not render service, nor to one who cavils at Me.

68) He who with supreme devotion to Me will teach this deeply profound philosophy to My devotees, shall doubtless come to Me alone.

69) Nor among men is there any who does dearer service to Me, nor shall there be another on earth dearer to Me, than he.

70) And he who will study this sacred dialogue of ours, by him shall I have been worshipped by the yajna of knowledge; such is My conviction.

71) And even that man who hears this, full of shraddha and free from malice, he too, liberated shall attain to the happy worlds of those of righteous deeds.

72) Has this been heard by you, O Partha, with an attentive mind? Has the delusion of your ignorance been destroyed, O Dhananjaya?

Arjuna said:

73) Destroyed is my delusion, and I have gained my memory through Your grace, O Achyuta. I am firm; my doubts are gone. I will do Your word.

Sanjaya said:

74) Thus have I heard this wonderful dialogue between Vasudeva and the high-souled Partha, causing my hair to stand on end.

75) Through the grace of Vyasa have I heard this supreme and most profound Yoga, direct from Krishna, the Lord of Yoga, Himself declaring it.

76) O King, as I remember and remember this wonderful and holy dialogue between Keshava and Arjuna, I rejoice again and

again.

77) And as I remember and remember that most wonderful form of Hari, great is my wonder, O King; and I rejoice again and again.

78) Wherever is Krishna, the Lord of Yoga, wherever is Partha, the wielder of the bow, there are prosperity, victory, expansion, and sound policy: such is my conviction.

Names of Sri Krishna in Gita

अच्युत : acyuta : The faultless, the immovable

अनन्त : ananta : Infinite

अनन्तरूप : anantarūpa : Infinite in form

अनन्तवीर्य : anantavīrya : Infinite in might

अप्रतिमप्रभाव : apratimaprabhava : Incomparable in might

अरसिूदन : arisūdana : Slayer of foes

कमलपत्राक्ष : kamalapatrākṣa : Lotus-eyed

कृष्ण : kṛṣṇa : The one who attracts all towards him/attractor of all beings

केशव : keśava : The one of luxuriant hair

केशिनिषूदन : keśiniṣūdana : Slayer of the demon Kesi

गोविन्द : govinda : The guardian of cows/light

जगत्पते : jagatpate : Master of the worlds

जगन्निवास : jagannivāsa : Refuge of all the worlds

जनार्दन : janārdana : One who has no birth and puts an end to the birth of other beings

देव : deva : God

देवदेव : deva deva : God of the gods

देववर : devavara : Great godhead

देवेश : deveśa : Lord of the gods

परमेश्वर : parameśvara : Supreme Lord

पुरुषोत्तम : puruṣottama : Supreme Self

प्रभो : prabho : Lord

भगवन् : Bhagavan : The Blessed Lord

भूतभावन : bhūtabhāvana : Source of beings

भूतेश : bhuteśa : Lord of beings

मधुसूदन : madhusūdana : Slayer of demon Madhu

महात्मन् : mahātman : Great spiriti/Mighty spirit

महाबाहो : mahabāho : Mighty-armed

माधव : mādhava : Consort of Lakshmi

यादव : yādava : Descendant on Yadu clan

योगिन् : yogin : Yogin

योगेश्वर : yogeśvara : Master of Yoga

वार्ष्णेय : vārṣṇeya : Descendant of Vrishni family

विश्वमूर्ते : viśvamūrte : Form universal

विश्वरूप : viśvarūpa : Form universal

विश्वेश्वर : viśveśvara : Lord of the universe

विष्णो : viṣṇo : All-pervading Lord

सखे : sakhe : Comrade

सर्व : sarva : All

सहस्रबाहो : sahasrabāho : Thousand-armed

हृषीकेश : hṛṣīkeśa : Master of the sense organs

Names of Arjuna in Gita

अनघ : anagha : Sinless

अर्जुन : arjuna : The sattwic or purified and light-filled

कुरुनन्दन : kurunandana : Joy of the Kurus

कुरुप्रवीर : kurupravīra : Foremost of the Kurus

कुरुश्रेष्ठ : kuruśreṣṭha : Best of the Kurus

कुरुसत्तम : kurusattama : Excellent among the Kurus

कौन्तेय : kaunteya : Son of Kunti

गुडाकेश : guḍākeśa : The one who has conquered sleep

तात : tata : Beloved

देहभृतां वर : dehabhṛtāṁ vara : Best of the embodied beings

धनञ्जय : dhanañjaya : Conqueror of riches

परन्तप : parantapa : Scourge of foes

पाण्डव : pāṇḍava : Son of Pandu

पार्थं : pārtha : Son of Pritna

पुरुषर्षभ : puruṣarṣabha : Excellent among men

पुरुषव्याघ्र : puruṣavyāghra : Tiger of men

भरतर्षभ : bharatarṣabha : Best of the Bharatas

भरतश्रेष्ठ : bharataśreṣṭha : Best of the Bharatas

भरतसत्तम : bharatasattama : Best of the Bharatas

भारत : bhārata : The one born in Bharata

महाबाहो : mahābāho : Mighty-armed

सव्यसाचिन् : savyasācin : Skilled in throwing arrows by left hand

Glossary of terms
[from Sri Aurobindo's Gita book]

abhayam—fearlessness.
abhyasa—Yogic practice.
acharya—teacher.
ahankara—the ego-sense, egoism.
ahinsa—non-violence.
akarta—a non-doer.
Akshara—the immobile, the immutable.
ananda—spiritual delight, the bliss of the Spirit.
anisha—not lord, not master of but subject to the nature.
anumanta—giver of sanction.
apana—the incoming breath.
artha—self-interest.
Asura—a hostile being of the mental world.
Asuric—relating to, of the nature of the Asuras.
Atman—the Self or Spirit.
avatara—descent or incarnation of God.
avikarya—free from all change.
avyaktam—the unmanifest.
bhakti—emotional devotion felt for the Divine.
bharta—upholder, maintainer of the nature.
bhava—subjective state or feeling ; becoming.
bhuta—any one of the five elements — earth, water, fire, air, ether—which form part of the list of tattwas.
bhutani—becomings, existences.
brahmacharya—sexual purity.
Brahman—the Supreme Reality that is one and indivisible and infinite, besides which nothing else really exists.
Brahmic—relating to Brahman.
buddhi—the reason, intelligence, mental power of understanding.
Chandala—pariah, outcaste.
chaturvarnya—the four orders—Brahmin, Kshatriya, Vaishya, Shudra — of the old Indian social culture.
Daivic—relating to, of the nature of the Devas.
dakshina—giving.

Danava—a Titan.
Deva—a god.
dhama—status, place.
dharma—action governed by the essential law of one's nature; right moral law.
dhirah—the self-composed.
dhriti—spiritual patience, persistence.
dhyana—meditation.
Dwaita—dualism.
dwandwa—duality, pair of opposites.
GUDAKESHA—an epithet applied to Arjuna which means 'one who has conquered sleep.'
guna—any one of the three essential modes of energy, of the three primal qualities that form the nature of things.
guru—spiritual guide and teacher.
HRISHIKESHA—an epithet applied to Krishna which means 'Lord of the senses.'
indriya—any one of the ten senses (five of knowledge and five of action).
Ishwara—lord; God, as lord of Nature.
jagat—world, universe (lit. "the moving").
JANARDANA—an epithet applied to Krishna which means 'one who has no birth and puts an end to the birth of other beings.'
jiva—the individual soul.
jnana—knowledge.
jnata—knower.
kama—desire.
karana—cause.
karma—action entailing its consequences.
karta—a doer.
KAUNTEYA—an epithet applied to Arjuna which means 'son of Kunti' (one of his mother's names).
KESHAVA—an epithet applied to Krishna which means 'one who has long hair.'
Kshara—the mobile, the mutable.
Kutastha—stable; high-seated.
laya—dissolution of the individual being in the Brahman.
lila—creation as the play of God.

manas—the sense-mind as opposed to the reason.
mantra—the revealing word.
Maya—the lower Prakriti (as distinguished from the Para Prakriti).
Mayavada—the doctrine which holds that the world is unreal and that it is created by the power of illusion.
moha—delusion.
moksha—liberation from Maya.
naishkarmya—actionlessness.
NARAYANA—an epithet applied to Krishna which means 'one who has made the water his abode'.
nigraha—coercion of the nature.
nirguna—without qualities.
nishkama—free from desire, desireless.
nivritti—inaction.
niyamya—controlling.
niyata—controlled, regulated.
Param—supreme.
PARANTAPA—an epithet applied to Arjuna which means 'subjugator of all enemies'.
PARTHA—an epithet applied to Arjuna which means 'son of Pritha' (one of his mother's names).
Pisacha—a hostile being of the lower vital world.
Prabhu— master.
prakasha—light, illumination.
Prakriti—Nature, creative energy (being more or less a synonym for Shakti).
pralaya—dissolution.
prana—the nervous energy, the vital breath, the half-mental, half-material dynamism which links mind and matter; the outgoing breath.
pranayama—the Yogic exercise of the control of the respiration.
prasada—clearness and happy tranquillity.
pravritti—impulsion to works.
Purusha—Being or Soul as opposed to Prakriti which is Becoming.
Purushottama—the Supreme Personality.
rahasyam—a secret.
Rakshasa—a hostile being of the middle vital world.
rajas—the guna that drives to action.

rajasic—belonging to the guna of action and passion.
rasa—affection of the senses (especially of pleasure).
Rishi—Seer.
sadhana—spiritual self-training and exercise.
sadharmya—becoming of one law of being with the Divine; oneness in nature with the Divine.
sadrishya—a synonym for sadharmya.
saguna—with the qualities.
sahaja—inborn, innate.
sakshi—a witness, the soul as a detached witness of the actions of the nature.
salokya—dwelling in the Divine.
samadhi—the Yogic trance.
samagra—integral.
samata—equality of soul and mind to all things and happenings.
samipya—nearness to the Divine.
Sannyasa—(outward) renunciation.
sanyama—a spiritual control of the nature; a concentration or directing of the consciousness.
sat—Being, existence, good.
sattwa—the guna that illumines, clarity, intelligence.
sattwic—belonging to the guna of light and happiness.
satyam—truth.
sayujya—contact with the Divine.
shabda—sound, word.
shakti—force, energy; the divine or cosmic Energy (being more or less a synonym for Prakriti).
shastra—the scriptures, theory, prescribed rule.
shraddha—faith.
siddhi—Yogic perfection.
sloka—verse.
Sruti—revealed scripture (a general term for the Vedas and the Upanishads).
sthiti—status.
sukha—happiness, pleasure.
swabhava—the nature proper to each being.
swadharma—one's own law of action.
tamas—the guna. that hides or darkens, inertia, non-intelligence.

tamasic—belonging to the guna of ignorance and inertia.
tanmatra—any one of the five subtle energies which underlie the respective sense-experiences of smell, taste, sight, touch, hearing.
tapas—concentration of spiritual will force.
tapasya—a synonym for tapas.
Tat—That.
tattwa—any one of the twenty-four principles of the cosmic Energy which are enumerated by Sankhya.
tejah—force, energy.
traigunya—the state of being bound to the three gunas.
trigunatita—beyond the control of the three gunas.
turiya—the superconscient state.
tyaga— (inner) renunciation.
uttama—highest.
vairagya—distaste for the world and life.
vak—speech.
VASUDEVA—an epithet applied to Krishna which means 'son of Vasudeva'.
Vedanta—a general term for all the Upanishads; a monistic philosophy based on the Upanishads.
Vedavada—traditionary lore of the Vedic hymns and the Vedic sacrifice.
Vibhu-'-the all-pervading Impersonal.
Vibhuti—divine power as manifested in the world.
vichara—reflective thought.
vidhi—order, rule.
vijnana—comprehensive knowledge.
vikara—deformation, distortion.
viveka—direct intuitive discrimination.
Yajna—sacrifice.
Yoga—union or oneness of the whole subjective being with the Supreme. Aishwara Yoga (the divine Yoga)—that by which the Transcendent is one with all existences even while more than them all and dwells in them and contains them as becomings of His own Nature.
Yuga—a cycle, age.

Gita Translator's Index

Adidevananda, Swami: 1992; Sri Ramanuja Gita Bhasya transl.
Ananda S.S. ; 1900; translation
Arnold, Edwin: 1885; translation
Aurobindo: 1922, 1938. 1995; essays, translation and commentary
Baijnath, Lala, Rai Bahadur; 1908; essay
Barnett, Lionel D. ; 1905; translation with notes
Basak, Radhanath:1888; Essay on Philosophy of BG
Besant, Annie:1894; translation
Bhaktivedanta, AC: 1968; translation and commentary
Bhawani Shankar; 1916; lectures
Bolle, Kees: 1979; translation
Books, F.T.; 1909; translation
Bower, A: Lecture comparative with Christianity
Browning, Katherine; 1916; notes and index
Burway, Mukund Wamanarao; 1916; translation with notes
Caldwell, Robert:1894; Christian polemic
Caleb, C.C.;1911; metrical translation
Chakravarti, Rai Bahadur Biresvar; 1906; translation
Chatterji, Mojini {Mohani} Mohan: 1880; translation and commentary with references to Christian scriptures
Chintamon, Hurrychund:1874; commentary with Cockburn's trans.
Das, Ram: 2004; Paths to God: Living the BG
Davies, John:1882; translation with notes
Davies, Roy Eugene: 1996; translation commentary
Dew, John: 1898; essay
Edgerton, Franklin: 1944; translation
Farquhar, John Nicol: 1904; essay on age and origin of BG
Feurstein, Georg: 2011; A new translation
Gaijar, Irina: 2000; translation
Gamhirananda, Swami: 1984; Translation of Sankaracharya
Goswami, P.K: 1889; translation with notes and commentary
Govindacharya, A.: 1898; translation of Ramanuja's commentary
Hawley, Jack: 2001; translation and commentary
Humboldt, Wilhelm: Essay in German translated into English
Jagannandaswami, S.P.S: 1894; index only

Jinarajadasa, Curuppumullage; 1915; essay
Johnston, Charles; 1908; translation
Judge, William Q.: 1890; translation
Kaji, Chhaganlal G; 1909; translation
Kitai, Pakavat: 1889; translation
Lahiri, Subodh Chandra; 1900; translation
Lalan, F.K: 1897; essay
Lall, Maheshee: 1870; translation
Legget, Trevor: 1995; translation and notes
Malik, Balaram: 1894; Essay on Ethics of BG
Marjanovic, Boris: 2004; translation of Abhinavagupta's Gita
Mascaro, Juan: 1962; translation
Misra, Pandit Adya Prasada; 1910; translation with notes
Mittchell, Stephen: 2000; translation
Mitra, Pramada Dasa: 1806; translation
Morgan, Les: 2017; Study Guide
Mukhopadhyaya, Shiboprosanna ; 1915; lecture
Murdoch, John: 1894; Essay on Krishna from Christian perspective
Nath, PV: 1998; translation and commentary
Nikhilananda, Swami: 1944; translation and commentary
Oxley, William; 1881; translation
Pandit, Shridhar; 1880; commentary
Philips, Maurice: 1893; Christian polemic
Phillips, George Searle; 1851; essay
Paramananda, Swami; 1913; translation
Prabhavananda, Swami:1944; translation
Prasad, Ramananda: 1989; translation and commentary
Prem, Krishna: 1938; translation and commentary
Premananda, Swami: 1949; Translation and commentary
Radhakrishnan, S.: 1947; translation
Rama, Babu; 1808; translation; manuscript only
Rama, Swami: 1885; Perennial Pschology of BG
Ramamurti, K; 1915; essay
Rangacharya, M; 1905; lecture with translation and notes
Rangacharya, Malur; 1915; lectures
Row, R. Narasinga; 1909; translation
Sahaya, Devi: 1874

Sargeant, Winthrop: 1994; Word for world translation
Sastri, A. Mahadeva:1897; translation of BG plus translation of commentary by Shankaracharya
Sastri, A. Mahadeva; 1908; essay
Schweig, Graham: 2007; translation
Shankarnanda: 1880; commentary
Sharma, Shailendra: 2012; translation and commentary
Sivananda, Swami:1949; translation and commentary
Sridhar Swami: 1894; commentary
Sonde, Nagesh D:1995; transl. of Sri Madhva's Bhasya
Subba Row, Tiruvalum: 1888; Lectures on BG
Swami, Purohit: 1935; translation
Swarupananda, Swami; 1909; translation, comments, notes, index
Tapasyananda, Swami: 1984; translation
Telang,Kashinath Trimbak:1875; transl., notes, introduction;1882; Sacred Books of the East; with the Sanatsugatiya and the Anugita
Thandani, Nanikram Vasamal; 1900; transl with intro and notes
Thomson, J. Cockburn:1855; translation with lots of notes
Van Buitanen, JAB: 1979; translation
Vasvani, Thanwardas; 1900; translation with notes
Wilkins, Charles:1785; translation
Wilmhurst, Walter Leslie; 1906; essay
Wood, Earnest: 1961; translation
Yogananda, Paramhansa: 1995; two volume guide to BG
Yogi Ramacharaka; 1907; translation
Zaehner, RC: 1969; translation and commentary

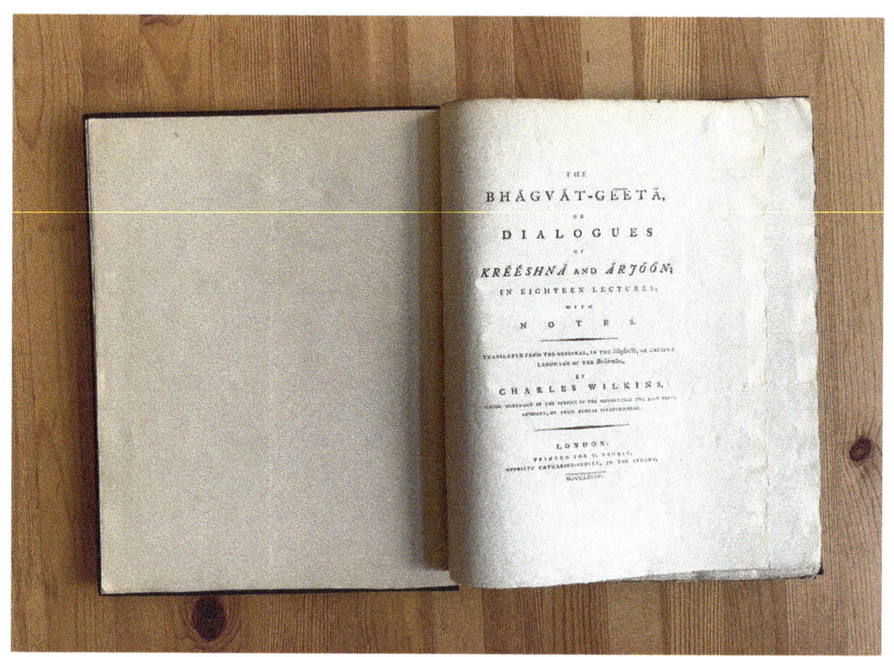

THE

BHĂGVĂT-GEĒTĀ,

OR

DIALOGUES

OF

KRĔĔSHNĂ AND *ĂRJŌŌN*;

IN EIGHTEEN LECTURES;

WITH

NOTES.

BY

CHARLES WILKINS,

LONDON:

Figure 7

The first English Translaton of the Gita by Charles Wilkins

Figure 8
A few more noteworthy or interesting translations of the Gita

A Bibliography of the English Translations of the Bhagavad Gita
Based on the pioneering work by J.C. Kapoor in: Bhagavad-Gita: An International Bibliography of 1785-1979 Imprints; Garland Publishing Inc .[1983]

Although I was not able to obtain a copy of the above work, some booksellers that I contacted in the 1990s had photocopies of a few pages that I could refer to.

There have been more translations of the Gita since 1979, and some are included. I've also put in bold some of the books that I feel are noteworthy or that I personally liked.

1785

1. **The Bhagvat-geeta, or Dialogues of Kreeshna and Arjoon, in eighteen lectures; with notes. Translated from the original in the Sanskreet, or ancient language of the Brahmans, by Charles Wilkins,...[with a letter from Warren Hastings to Nathaniel Smith]. London: Printed for C. Nourse, MDCCLXXXV. 156 p.; 32.5 cm. " Published under the authority of the Court of directors of the East India company, by the particular desire and recommendation of the governor general of India (Warren Hastings)" who provided the introduction.**

1806

2. The Bhagavad Gita or the Divine Ode. Translated by Pramada Dasa Mitra. Benares: Freeman and Co. xxiii, 192 p.

1808

3. Bhagavadgita. Edited by Babu Rama. Ms. Form. Kidderpore, [India]. Ff.60

1809

4. Bhagavad-geeta, or dialogues between Krishna and Arjuna, extracted from the Mahabarut. Printed at Khizupoor near Calcutta. [A new and improved edition of the English translation.]

1845

5. The Bhagvat-geeta or Dialogues of Kreeshna and Arjoon in eighteen lectures; with notes...[Wilkins' translation] Revised and improved by G.P.C. Calcutta; Bengal Superior Press. Iii,xiii, 62p.

1846

6. The Bhagavat-Geeta, or Dialogues of Krishna and Arjoon, in eighteen lectures. Sanscrit, Canarese, and English in parallel columns. The Canarese newly translated from the Sanscrit, and the English from the translation by Sir Charles Wilkins, with his preface and notes, etc.; and the introduction by the Hon. Warren Hastings, esq. With an appendix containing Schlegel's text and Latin translation of the Geeta, notes from the German of Baron Humboldt [various readings collected from several good Malayalam manuscripts and commentaries, an essay by H.D. Griffith] etc. Edited by Rev. J. Garrett, Bangalore: Wesleyan Mission Press, 1846-48. xvi, 147 p., 29, lvii; 4*. [Outside measure 230 x180mm. and inside measure 152x120mm. Title within broad ornamental borders.]

1847

7. The Bhagaad-Gita. The text of Lassen and Schlegel. Bombay: American Mission Press. 88p. [A few copies printed for private use.]

8. The Bhagvat-geeta, or Dialogues of Kreeshna and Arjoon, in eighteen lectures; with notes....Another ed. of item 1.

1849

9. The Bhagavat-geeta, or dialogues of Krishna and Arjoon; in eighteen lectures. Sanscrit, Canarese, and English; in parallel columns. The Sanscrit text from Schlegel's edition; the Canarase newly translated from the Sanscrit; the English translation by Sir Charles Wilkins, with his Preface and Notes, and commentary, and the Introduction by the Hon. Warren Hastings, Esq. With an Appendix containing additional Notes from Professor Wilson, Rev. H. Milman, and [others]; and an essay on the Philosophy and Poetry of the Bhagavat-Gita, by Baron William von Humboldt, translated from the German

by Rev. G.H. Weigle; the second edition of Schlegel's Latin Version of the Geeta, with the Sanscrit Text revised by Professor Lassen and [others]. Edited by the Rev. J. Garrett. Kanada Characters. Bangalore; Wesleyan Mission Press. Xvi, 147p., [2], 29 p., lvii,; 23x28 cm.

10. Humboldt, Wilhelm, Freiherr Von. Essay on the Episode of the Mahabharat known by the Name of Bhagavat-Geeta. (A Lecture delivered in the Berlin academy of science on the 30th June, 1825; and 15th June, 1826). Translated from the German, by G.H. Weigle. The Bhagavat-Geeta, etc. pp. 121-147;

1850

11. Bhagavat-geetta, or dialogues of Krishna and Arjoon, in eighteen lectures. Another ed. of item 9. Bombay. 116 leaves, oblong;

12. Bhagavat-geetta, or dialogues of Krishna and Arjoon, in eighteen lectures. Another ed. of item 9. Indore, [India]. 146 leaves, oblong;

1851

13. The Bhagavat-geeta, or dialogues of Krishna and Arjoon; in eighteen lectures. Another ed. of item 9. Mirath [Meerut, India]. 163 p., oblong;

14. Phillips, George Searle. Essays, poems, allegories, and fables; with an elucidation and analysis of the "Bhagavat Geeta". By January Searle [pseudo.]. London: Chapman. 188 p.; 20.5 cm.

1855

15. Bhagavad-Gita; or a discourse between Krishna and Arjuna on

divine matters. A Sanskrit philosophical poem: translated, with copious notes, and introduction on Sanskrit philosophy, and other matters, by J. Cockburn Thomson. Hertford: Stephen Austin. 4 p.l., [v]-cxix, 155 p.; 21 cm.

16. Bhagavad-gita; or the sacred lay; a colloquy between Krishna and Arjuna on divine matters. An episode from the Mahabharata. A new edition of the Sanskrit text, with a vocabulary, by J. Cockburn Thomson. Hertford; Stephen Austin. Xii, 92 p.; 20x14 cm. [Has Sanskrit title at head of title-page.3

1858

17. Crofton, Denis. On the collation of a MS. Of the Bhagavad-Gita. [Dublin, 1858.} 12p. (In royal Irish Academy. Dublin. Polite Literature. Vol. 24, 1864)

1860

18. The Bhagavad-Gita; or a discourse between Krishna and Arjuna on divine matters. Another imprint of item 15. cxxxviii, 158 p.: 22.5 cm.

19. Phillips, George Searle. Essays, poems, allegories, and fables... Another ed. of item 14. Hertford; Printed and published by Stephen Austin. Cxxxvii, 158 p.; 22.5 cm.

1864

20. Wilson, Horace Hayman. Essays, analytical, critical and philosophical on subjects connected with Sanskrit literature. By the late H.H. Wilson ..Collected and edited by Dr. Reinhold Rost. London; Trübner & Co., 1864-65. 3 vols.; 23 cm. Vol. 3; Review of

A.W. Schlegel's edition of the Bhagavadgita, Bonn: 1823.

1865

21. Wilson, Horace Hayman. Works....London: Trübner & Co.; 1861-77. 12 v.; 22.5 cm. Vol. 5: Review of Schlegel's edition of the Bhagavad-gita. Pp. 99-157.

1867

22. Bhagavad-gita; or the sacred lay: a colloquy between Krishna and Arjuna on divine matters.... Another ed. of item 16. London: W.H. Allen. Xii, 92 p.; 20 cm.

23. The Bhagvat-Geeta, or dialogue of Kreeshna and Arjoon.... Translated by Charles Wilkins. New York: Reprinted for G.P.Philes, New York University, MDCCCLXVII. 3 p. l., [53-117 p.; 21 cm. "261 copies printed for subscribers." A reprint of the original edition published under the authority of the East India Company "by the particular desire and recommendation of the governor general of India" (Warren Hastings), London: C. Nourse, 1785; with the addition of new t.p. (See item 1)

1870

24. The "BHAGWAT MAHATMA". Translated by Maheshee Lall. Fyzabad, [India]

1871

25. The Bhagvat-geeta, or Dialogues of Kreeshna and Arjoon, in eighteen lectures; with notes. Translated from the original in the Sanskreet, or ancient language of the Brahmans, by Charles Wilkins. Chicago: Religion-Philosophical Publishing House. 129 p.; 19 cm.

1872

26. Crofton, Denis. On the collation of a MS. of the Bhagavad-Gita. Dublin. (In Royal Irish Academy, Dublin. Transactions. Vol. 24, part 2, pp. 3-12. [1872]) (See item 17)

1874

27. The Bhagavad-Gita; or a Discourse on divine matters between Krishna and Arjuna. A Sanskrit philosophical poem translated with copious notes, an introduction on Sanskrit philosophy, and other matters, by J. Cockburn Thomson. Chicago: Religion-Philosophical Publishing House. Viii, 278 p. ; 20 cm. (See also item 15)

28. Chintamon, Hurrychund. A commentary on the text of the Bhagavad-Gita; or the discourse between Krishna and Arjuna on divine matters... With [the text in J.C. Thomson's English Translation and] a few introductory papers. London: Trübner & Co. xxxiv, 83 p.; 21x14 cm. (See also items 15 and 27)

29. Gita-Sar. An Epitome of the Bhagavad-gita. By Devi Sahaya. Sialkot, {Pakistan}. 32p.

1875

30. Bhagavad-gita. Translated into English blank verse, with notes and an introductory essay, by Kashinath Trimbak Telang, M.A., LL. B. Bombay: Atmaram Sagoon & co. 12, cxix, 144 p.; 22x13 cm.

31. Bower, A. Lectures on the Bhagavad-Gita; its Doctrines compared with Christianity. 2d ed. Madras.

32. Gita-Sar. 3d ed. of item 29.

1879

33. Gita-Sar. An Epitome of the Bhagavad-gita. 4th ed. of item 29.

1880

34. **The Bhagavad-gita; or The Lord's lay, with commentary and notes, as well as references to the Christian Scriptures. Translated from the Sanskrit, for the benefit of those in search of spiritual light, by Mojini {Mohani} Mohan Chatterji. London. X, 283 p.**

35. Bhagavat-Gita; with commentary by Shankarnanda. Bombay: Printed with moveable types [Trübners]. 300 leaves, oblong folio.

36. Bhagavat-Gita; with commentary by Shridhar Pandit. Bombay; [Trübners] 110 leaves, oblong;

37. Bhagawat-Gita; and four other extracts (The Wishnu Sahausranama-Bishma Stawaraj-Anubhuti-Gajendra Moksha from the Mahabharata). Bombay: Printed with moveable types [Trübners]. 142 leaves.

1881

38. Oxley, William. The philosophy of spirit, illustrated by a new version of the Bhagavat gita. An epitome of the Mahabharat, one of the epic poems of ancient India. Glasgow;: Hay Nisbet & Co.: London: E.W. Allen. Vi+[2], 306 p., 2 plates; 19x13 cm.

1882

39. The Bhagavad Gita; or, The sacred lay. Translated with notes by John Davies. London: Trübner & Co. vi, 208 p.; 21x14 cm.

40. **The Bhagavadgita, with the Sanatsugatiya and the Anugita; translated by Kashinath Trimbak Telang, M.A. Oxford: The Clarendon Press. V p. l., 446 p.; 22.5 cm. (Added title-page: The sacred books of the East...v.8)**

41. Hindu philosophy. The Bhagavad Gita, or the sacred lay. A Sanskrit-philosophical poem. Translated with notes by John Davies. Boston: Houghton, Mifflin & Co. vi, 208 p.; (The English and Foreign Philosophical Library, 31)

42. Hindu philosophy. The Bhagavad Gita, or the sacred lay Another ed. London: Trübner & Co. vi, 208 p.; 22 cm. (Half-title: Trübner's Oriental series) Errata slip laid in after p. vi.

1885

43. Bhagwat gita; or Dialogues of Krishna and Arjun, translated from Sanskrit by Charles Wilkins....with notes. [Bombay]: Revised and reprinted for the Bombay Theosophical Publication Fund by Tukaram Tatis, [1885]. 121 p.; 15 cm.

44. Bhagwatgita.........translated from Sanskrit by Charles Wilkins.... with notes. Revised [by Janardana Damodara Kolatkara] and reprinted for the Bombay Theosophical Publication Fund. Bombay: Subodha-Prakash Press. [7], 39, 121 p.; 15x10 cm.

45. **The Song Celestial or Bhagavad-gita (from the Mahabharata), being a discourse between Arjuna, Prince of India, and Supreme Being under the form of Krishna**
Translated from the Sanskrit text by Edwin Arnold....Boston: Roberts Bros. 185 p.: 18 cm.

46. The Song Celestial or Bhagavad-gita (from the Mahabharata), being a discourse between Arjuna, Prince of India, and Supreme Being under the form of Krishna
Translated from the Sanskrit text by Edwin Arnold 2d ed. London: Trübner & Co. xiv, 173 p.;

1886

47. The song Celestial; or Bhagavad-gita (from the Mahabharata), Being a discourse between Arjuna, Prince of India, and the Supreme Being under the form of Krishna--- 3d ed. of item 45.

1887

48. The Bhagavad gita; or, The Lord's lay, with commentary and notes, as well as references to the Christian Scriptures… Another ed. of item 34. Boston: Tickner & Co. [Cambridge, Mass., printed 1887] 2 p. l., [iii]-ix p., 1 l., 283 p.; 22.5 cm.

49. The Bhagavad gita; or, The Lord's lay, with commentary and notes, as well as references to the Christian Scriptures. Another imprint od item 48. Boston and New York: Houghton Mifflin & Co., [c1887].

50. The Bhagavad gita; or, The Lord's lay, with commentary and notes, as well as references to the Christian Scriptures Another ed. of item 48. London: Trŭbner & Co., [Cambridge, Mass., printed. 1887]. Ex, 283 p.;

51. The Bhagavad gita; or, The Lord's lay, with commentary and notes, as well as references to the Christian Scriptures Another imprint of item 48 with a new title-page.

52. Bhagwatgita; or Dialogues of Krishna and Arjun, translated from Sanskrit by Charles Wilkins….Another ed. of item 43. Reprinted for the Bombay Theosophical Publishing Fund Society. Bombay: Tukaram Tatya [Tatia]. Vi, 64, 232 p.; 32*.

53. Bhagwatgita; or Dialogues of Krishna and Arjun, translated from Sanskrit by Charles Wilkins, with notes. Another ed. of item 44. Revised and edited [by Janardana Damodara Kolatkara. Bombay: Theosophical Publications Fund Society, [1887]. [2], iii, [2], 232 p.

1888

54. Basak, Radhanath, Philosophy of the Bhagavadgita. Calcutta.

55. The Bhagavad gita; or, The Lord's lay, with commentary and notes, as well as references to the Christian Scriptures. [2d ed. of item 49. Boston, New York: Houghton. Mifflin & Co., [1883], 283 p.

56. The Bhagavad gita; or, The Lord's lay, with commentary and notes, as well as references to the Christian Scriptures; 2d ed. of item 34. Calcutta.

57. The Bhagavad gita; or, The Lord's lay, with commentary and notes, as well as references to the Christian Scriptures; Another imprint of item 50. ix, [i], 283 p.; 23x15 cm.

58. The Song Celestial or Bhagavad-gita (from the Mahabharata), ...Another ed. of item 45.

59. Shrimad Bhagavad-gita. [Bombay, 1883] , 109 p.

60. **Subba Row, Tiruvalum. Discourses on the Bhagavat gita, to help students in studying its philosophy. Bombay: Printed at the Joint-Stock Printing Press. 1 p.l.,viii,95 p.; 21 cm. "Printed for the Bombay Theosophical Publications Fund by Tookaram Tatya [Tukaram Tatia]."**

1889

61. Bhagabadgita. With Sanscrit and English notes, translation and an esoteric exposition in English by P.K. Goswami. Calcutta.

62. Hindu Philosophy. The Bhagavad Gita 2d ed. of item 41. vi, 216 p.

63. Pakavat Kitai. A Sanskrit philosophical poem, in the form of dialogues between Krishna and Arjuna, translated into English and Tamil [Press rendering printed in parallel column], with an

introduction by the late Rev. Henry Bower. Madras: Higgin Bothan & Co. lvi, 137 p.: 21 cm.

64. The Song Celestial; or, Bhagavad-gita (from Mahabharata)...4th ed. of item 45. 18 cm. (On cover: Sir Edwin Arnold's Poetical Works (v.73)

1890

65. **The Bhagavad-Gita; the book of devotion, Dialogues between Krishna, Lord of Devotion, and Arjuna, Prince of India. New York: The Path; London: Theosophical Publishing Society, [1890]. xii, 133p.; 14.5 cm. (Theosophical series, 5) [Translated by William Q. Judge]**

66. The Bhagavad-Gita..Another Ed. of item 65; New York: Theosophical Publishing co., [1890]. xii, 133 p; 14 cm. William Q. Judge. Eighth edition.

67. The Song Celestial; or, Bhagavad-gita (from the Mahabharata)... Another ed. of item 64. London: Kegan Paul, Trench, Trübner. 173 p. (Title on spine: Poetical Works)

1891

68. Jacob, George Adolphus. A concordance to the principal Upanishads and Bhagavadgita. Bombay: Government Central Book Depot. Viii p.l.,1083 p.; 25 cm. (Bombay Sanskrit series. 39) At head of title: The Department of Public Instruction, Bombay.

69. The Song Celestial; or, Bhagavad-gita (from the Mahabharata)... Another ed. of item 45

70. The Song Celestial; or, Bhagavad-gita (from Mahabharata) Another ed. of item 67. xiv, 173 p.

1892

71. The Bhagavad Gita or the Lord's lay, with commentary and notes as well as references to the Christian Scriptures....Another ed. of item 49. xv, 283 p.

1893

72. Bhagavad Gita or the Lord's lay, with commentary and notes as well as references to the Christian Scriptures...Another ed. of item 49. xv, 283 p.

73. The Bhagavad gita; or, the sacred lay...... 2d ed. of item 39. London: Kegan Paul, Trench, Trübner & Co. vi, 216 p.; 23.5 cm.

74. The Bhagavad Gita; or, The sacred lay. 3d ed. of item 39. 21.5 cm. Half-title: Trübner's Oriental series.

75. The Bhagavad-Gita, the book of devotion... [Translated by William Q. Judge. 4th ed. of item 65.

76. Krishnasami Aiyar, M.C. Some thoughts on Bhagavad Gita. Kumbakonam, {India}. 164p.

77. Philips, Maurice. The Bhagavad-Gita. Its doctrines stated and refuted. Madras: Religious Tract and Book Society. 34p.

78. The Song Celestial; or, Bhagavad-Gita (from the Mahabharata)...6th ed. of item 45. 19.5 cm.

79. Thoughts on Bagavad Gita. A series of twelve lectures read before the Branch Theosophical Society, Kumbhakonam. By a Brahmin F.T.S. Vol. 1-. Kumbhakonam, [India]: Kumbhakonam Branch Theosophical Society. 8* [This is stated on the title-page to be volume 1, though containing all the twelve lectures.]

1894

80. The Bhagavad-gita; the book of devotion, Dialogue between Krishna, Lord of Devotion, and Arjuna, Prince of India. New York: The Path. 5th ed. of item 65.

81. Caldwell, Robert. Bishop Caldwell on Krishna and the Bhagavad Gita. Madras; C.L.S.I. 32 p. ; 18 cm. (Papers for thoughtful Hindus, no. 7)

82. Malik, Balaram. The land-marks of Ethics according to the Gita. Calcutta.

83. [Murdoch, John]...Krishna as described in the Vishnu Purana, Bhagavata Purana, and the Mahabharata, especially the Bhagavad gita; with a letter to Mrs. Annie Besant...Madras; The Christian Literature Society. Ix 62 p., illus, 1st ed.; Letter signed: J. Murdoch. (Papers on Indian Religious Reform for Thoughtful Hindus)

84. Srimath Bhagabath Gita, or the Song Celestial. With the original Sanskrit, English, and Bengali translation. Commentary by Sridhar Swami, including copious footnotes in English and Bengali from Book 1 to Book VI. Compiled and published by Kaliprasanna Sarker. Comilla, (India), 1894-1901. 3 vols. [in 1.] Vols. 2, 3 published at Faridpur, [India]: Sanjay Press, 1900-1901. Added title-page in Bengali.

86. **The Bhagavad Gita; or The Lord's Song. Translated [into English] by Annie Besant.**
London: Theosophical Publishing Society.
xii, 168 p.; 14x10 cm. (Lotus Leaves, II)

87. The Bhagavad Gita; with an English trans. [based on that of Wilkins], explanatory notes, and an examination of its doctrines, Compiled from various writers. 1st ed. Madras; The Christian Literature Society; S.P.C. K. Press. Vi, 90 p.; 22cm. (The Sacred books of the East described and examined. Hindu Series, vol. 2, part 2)

88. Gita. A press English translation from the original Sanskrit; the teachings of Sri Krishna on the fields of Kurushetra. 2d ed. Edited and published by Manmatha Nath Dutt. Calcutta. 2 p. l., 88 p.; (Cheap Sanskrit translation Series)

89. The Bhagavad-gita; the book of devotion, Dialogue between Lord Krishna and Arjuna, Prince of India. 6th ed. of item 65. xii, 133 p., pl.; 14.5 cm.

90. The Bhagavad Gita, or The Divine Ode. Translated by Pramada Dasa Mitra. Another imprint of item 2.

91. The Bhagavad Gita, or The Divine Ode. Translated by Pramada Dasa Mitra. Another imprint of item 2. Another imprint. New York: Vedanta Society. [n.d.] 180 p.

92. The Bhagavad gita; or The Lord's lay, with commentary and notes, as well as references to the Christian Scriptures... Another ed. of item 48. xv, 283 p.; 23 cm.

93. The Bhagavadgita; or the Lord's Song.....New and revised ed. of item 86. London, New York. Xii, 176 p.; 14.5 cm.

94. Jagannandaswami, S.P.S. Bhagavadgita pada suchika: Index to the Bhagavadgita. Vizagaptam, [India]: The author. 48p.

1897

95. The Bhagavadgita or the Divine Ode. Translated by Pramada Dasa Mitra. 2d ed. of item 2.

96. Bhagavad Gita Sara Bodhini. The essential teachings of the Bhagavad Gita. Containing the grand truths of Hinduism treasured up in the most excellent Sanskrit stanzas selected from the Bhagavad Gita with English translations and explanations [sic]. Edited by Brahmsari Satchdananda Yogi R. Sivasankara Pandiyaji. 2d ed. Madras. Xii, 36 p., 12. [Forms no. 15 of the editor's Hindu Excelsior Series. The text is printed first in Devanagari in the 2d folio and each stanza is printed first in Telugu and again in Grantham in the 3d folio, and is followed by its English translation.]

97. **The Bhagavad-gita, with the commentary of Shri Shankaracharya. [Footnotes, derived in part from the gloss of Anandagiri] Translated by A. Mahadeva Sastri. Part 1. Madras: Minerva Press. Xvi, 360 p.; 22x14 cm. (This volume is no. 1 of the Vedic Religious Series, and contains the whole text of the Gita and the commentary in translation.)**

98. The Bhagavad-gita, with the commentary of Shri Shankaracharya. Another ed. fo item 97; Madras: Thompson & Co.

99. Lalan, F.K. [Fathehand Karpurchand] Key to the esoteric meaning of the Bhagavad gita. Chicago: Randall, [1897] 10p.;

100. The Sacred books of the East. Translated by various Oriental scholars, and edited by F. Max Mṻller. American ed. [New York: Scribner, 1897-1901] 12 volc., fold, plates, port.; 23cm. Vol. 8; The Institiute of Visnu, translated by J.Jolly. The Bhagavadgita, with the Sanatsugatiya and the Anugita, translated by Kashinath Trimbak Telang. (See also item 40)

101. The Song Celestial or Bhagavad-gita (from the Mahabharata)… 8th ed. of item 45. London : Kegan Paul, Trench, Trṻbner & Co. xiv, 173 p.;

102. Subba Row, Tiruvalum. Lectures on the study of the Bhagavad Gita ..Bombay: Theosophical Publishing FundXviii, 216p.; 14cm. (See also item 60)

1898

103. Gita. [A prose English translation from the original Sanskrit.] The teachings of Sri Krishna on the field of Kurukshetra. 3d ed. (See item 88) Edited and published by Shastri Manmatha Nath Dutt. Calcutta: [Printed by H.C. Dadd.] 2 p. l., 66 p.; 15.5 cm.

104. The Sacred books of the East….2d ed. Oxford: Clarendon Press, 1898- (See items 40 and 100)

105. The Sacred Books of the East described and examined. Hindu Series. London: Christian Literature Society for India. 3 vols., illus.; 22 cm. Vol. 2: Philosophic and law books: Selections from the Upanishads. Bhagavad Gita. Vedanta Sara. Yoga Satrap. Laws of Manu. Each part has also separate t.p. Includes bibliography. (See also item 87)

106. Sacred symbols of Bhagavad-gita. Translated by John Dew.... known as Kedpa.

107. Sri Bhagavad-gita. With Sri Ramanujacharya's Visishtadvaita commentary. Translated into English [and annotated] by A. Govindacharya. Madras: Printed at the Vaijayanati Press xxii, 582 p.; 22cm.

1899

108. The Sacred books of the East described and examined. Compiled from various writers....2d ed. Madras: Christian Literature Society for India. Vol. I: The Bhagavad Gita....98 p.; 21 cm.

109. The Song Celestial or Bhagavad-gita (from the Mahabharata)...9th ed. of item 45.

1900

110. The Bhagavad Gita. Translated into English verse with introduction and notes by Nanikram Vasamal Thandani. Krachi: Bharat Publishing House.

111. The Bhagavad-Gita; the book of devotion, Dialogues between Krishna, Lord of Devotion, and Arjuna, Prince of India. Translated by William Q. Judge; 7th ed. of item 65. New York: Theosophical Publishing Co., [4], xii, 133p., pl.; 15 cm.

112. The Bhagavad Gita: The Song of Life. English translation and explanatory notes by Thanwardas Lilaram Vaswani; edited by J.P. Vaswani. Poona, [India]; Gita Publishing House. 246 p.; 22cm.

113. The Bhagavat gita jeevan mukti saar, or the Hindus' book of life and salvation, with the text in Devannagari and translation in simple, easy English by S.S. Ananda. [Lahore, Pakistan]: N.N. Vaid. 106 p.

114. The Divine psalm: the poetical trans. of the Srimad Bhagbad Geeta in English. [By] Subodh Chandra Lahiri. Varanasi City. 106 p.

115. The Song Celestial or Bhagavad-gita (from the Mahabharata).... Another ed. of item 45. Boston: Little Brown & Co.

116. The Young Men's Gita. An English translation with introduction, notes, index and glossary. Edited by Joginadranath Mukharji. Calcutta: S.K. Lahiri. Ii, xiii, 179 p.

117. The Bhagavad-Gita, with the commentary of Sri Sankaracharya; translated into English by A. Mahadeva Sastri....24 ed. of item 97. Revised and improved, with additional notes. Mysore: [G.T.A.Printing Works]. Xx, 479 p.;19 cm. (Vedic religion series) Errata slip inserted after p [x].

118. The Bhagavad Gita. Part 1, chapters 1-VI, with Hindi and English translations....by Pandit Ramaranga Shastri. Lahore, [Pakistan]: Enad Bros. 160 p.

119. Raya, Muralidhara. Sree Krishna etc. [An epitome of the legends of Krishna contained in the Bhagavadgita and Bhagavatapurana.] Calcutta: Indian Publication society. xiii, vi, 393 p.

120. STRAY THOUGHTS on the Bhagabad Gita. By the Dreamer. First series. Calcutta.

1902

121. The Bhagabat Gita [in Sanskrit and English] with [English translation of] the commentary by Shri Shankaracharya.... Edited by S.C. Mukhaopadhaya [Sic.]. Calcutta. 32, 402 p.

122. The Bhagavad-Gita; the book of devotion....7th ed. of item 65. New York: Alliance Publishing Co.

123. Dreamer [Pseud.]. The Dreamer Studies in the Bhagavad-Gita [by William King]. London: Theosophical Publishing Society. 112 p.

124. Murdoch, John. The Religious and moral teachings of the Bhagavad Gita examined; an appeal to educated Hindus....London: Christian Literature Society for India. [2], 61 p.; 21 cm. (Great Indian questions of the day, no.1) Prefatory note signed by John Murdoch. Running title: The teachings of the Bhagavad Gita.

125. Kalidasa. Sakuntala [translated by Sir W.Jones]...To which is added Meghaduta; or the Cloud Messenger [translated by H.W. Wilson], the Bhagavad-gita or Sacred Song [from the Mahabharata translated by Sir Charles Wilkins]. Edited with an introduction by T. Holme. London: Walter Scott Publishing Co., [1902] 240 p.; 8*. (The Scott Library, vol. 117) prose translation of the Bhagavad-Gita is a reprint of Charles Wilkin's 1785 edition.

1903

126. The Bhagavad-Gita or the Lord's Song....3d and newly revised ed. of item 86. 186 p.; 14.5 cm.

127. The Bhagavad-Gita or the Lord's Song....3d and newly revised ed. of item 86 Another imprint. Benares: Tara Printing Works.

128. Gita....Edited and published [text and translation] by Manmathnath Shastri. Calcutta: Society for the Resuscitation of Indian Literature. 108, 126 p. (See items 88 and 103)

129. Omley, William. The Philosophy of Spirit....2d ed. of item n 38. Manchester and London: John Heywood. Vi [4], 282 p.

1904

130. The Bhagavad-Gita; or the Lord's Song; 4th and newly revised ed. of item 86. Benares and London: Theosophical Publishing Society.

180 p.; 13.5 cm

131. Farquhar, John Nicol. The Age and Origin of the Gita. London: Christian Literature Society. 24 p. (Pice Pamphlets, no. 3) "Reprinted from East and West."

1905

132. Bhagavad-gita: or the Lord's Song. Translated {with introduction and notes} by Lionel D. Barnett. London: J.M. Dent & Co. vi, 211, [1]p., front, diagr.; 15.5cm. [In case 16.5 cm.] Half-title: The Temple Classics. Title in red and blue within ornamental border. Original blue cloth top edges gilt in blue cloth case.

133. **The Bhagavad-gita, with Sanskrit text, free translation into English, a word-for- word translation and an introduction on Sanskrit grammar, by Annie Besant and Bhagavan Das. London and Benares: Theosophical Publishing Society. 4p.l., xxxiii, 348 p.; 19 cm**

134. Rangacharya, M. Bhagavad-gita lectures in English...[with the text and an English translation] Sanskrit and English. Madras; Oriental Press.

135. Shrimad Bhagavadgita navpushparvah bhashya. The illustrated Bhagwad Gita. Containing text. Prose order. Word meaning. Prose and poetical. Translations in Hindi, Urdu, Persian, Bengali, English. Commentaries by Shakaracharya,
Ananda Gir, Sri Dhar Swami. Short history of the Bhagwad Gita. Chronological table of Lunar dynasty, and copious notes.... Pandit Adya Prasada Misra, editor. 3 parts, containing adhyayas 2 and 3. Benares, [1905]-09. 60-98, [4], 4; 104-131 p., pl., 8, 44, 8 p.; 21x17 cm. [Imperfect and incomplete]. The Bengali is in Nagri characters.

136. The Song Celestial....New ed. of item 45. London: K.Paul, Trench, Trübner. xii, 111 p.

1906

137. Besant, Annie (Wood). Hints on the Study of the Bhagavad Gita; four lectures delivered at the thirtieth anniversary meeting of the Theosophical Society at Adyar, Madras, December 1905. Benares and London; Theosophical Publishing Society. 131 p.;

138. The Bhagavad gita. Translation and commentaries in English according to Sri Madhawacharaya's bhashyas by S. Subba Rau. Madras: Minerava Press. Lxxviii, 317 p., vi; 22x14 cm.

139. (The Bhagavadd-gita) [Translated into English.] Moradabad. 166 p.; 14x9 cm. No title page.

140. The Bhagavad-Gita, or the Lord's Song. Another imprint of item 130. (See item 86). (Lotus Leaver,2)

141. Farquhar, John Nicol. Gita and Gospel...2d ed. London Christian Literature Society; Madras [printed]. 92 p.;

142. Rai Bahadur Biresvar Chakravarti's translation of the Bhagavad Gita in English rhyme. Edited....by J.S. Charavarti. London: Kegan Paul, Trench, Trübner andCo.; Calcutta: S.K. Lahiri and Co. lxvi, 193 p.

143. The Song Celestial ..... 10th ed. of item 45. 20 cm. (In Arnold, Sir Edwin. Poetical works, 1981-1904, V. 7)

144. Wilmhurst, Walter Leslie. The Chief Scripture of India, the Bhagavad Gita and its relation to present events. London: Philip Wellby. 84 p.; 8*

1907

145. The Bhagavad Gita or the Divine Ode. New ed. of item 2. (See also item 95) New York: Vedanta Society, [1907]

146. Bhagavad-gita....Edited with an English Translation,...Notes, a Preface and a Summary....By Janardan Sakharam Kudalkar, M.A.

Lahore, [Pakistan]: Anglo-Sanskrit Press. [iii], lxv, 151 p., covers; 18x13 cm.

147. The Bhagavad gita; or the message of the master. Compiled and adapted from numerous old and new translations of the original Sanscrit text, by Yogi Ramacharaka [William Walker Atkinson]. Chicago, Illinois: The Yogi Publication Society. 151 p.; 20 cm.

148. The Bhagavad-gita or The Lord's Song, with the text in Devanagri and an English translation by Annie Besant. 1st ed. Madras: G.A/ Natesan, [1907], [iii], v, 212 p., covers; 17x11 cm.

149. Hindu Philosophy…4th ed. of item 41. London: Trŭbner & Co. vi, 216 p.; 22x15 cm. (Trŭbner's Oriental Series)

1908

150. Baijnath, Lala, Rai Bahadur. The Bhagavad Gita in Modern Life. Being a concise exposition of its religion and philosophy as applicable to different aspects of modern society, with illustrations from the life of the teacher- Sri Krishna- and the thoughts of eminent men of India and other countries. Meerut, [India]: Vaishya Hitkari. Iii, 110 p.

151. Besant, Annie (Wood). Hints on the Study of the Bhagavad Gita. Another imprint of item 137. 129 p.; 19 cm.

152. Bhagavad gita "The songs of the master", translated with an introduction and commentary by Charles Johnston….Flushing, New York: C. Johnston. Lxii, 61 p.; 24.5 cm.

153. _______. Another edition. New York: Quarterly Book Department, [c1908]. Viii p., 1 l., 200p., incl. front.; 15cm.

154. Bhagavad-Gita or the Lord's Song…. 2d ed. of item 148. Madras: G.A. Natesan & Co.

155. The Bhagavadgita, with the Sanatsugatiya and the Anugita…2d ed. of item 40. [5], 442, 18 p.; 23x15 cm.

156. Sastri, A. Mahadeva. Vedic religion and casts, or the basis of united humanity. An introduction to the study of the Bhagavad-Gita. Mysore: Published by the author.
70 p; 21 cm.

157. Shri Gitamrita Bodhini [i.e., the Bhagavad-gita in the translation of Annie Besant, rearranged under 27 headings], compiled by Vanaparti Rama Prapanna Das, alias Lt. Henry Wahab. Madras: Hoe and Co. iii, iii, 99 p.

158. Srimadbhagavad gita with Shankar's commentary. Translated by A. Mahadeva Sastrai. Edited by Hari N. Apte and others. Poon. (Anandasrama Sanskrit Series, no. 34)

1909

159. The Bhagavad gita. Text and translation by F.T. Books. Srirangam, [India]: Sri Vani-vilas Press. [ii], iv, iv, 139, [1] p. covers.

160. The Bhagavad-gita; or The Chant of the Blessed One. Translated into rhythmical English by F.T. Brooks. Ajmer, [India]: Syama Behari Misra, [1909]. I, 143 p. 23 cm.

161. The Bhagavad-gita; or the Lord's Song.... Another imprint of item 130. 14.5x11 cm. (On cover; LOTUS LEAVES)

162. The Bhagavat Gita; or "The Celestial Song". A true literal translation with notes and arguments by R. Narasinga Row. Kumbakonam, [India]: Sri Vidya Press. 224 p.

163. Gopala Sastri, Susarla. The Jῆana-Lahari. [A collection of Sanskrit Vedantic texts, including the Bhagavad Gita, with commentaries of the Advaita School in Sanskrit, English, and Telugu, etc.] Edited and published by Susarla Gopalasastry. Madras: Ananda Press.

164. Kaji, Chhaganlal G. Philosophy of the Bhagavad Gita. As exposition [with text and translation]. Rajkot, [India]; Ganatra Printing Works, 1909-11. 2 vols.; vi, 1-244; 245- 628 p.

165. More, Paul Elmer. “The Bhagavad Gita”. In shelburne Essays. 6th series. (Studies of religious dualism) New York and London: G.P. Putnam’s sons. Pp. 43-64.

166. **Srimad-Bhagavad-Gita. With Sanskrit Text, Parapharase with word-by-word Literal Translation; English Rendering and Comments, Index, and Commentary. By The Swami Swarupananda. [1st ed.] Mayavati, Almora, [India]: Prabuddha Bharata Press. [iv], pl;l [iv], xii, 399, xiii-xvi p., covers; 19x13 cm. “Himalayan Series, 20.”**

1910

167. The Bhagavad gita, with Text, word-meaning, Paraphrase. Hindi and English prose translations and important notes. Adhyaya I. Edited…by Pt. [Pandit] Adya Prasada Misra…Benares, [India]: Purana-prakasa Press. [1], 16 p., covers; 27x18 cm.

168. The Bhagavad-Gita, or The chant of the blessed one…. Another ed. of item 160. Ajmer, [India].: Printed by S.M. Industries Co., Ltd. [4], 143p.; 22x14 cm.

169. The Bhagavat gita or ‘The Celestial Song”, … Another imprint of item 162.

170. “Bhagavad Gita”. In Sacred Writings. (Harvard Classic, v. 44-45) New York: P.F. Collier, [c1910]. 2 vols. V. 2, pp. 799-884.

171. The Song Celestial….New Ed. of item 45. London: Kegan Paul. 111p.

172. Srimad Bhagavad-gita pakita. Pakit saiz Bhagwat Gita. Sanskrit shlokwar. Hindi tarjumah shlokwar. Urdu tarjumah shlokwar. Angrezi tarjumah shlokwar. Mu’alafah Diwan Maya Das Gharib munshi. [The English translation is Mrs. Annie Besnat’s, reprinted.] Nagri and Urdu characters. Lahore, [Pakistan]: Nawalkishor Printing Works and Commercial Printing Works, [1910]. 10, 149, p1., 4, 4, 28, 605 p.; 14x9 cm.

173. Subba Row, Tiruvalum. Lectures on the study of the Bhagavad Gita. Being a help to students of its philosophy...printed for the Bombay Theosophical Publication Fund, by Rajaram Tukaram... [2d ed.] Bombay: Bhivaji Hari Shinde. xviii, 211 p.; (See item 102) First published under title: Discourses on the Bhagavat Gita. 1888. (See item 60)

1911

174. The Bhagavad Gita; or the Message of the master...Revised ed. of item 147. 184 p.; 14 cm.

175. Bhagavad-Gita, or the Lord's Song.... 3d ed. of item 148. 3p.l., ix, 254 p.; 12 cm.

176. Passage from the song celestial, by Sir Edwin Arnold. Portland, Maine: T.B. Mosher. Vii, [3], 3=37 p., [1] p., 1 l.; 18 cm." Nine hundred and fifty copies of this book printed on Van gelder hand made paper."

177. The Song Divine, or The Bhagavad-Gita. A metrical rendering (with annotations) by C.C. Caleb. London: Luzac & Co. xi, 168 p.: 17x13 cm.

178. Sri Geetha Ratnamulu. A selection of the Bhagavad Gita {with English translation]. By T. Ramakristna Rao Gupta. Narasarowpet, [India]: Bharati-vilasa Press. [4], 2, 2+[1], 2, 10+ [1], 98, 4+{2} p., covers; 11x7 cm. [Text in Telugu Characters.]

179. Subba Rao, A. The theory of Sri Krishna of Srimad Bhagavata, Narsapur, [India]. xii, 94 p.

1912

180. The Bhagavad-Gita; or The Lord's Song...4th and revised ed. of item 86. 180 p.; 14x10.5 cm

181. The Bhagavad-gita, the book of devotion.....8th ed. of item 65

182. Farquhar, John Nicol. Permanent Lessons of the Gita. 2d ed. London; Madras: Christian Literature Society for India. 31p.; 19 cm

183. Narasinga Row Sahib, C.V. The Introductory Study of the Bhagavadgita. (A systematic exposition of the Gita.) Madras: Brahma-Vadin Press. [1], ii, iii, vii, 247 p.; 18x13 cm.

184. Subba Row, Tiruvalum. Philosophy of the Bhagavad-gita. Madras: The Theosophical Office. 2 p.l., 137 p., [1]; 19 cm. "Four lectures delivered at the Eleventh annual convention of the theosophical society, held at Adyar on December 27, 28, 29, and 30, 1886."

1913

185. The Bhagavad-Gita; the book of devotion....From the Sanscrit by William Q. Judge. 9th ed. of item 65. 4 p.l., [vii]-xviii, 133 p., pl.; 14.5 cm.

186. Bhandarkar, Ramkrishna] Gopal]. Vaisnavism, Saivism and minor religious systems. Strassburg: K.J. Trübner. 1 p.l., 169. (Grundriss der Indo-Arischen Philologie und Altertumskunde. Vol. 3, part 6

187. Srimad-Bhagavad-gita; or The Blessed Lord's song; translated from the original Sanskrit text by Swami Paramananda. Boston, Massachusetts; The Vedanta Centre. xv, 144 p.' 14.5 cm.

1914

188. The Bhagavad-gita or The Lord's Song. Translated [into English] by Annie Besant (with the text in Devananagri). Another ed. of item 86. Adyar (Madras): Theosophical Publishing House. [iii], xii, 334 p.; 11x7 cm

189. Brooks, F.T. "Whom does the Bhagavad Gita belong to?" A lecture. (2d edition.) Madras: Vyasasharma Book Shop. 54 p.

1915

190. The Bhagavad-gita; or, The divine ode....A new ed. of item 2. New York: The Vedanta Society. 180 p.

191. The Bhagavad-gita; or, The Lord's song....Another ed. of item 86. 180 p. On cover: Lotus leaves II

192. Jinarajadasa, Curuppumullage. The Bhagavad Gita. Adyar, [India}: Theosophical Publishing House. 30 p.; 19 cm. (Adyar Pamphlets, no. 59) "From the Proceedings of the Federation of the European Sections of the Theosophical Society, Amsterdam, 1904."

193. Lingesa Mahabhagawat. "The Significance of the Bhagavad-gita". Poona. Sanskrit Research, v. l, pp. 81-88.

194. Ramamurti, K. The essential analysis of the Bhagavad-Gita and the Anu-Gita. Vizagapatam, [India]. ii, 54 p.

195. Rangacharya, Malur. The Hindu Philosophy of Conduct. Being class lectures on the Bhagavadgita by M. Rangacharya, M.A., Rao Bhadur. Revised reprint. (Vols. 2,3 edited by M.B. Varadaraja Iyengar and M.R. Sampatkumaran). Madras: Law Printing House, 1915-1939. 3v. (Vol. 1 only is a "revised reprint". Vols. 2,3 were published by G.A. Natesan & Co., Madras). 25x17 cm. {Includes text and translation of the Bhagavadgita]

196. Srimad-bhagavad-gita, a treatise on Yoga philosophy of the Aryans, with explanations in Bengalee and English by Shiboprosanna Mukhopadhyaya. Calcutta: Laksmi-narayana Press, 1915-. Adhyaya I. 49 p. [1915]. Adhyaya IV. pp. 181-229. [1916]. Adhyaya VI. Pp. 269-315. [1918]. 24x15 cm.

1916

197. Bhawani Shankar. Lectures on Bhagavad Gita, delivered....at Calcutta in 1914. Benares City, [India, 1916]. (i), 42 p.

198. Browning, Katherine. Notes and Index to the Bhagavadd Gita. London: Theosophical Publishing Society. 104 p.

199. Burway, Mukund Wamanarao. Glimpses of the Bhagawatgita and the Vedanta philophy. Bombay: Vaibhav Press. 2 p. l., ix p., 11, 310, 3 p.; 21 cm. [Includes text with English introduction and translation by Mukund Wamanarao Burway.] (Bibilographical footnotes. Text and translation of the Bhagavat-gita, pp. 129-262.)

200. Joshi, V.M. A gist of Mr. Tilak's Gita-Tahasya; or, Karmayoga-shastra (the Hindu philosophy of life, ethics and religion). Benares, [India]. iv, 15, 88 p.

201. Padmanabhachar, C.M. A critical study of Bhagavad Geeta. First six chapters only in the light of Sri Madhava's commentaries compared with those of other schools. [Foreword by K.Krishnaswami rao, Dewan Bhadur.] Madras: The Law Printing House. [i], pl., [i], 1`0, xvii, 1108, 110 p.; 23x14 cm.

1917

202. Bhagavad-geeta of Bhagavan Sri Krishna and the Geetartha-Sangraha of Maharshi Gobhila. Edited by....K.T. Sreenivasachariar...with a preface by him and an English foreword by Dr. Sir S. Subrahmanya Iyer. [This recension of the text has some 70 verses not found in the vulgate.] Madras: Law Printing House. Viii, xliii, 100p. (Suddha-dharma-sandals series, No.3)

203. Dhar, Mohini Mohan. Krishna the charioteer; or the teachings of Bhagavad Gita. London: Theosophical Publishing House. 173 p., 1l.; 14 cm.

204. Farquhar, John Nicol. Gita and Gospel. 3d ed. (See item 141) Madras: Christian Literature society for India. (1), 106 p.; 8*.

205. Jagannatha, P. "The text of the Gita". Bangalore City. Sanskrit Research, v. 2, pp. 195-215.

206. Joshi, V.M. A gist of Mr. Tilak's Gita-Rahasya... Another ed. of item 200. Bombay. Iv, 14, 73 p.

207. Kannoomal, L. Lord Krishna's message based on the Bhagavad Gita. Agra. Ii, 22p.

1918

208. The Bhagavad-gita; or the battle of life, the ancient poem of India.... Chicago, Illinois: The Abstract Truth Society, [1918]. 128 p.; 17.5 cm. (The Impersonal series) [Translated by Arthur and Frank Crane.

209. The Bhagavad-gita on the Lor's Song... Another ed. of item 188. [i], xii, 383+[1] p.; 12x7 cm.

210. The Bhagavad-gita with the commentary of Sri Sankaracharya, translated from Sanskrit into English. 3d ed. of item 97. Madras: V. Ramaswamy Sastrulu and Sons. Xii, 522 p.; 19x13 cm.

211. Garbe, Richard von. Garbe's introduction to the Bhagavadgita. Translated from the German by N.B. Utgikar. [Bombay, 1918-]. Pp. 1-8, and latter sheets;. "Issued in sheets in successive numbers of the Indian Antiquary."

212. ____. Introductionn to the Bhagavadgita. Translated by the Rev. D. Mackichan ...[Bombay]: The University of Bombay. 1 p. 1, 50 p.; 24 cm. cover has imprint: Bombay, Printed at the Government Central Press.

213. Judge, William Quan. Notes on the Bhagavad-gita, the first seven chapters by William Q. Judge, the remaining chapters by a student taught by him. Los Angeles, California: The magazine Theosophy. 3p. l., 237 p.; 15 cm. "Appeared in the magazine Theosophy from November, 1913, to February, 1917. Notes upon chapters one to seven, inclusive were first printed in The Path...From 1887 to 1895."

214. Lingesa Mahabhagawat. The Heart of the Bhagavad-Gita. [With a preface by Sir S. Subrahmanya Aiyer.] Baroda: A.G. Widgery. Liii,230 p.; 19.5 cm. (The Gakewad Studies in religion and philosophy, 3) (The author is also known as Lingesa Vidyabhushana Vedanta-Vachaspati....now His Holiness Sri Vidya Shankar Bharati Swami.)

215. Ramaswamy Sastrigal, K.S. Our social problems and the Bhagavad Gita. Srirangam, {India}. 72 p.

216. Sampson, Holden Edward. The Bhagavad-Gita interpreted in the light of Christian tradition. London: William Rider & Son, Ltd. Xxii, 165 p.; 32*. Foreword by Robert Frederick Hall.

217. Srimad-Bhagavad-gita; with Text, Word-for-word Translation English Rendering, comments and Index. By The Swami Swarupananda. 2d ed. of item 166. Calcutta: Sri Gauranga Press. [ii], [iii], pl., xiii, 418 p.; 18x13 cm. (Himalayan Series, no. 20)

218. ______. Another ed. [Mayavati, Almora, India: Prabudha Bharata Office.]

219. Stephen, Dorothea Jane. Studies in the early Indian thought. Cambridge: University Press. 4 p.l., 176 p:

1919

220. Dhar, Mohini Mohan. Krishna the Charioteer; or the teachings of Bhagavad Gita. 2d ed. of item 203. 186 p.; 20 cm.

221. Mehta, S.S. A manual of Vedanta philosophy as revealed in the Upanishadas and the Bhagavadgita. Bombay. Xvii, 12. 61, 85 p.; 21 cm. "Based on the Sarirakaminanasabhasya of Sankaracarya which is a commentary on the Brahmasutra of Badarayana."

222. The Song Celestial or Bhagavad-gita (from the Mahabharata)... New ed. of item 45. London; Kegan Paul, Trnch, Trϋbner & Co., Ltd. Xii, lll p.; 15 cm.

1920

223. The Bhagavad-gita; or, the Lord's song...Another imprint of item 130.

224. The Bhagavad-Gita; or, The Lord's song, translated by Lionel D. Barnett...Another imprint of item 132.

225. The Bhagavad-Gita; the book of devotion... 10th ed. of item 65. Los Angeles, California: United Lodge of Theosophists. Xviii, 133 p.;

14.5 cm. (Imprint covered by label : For sale by the quarterly Book Dept., New York.)

226. The Bhagavadgita, The Song of the Divine One, the Lord, with copious annotations by Tookaram Tatya [Tatia]. Bombay: Theosophical Publications Fund. Contains the Sanskrit text along with the English translation.

1921

227. Crittenden, Charmain. Ethics of the Bhagavad Gita and of Buddhism, parts I and II. Berkeley, California; University of California Press. [40 p.]; 26.3 cm. (University of California chronicle, vol. xxiii, pp, 72-94, 150-168.)

228. Lajpat Raya; The Message of the Bhagavad Gita. Bombay. [1921]. 68 p.;

229. Sarma, Durga Sahaya. The Reality of Life in the Bhagavadgita. Agra. Iv, 193 p.;

230. The Song Celestial or Bhagavad-gita (from the Mahabharata)... Another ed. of item 222. lllp.; 15 cm.

231. Subba Row, Tiruvalum. The Philosophy of the Bhagavad-Gita. Another ed. of item 184.

1922

232. **Ghose, Aurobindo. Essays on the Gita. Madras: V. Ramaswamy Sastrulu & Sons. [iii], 332 p., pl., port.; 20 cm.**

233. Gode, P.K. The Bhakti-Sutras of Narada and the Bhagavadgita; A study in parallelism of thought and expression. Poona, [India]: Bhandarkar Oriental Research Institute, 1922.23. [32p.] (Bhandarkar Oriental Research Institute, Annals, vol. IV, pp. 63-95.)

234. Haas, George Christian Otto. Recurrent and Parallel Passages in the Principal Upanishads and the Bhagavad-Gita with references to other Sanskrit texts. Boston, Massachusette. 43 p.; 8*. (Reprinted from the Journal of the American Oriental Society, etc.)

235. Introduction to the Bhagavad-Gita. By Dewan Bhadur V.K. Ramanujacharya. London, Madras, Chicago: Theosophical Publishing House. x+[1], 257 p.; 18.5 cm. "With the Sanskrit text and English translation.:"

1923

236. The Bhagavad-Gita; or, The Lord's song. Another ed. of item 86. Chicago: Theosophical Press. 176 p.; 15 cm.

237. Gopalasastry, Susarla. The century questions on the Bhagavat Gita. Amalapuram, [India]. (1), 147 p., illus.

238. Sampson, Holden Edward. The Bhagavad-Gita interpreted in the light of Christian tradition. Another ed. of item 216. 16 cm.

239. Taki, Ramachandra Shankar. De carmine dei decrum, or On the Song of the God of Gods. Being a commentary in English on the Bhagavad-Gita. [With Sanskrit text and English translation.] Bombay: Sadbhakti Prasarak Mandall, [printed at] Tutorial Press, 1923-1925. 3 v.; 19 cm. Vol. 1 lacks t.p.

1924

240. The Bhagavad-gita, or The Lord's Song.... 4th Adyar ed. of item 188. xvi, 276 p.; 11x7 cm.

241. ____. 5th ed. of item 148. vii, 264 p.

242. The Sacred Books of the East... Another ed. of item 100.

243. Sharpe, Elizabeth. Shri Ganeshya Namah: Shri Krishna and the Bhagavad-Gita. London: A.H. Stockwell. 44p.: 19 cm.

244. Shrimad Bhagavadd Gita. (Metrical English Translation) by Vedantacharya Swami Tulsiram Misra Vidyanidhi. Lucknow: Newal Kishore Press. [ii], 14, iv+(1), 143, 43 p., pl.; 16x10 cm.

245. Sri-Bhagavad-Geeta; with the commentary of Sri-Hamsa-Yogin. Edited and published by K.T. Sreenivasachariar. Madras: Mudaliar, 1924 (Suddha Dharma Mandala's series, no. 8)

246. Visvasa Gangadhara Bhatta. Bhagavadgita, a Study. Dharwar, [India]: Karnatak Printing Works. 86 p.;

1925

247. Besant, Annie (Wood). Hints on the Study of the Bhagavad-Gita. 3d ed. of item 137. Adyar, [India]: Theosophical Publishing House. 3 p.l, 123 p.; 19 cm.

248. The Bhagavad gita; or, Song of the blessed one, India's favorite Bible. Interrupted by Franklin Edgerton...Chicago; The Open Court Publishing Company. 3 p.l., iii, 2 l., 106 p.; 22.5 cm.

249. The Bhagavad-gita; or, The Lord's Song... 5th revised ed. of item 86. Reprinted from the 1904 edition. London; The Theosophical Publishing House Limited, [1925]. 150 p; 14x11 cm. (See item 130)

250. The Bhagawadgita, the divine path to God. [By] K.S. Ramaswami Sastri. Madras: Ganesh & Co., [1925]. [6], 174 p.

251. Sarma, Dittskavi Subrahmanya. Introduction to the Bhagavad Gita. Madras: Ganesh & Co., viii, 106p.; 19.5 cm. (Italian Renaissance Library series, no. 4)

252. The Song Celestial or Bhagavad-gita (from the Mahabharata)... Another imprint of item 222.

253. Steiner, Rudolf. The Bhagavad-Gita and the Epistles of St. Paul, five lectures... London: Anthroposophical Society, [1925]. 70 p.;

254. Yogananda, Paramhansa. Songs of the soul, including "Visions of

visions" from the Bhagavad Gita. 3d enlarged ed. Los Angeles, California: Sat Sanga, [c1925]. 121 p.; 19 cm.

1926

255. The Bhagavad-gita. With Saṃskṛṭ text...2d revised ed. of item 133. Adyar, [India]: Theosophical Publishing House; Madras: Hindipracara Press. 73 l., 319+[1], 73 p.; 19x13 cm.

256. Bhagavaddgita: or, The Lord's Song....Another ed. of 132.

257. Brahmananda, Brahmarshi Bhai. The Blunders of the Bhagabath Gita. Telinipara, [India]: The Author. Part 1. 192 p.

258. Ghose, Aurobindo. Essays on the Gita. Series 1-2. Calcutta: Arya Publishing House, [1926-28]. 2v.; . (See also item 232)

259. Metric translation of Bhagabad Gita. By Bilash Chandra Roy. Dacca, [Bangladesh]: Ajit Chandra Roy. [3], ii, ii, [1], 136 p.; 13.5 cm

260. Srimad-Bhagavad-gita. With text, word-for-word Translation... 4th ed. of item 166. [6], pl., xiii, 418p.; 19x13 cm.

261. _____. Another ed. Almora, [India]: Advaita Ashram.

262. Trimargaya Gita arthat Gita-jn̄ana-Gaṃga ki Triveṃi (Samskrta-Hindi-Anṃgreji[English])... Lekhaka Vedantacarya Svami Tulasirama Misra. Agra: Santi Press. [3], 3,2, 261+[1] p.; 18x12 cm. (Gita-grantha-mala, no. 4)

1927

263. The Bhagavad-gita: with translation and notes. By K.S. Ramaswamy Sastrigal. Vol. I, chapters 1-6. Srirangam, (India): Sri Vanivilas Press. [1], ii, 384 p.; 18x12 cm.

264. The Bhagavad-Gita, or the Lord's Song...Another imprint of item 86. London: Theosophical Publishing House. 180 p..

265. Leidecker, Kurt Friedrich. "The Noetical terminologyin Upanisads and Bhagavad Gita". Ph.D. Thesis, University of Chicago. (Typescript-carbon copy) xvii, 140, l.p.; 29 cm. Bibliography: Leaves 135-140.

266. Rele, Vasant Gangaram. Bhagavad-Gita; an exposition on the basis of psycho-philosphy and psycho-analysis. With forewords by N.D. Mehta and C.V. Vaidya. 3d ed. Bombay: D.B. Taraporevala, [1927].

267. A synthesis of the Bhagavad-Gita. An arrangement of the teachings of the Gita in their relation to the five paths of attainment, with comments by the editors of the Shrine of Wisdom. London: Shrine of Wisdom. 71 p.; 8*. (Shrine of Wisdom, Manual no. 9)

1928

268. The Bhagavad-gita; or the Lord's song….5th Adyar ed. of item 188. xvi, 276 p.; 11 cm. (Imprint on label mounted on t.p.: Wheaton, Ill. Sold by the Theosophical Press.)

269. Bhagavad-Gita: or, the Lord's song… Translated by Lionel D. Barnett. Another ed. of item 132. London: J.M. Dent & Sons. Vi, 211 p., front.' 16 cm.

270. The Bhagavad-Gita. The book of devotion…11th ed. of item 65. Los Angeles: The Theosophy Co. xviii, 133 p.; 16*.

271. The Bhagavadgita, translated from the Sanskrit with an introduction, an argument and a commentary by W.Douglas P. Hill… London: Oxford University Press. Xii, 303, [1] p.; 23 cm. (Translation at foot of text). "Bibliographic notes": p. 273-278. Errata Slip inserted. Text in Sanskrit and English.

272. Bhagawat Gita with Sanskrit text, Padachhchheda, word-meaning, literal translation, notes and quotations from the Hindu scriptures and a metaphysical preface. Compiled by Babu Radha Charan… Allahabad, [India]: Dr. Lalit Mohan Basu, M.B., Panini Office, [pref. 1928]. 1p. l., xxii (i.e. xxxii), 591 p.; 18.5 cm. (The Sacred books of the Hindus. Extra V. [6]). Sanskrit and English texts.

‘First edition.” “Errata statement” :p. xxx-[xxxii].

273. Ghose, Aurobindo. Essays on the Gita. Second Series. Calcutta: Arya Publishing House, [1928]. 4 p.l., 501 p., 1 l.’ 22 cm. (See also items 232 and 258)

274. Gitanand, Brahmanchari. The dialogue divine and dramatic (between Lord Sri Krishna and heroic warrior Arjuna). Chapters first and second (retold and rewritten in the language and expression suitable to modern Arjunas). Madras: B.G. Paul. Vi, 89 p.: 19 cm.

275. Judge, William Quan, and Crosbie, Robert. Notes on the Bhagavad Gita. Los Angeles: The Theosophy Co. 239 p.;

276. Rele, Vasant Gangaras. Bhagavad-Gita; an exposition on the basis of psycho-philosophy and psycho-analysis. With forewords by N.D. Mehta and C.V. Vaidya. Bombay: D.B. Taraporevala Sons & Co. 186 p.:. (See item 266)

277. Saunders, Kenneth James. The gospel for Asia; a study of three religious masterpieces: Gita, Lotus, and Fourth Gospel. London: Society for Promoting Christian Knowledge. Xv, 245 p.; (Printed in the U.S.A)

278. ____. Another ed. New York: The Macmillan Company. Xv p., 2 l., 245 p.: 22.5 cm. “Footnotes by chapters”: 226-254.

279. Vadekar, Devidas Dattatraya. Bhagawad-Gita: a fresh study; being a plea for the historical study and interpretation of the Gita. An essay by D.D. Vadekar with a foreword by Prof. S.V. Dandekar. Poona: Oriental Book Agency. Xv, 100 p.; 19 cm.

280. Wise words from the Gita [by M.N. Patil…Revised and enlarged. Gujarati-English edition…by N.H. Metha(sic) & Patil. Bombay: M.N. Patil, [1928]. 112 p.; 19.5 cm. Title supplied in part from publisher’s label, inserted. Bound with its: Wise words from the Gita. Bombay, 1935. (See item 334)

1929

281. The Bhagavad-Gita, [translated into English verse] by Arthur W. Ryder. Chicago, Ill.: The University of Chicago Press. [1929]. Xxiv, 139 p., 1 l.; 20 cm. At head of title: Arthur W. Ryder.

282. The Bhagavadgita; with easy Sanskrit annotations and literal English translation by Sitanath Tattvabhushan and Srischandra Vedantabhushan Bhagavataratna... Edited by Sitanath Tattvabhushan with an historical and philosophical introduction giving an expository and critical account of the contents of each chapter. Calcutta: Printed and Published by Trigunanth Roy at the Brahma Mission Press. Ii p.l., lxxvii, 336 p.; 19 cm. Text in Sanskrit and English.

283. Brooks, F.T. A synopsis of the Gita. Srirangam, (India). 43 p.; 10 cm.

284. Durrani, Fazal Karim Khan. The Bhagavadgita, a criticism. 1st ed. Lahore, [Pakistan]: Tabligh Literature Society. 112 p.

285. Narasimham, P. The Gita: a critique. Madras: Huxley Press. 270 p.;

286. Sircar, Mahendranath. Mysticism in Bhagavat Gita. Calcutta. New York: Longman, Green. 219 p.

287. Srimad Bhagavad-gita...Book XI,....with the commentaries of Sankaracharya and Sridhara Swamin ...and Translation in English and Bengali, together with the English rendering by Dr. Annie Besant ...and full explanatory and grammatical notes and an introduction in English by Sisir Kumar Mitra. [Canto XI only] Calcutta: Metcalfe Press, [1929]. [2], 18, 112 p.; 18x13 cm.

1930

288. The Bhagavad Gita (students' edition), the text [in Sanskrit] and translation with Introduction and notes by D.S. Sarma. Madras: Current Thought Press, xi, [1], 299 p.

289. The Bhagavad-Gita...Another ed. of item 281.

290. The Bhagavad gita: or, the message of the master. Rev. ed. of item 147. Chicago, Illinois: The Yogi Publication Society. 184 p.: 17 cm.

291. Charpentier, Jarl Hellen Robert Tousaint, Some remarks on the Bhagavadgita, Bombay. [20 p.] (Indian Antiquary, vol. 59, pp. 46-50, 77-80, 101-105, 121-126.)

292. Gitanand, Brahmachari. The Gita idea of God: or, The religion of life, beauty, love, truth and righteousness; being India's greatest contribution to the permanent and progressive thought of all mankind, expounded by Brahmachari Gitanand. Madras: B.G. Paul & Co. lxiv, 432 p.; 23 cm.

293. Jinarajadasa, Curuppumullage. The Bhagavad Gita [From the Proceedings of the European Secton of the Theosophical Society, Amsterdam, 1904]. 9ed ed.) Adyer. [India: Theosophical Publishing House]. 31 p.; 19 cm. (See item 192)

294. Kapali Sastri, T.V. Gospel of the Gita. Madras. [193} iii, 92 p.

295. The Kashmir Recension of the Bhagavadgita. [Varlant readings as compared with the vulgate; extracts from the commentaries Ramakantha and Abhinavagupta, translated] By Friedrich Otto Schrader. Stuttgart: W. Kohlhammer. 2p.l., 52 p.; 22.5 cm. (Added t.p.: Contributions to Indian philosophy and history of religion, v.3)

296. Ramanuja, founder of sect. Ramanuja's Commentary on the Bhagavadgita..Inaugural-Dissertation...Ludwig-Maximlians-Universitӓt su Mϋnchen [Hrsg. Undϋbersetzt] von Isvaradatta Vidyalankara. Hyderabad-Decca, [India]: K. Krishnaswamy; Chandrakanth Press. Xxxi, 360, iii p.; 25 cm. "An English translation of Ramanuja's Commentary on the Bhagavadgita, with introduction and notes."

297. Sarma, B.N. Krishnamurti. The grammar of the Gita-a vindication, Poona City, [India]. [161` p.] (Bhandarkar Oriental Research Institute, Poona, India. Annals. Vol. XI, PP. 284 – 299)

298. The Song Celestial...New ed. of item 45.

1931

299. The Bhagavad-gita with the commentary of Sri Sankaracharya. Critically edited by Prof. Dinkar Vishnu Gokhale. Poon: Oriental Book Agency. 8, 304 p.; 18 cm. "Title also in Sanskrit."

300. Jaisinghani, Amrita H. The Gita and the Koran, by A.H. Jaisinghani. Karachi. (i), 17 p.; 18 cm.

301. Schrader, Friedrich Otto. The Bhagavad-Gita in ancient Kashmir, Bombay. [6 p.] 8*. (Arya Path, vol. 2, pp. 748-753.)

302. The Song Celestial; verses from Sri Bhagavad-gita. Selected and reset by Ramana Maharashi. [4th ed.] Tiruvannamalai, [India]: Niranjananda Swami. 31 p.

303. The Song of God; translation of the Bhagavad-Gita, by Dhan Gopal Mukerji. New York: E.P. Dutton & co., Inc., [c1931]. Xxi p., 2 l., 3-166p; 22.5 cm. "First edition." "I as a Hindu have attempted to present the Gita…not inn arbitrary form but with great regard to its poetic significance…"

304. …..The Song of the Lord, Bhagavadgita; translated with introduction and notes by Edward J. Thomas…London: J[ohn]. Murray. 123, [1] p.; 17 cm. "Prose translation." (The Wisdom of the East Series, ed. by L. Cranmer-Byng and S.A. Kapadia). "First edition 1931."

305. Srimad bhagavadgita Srisankara bhagavatpada carya viracitenabhasyena sahita. The Bhagavad- Gita: with the commentary of Sri Snkaracharya. Critically edited by Dinkar Vishnu Gokhale. Poona: The Oriental Book Agency. Iv, 304 p. Sanaskrit. Prefacce in English.

306. Subba Row, Tiruvalum. The Philosophy of the Bhagavad-Gita…3d Adyar ed. of item 184. Adyar: Theosophical Publishing House. v-xxi, 140 p.; 19 cm.

307. Yamunacarya. Gitartha Sangraha – Summary of the Teachings of Bhagavad Gita by Yamunacarya, with translation into English and with explanatory notes by Diwan Bahadur V.K. Ramanujachari. Kumbakonam, [India]: The Author. Xv, 141 p.;.

1932

308. Bhat, Vishwas Ganagadhara. The Bhagavadgita; a study, by Viswas G.Bhat. (New edition) [with the Sanskrit text and an English translation]. With a foreword by S. Radhakrishanan. Poona: Aryasamskriti Press. 12, 276, 3 p.;

309. Jῆanadeva, fl, 1290. Gita explained. Rendered into Marathi by Govind Ramchandra Moghe. Translated into English by Manu Subedar. [Bandra: Manu Subedar]. 330 p.; 25 cm.

310. Modi, Prataprai Mohanlal. Aksara; a forgotten chapter in the history of Indian philosophy. A study of the term aksara with special references to the Bhagavad Gita. Inaugral-Dissertation-Kiel, 1931. Baroda: The Baroda State Press. 2 p.l., ii, xii, 178 p.; 25 cm.

311. Nanak…The Japji sahib, a masterpiece of Guru Nanak, with Hindi text, English translation & a copious commentary; also Discourses on the Bhagwadgita relation to important problems of life by Mehta Udhodas…[Dayalbagh, Agra: Printed by Har Narain at the Dayalbagh Press]. 306 p.; 19 cm. 'Discourses on the Bhagavaddgita', a revision of articles which appreared in 1928/29 in the Kalpaka (Tinnevelly S.I.), p. 197-306.

312. The Song Celestial… Another ed. of item 45. London: Routledge & Kegan Paul. Xii, 111 p.: 16 cm.

313. The Song of God…Another ed. of item 303. London: J.M. Dent & Sons, Ltd., [c1932]. Printed in the U.S. A.

1933

314. Athalye, D.V. The Song of Krishna. Poona City, [India]. (iii), 119p.; 19 cm.

315. The psalm of Krishna…by Richard [Fredric] Carlyle. Los Angeles, California: The Phoenix Press. [106] p., col. Front.; 20.5 cm. "Signed by the translator' [Richard Carlyle].

316. ___, 2d ed. Los Angeles, California: Hall Publishing Co. 116 p.;

317. **Rama-Dasa Svami. Gita-Sandesh, Message of Gita. [With a portrait.] Anandashram, [India]. ii, 222, vi p.; .**

318. Ray, K. Evolution of the thoughts in Bhagavadgita; or Evolution of Gita. Calcutta. 3, 3, 222 p.; 22 cm.

319. Sangeet Karma-Yoga Philosophy of Bhagwadgeeta in English, in Oriental tunes, and Commentary. By R.K. Kher. Jhansi, [India, 1933]. Iv, 18p.;

320. Sarvananda, Svami. The Religion and Philosphy of the Gita. New Delhi. Iv, 166 p.; The author is also known as Sharvanand Svami.

321. Srimad-Bhagavad-Gita, with text, word-for-word translation…5th ed. of item 166. Mayavati, Almora, Himalayas: Advaita Ashrama. 4 p.l., xiv p., 1l., 439 p., port.; 18.5 cm. "Swami Swarupananda… compiled the present edition…with the collaboration of his brother Sannyasins…and some of the Western disciples of Swami Vivekananda."

322. The Bhagavad-gita; or The Sacred Lay. Translated with notes… 4th ed. of item 39. Calcutta: Susil Gupta (India). [1934]. 152 p.; 22 cm.

323. The Bhagavad-Gita, or, The song divine…2d revised ed. of item 177. Lahore, [Pakistan]: R.Krishna & Sons [etc., etc.]. iii, 181 p.; 17.5 cm.

324. Kumarappa, Bharatan. The Hindu conception of the deity as culminating in Ramanuja…with a foreword by Dr. L[ionel]. D. Barnett. London: Luzac & Co. xv, 356 p.; 22cm. Thesis accepted by the University of London in June, 1930, under the title: "Ramanuja's conception of the Deity." Cf. Pref. Bibliography: p. 330-332

325. The Lights of Bhagavad Gita. By Baij Nath Khanna. [150 verses with an English translation and notes.] Delhi: New Lights Publishing Society, [1934]. 158 p.;.

326. The Song Celestial…Another ed. of item 45…illustrated by Willy

Pogany. Philadelphia: David McKay Company, {c1934]. 2p.l., iii-xii, 135 p., plates; 25.5 cm.

327. Subha Row, Tiruvalum. Notes on the Bhagavad gita, to help students in studying its philosophy. Point Loma, California: Theosophical University Press. 2 p.l., 127 p., 1 l., 42 p.; 20 cm. Slip attached to t.p.: Theosophical University Press... removed in June, 1942m to its new site near Corina, Los Angeles county California. Lectures given to the Theosophical Society in 1885 and 1886. First published in the Theosophist in 1886 and 1887. Published in book form by Tookaram Tatya in 1888 under title: Discourses on the Bhagavat gita...(See item 60). An edition, without the introductory chapter, was published in 1912 under title: Philosophy of the Bhagavad-gita (See item 184). The present ed. is from the lectures as originally published in the Theosophist, Cf. "Preface to Point Loma edition."

1935

328. The Bhagavad gita; or, the message of the master;....Revised ed. of item 147. (See also item 174) [c1935].

329. **The Geeta; the Gospel of the Lord Shri Krishna, translated from the original Sanskrit by Shri Purohit Swami, with a preface by His Highness Sir Sayaji Rao Gaskwar, the maharaja of Baroda...London: Faber and Faber, Limited, [1935]. 110 p. incl. col. Front.; 26 cm.**

"This edition is limited to seven hundred and fifty signed and numbered copies."

330. Modi, Prataparai Mohanlal. The doctrine of the Bhagavadgita: a triad of the three dyads. Madras. [14 p.] (All-India Oriental Conference. Proceedings and Transactions. No.7, pp. 377-390.)

331. Srimad Bhagavat Gita. Text of Suddha Dharma Mandalam edition with commentary of Sri Hamsa Yogi. Chapter the first. Translation of the text and summary of the commentary in English by R. Vasudeva Row. Published by T.M. Janardanam, for Suddha Dharma Mandalam Association. Mylapore, Madras: The Suddha Dharma Office, 1935...xciii, 57 p.; 18.5 cm. (Suddha Dharma Tract I)

332. Teachings from the Bhagawadgita. Translation, introduction and comments by Hari Prasad Shastri. [Woodchester, Stroud, Glos.: Arthurs Press Ltd., 1935]. 80 p.; 19 cm. At head of title: Om Tat Sat. "The passages from the Gita representing its chief teachings are translated from the original Sanskrit." p.16.

333. Tilak, Bal Gangadhar. The Hindu philosophy of life, ethics and religion. Om Tat Sat, Srimad Bhagavadgita rahasya; or Karmayoga-Sastra, including an external examinations of the Gita, the original Sanskrit stanzas, their English translation, commentaries on the stanzas, and a comparison of Eastern with Western doctrines, etc... Translated by Bhalchandra Sitaram Sukthankar...First edition. Poona, [India]: [Published for Tilak Bros. by R.B. Tilak], Saka year 1857; 1935-36. 2 v. front., illus., Plates (2 col.), ports (1 col.), facsims.; 22.5 cm. Paged continuously. "This edition has 8 indexes which the original Marathi edition lacks."

334. Wise words from the Gita. [By] M.N. Patil....Revised and enlarged. Marathi-English...Bombay: M.N. Patil. 16. 190 p.; 19.5 cm. Title supplied in part from publisher's label, inserted. With this is bound its: Wise Words from the Gita. Gujarat-English edition. Bombay, 1928. (See item 280)

335. The Adi Bhagwad Gita. [Comp., translated and commented by Surjan Lal Pande] Shanti Prakash. 1st ed. Fyzabad, [India], Sadharana Dharma Sangha, [1936]. 3. 73, viii p.; 19 cm. Cover title: In Sanskrit and English.

336. Bhagavad Gita abridged and explained, setting forth the Hindu creed, discipline and ideals, by C. Rajagopalachari. Delhi: Published by Hindustan Times Ltd. For the Federation of international Fellowships, Madras. 142, 5 p.; 19 cm.

337. Bhagavad-gita; or, the Lord's Song...Another ed. of item 132. London: J.M. Dent & Sons, Ltd. Vi, 211 p., front., pl.; 15.5 cm. (The Temple Classics).

338. Divanji Prahlada Chandrashekhar, Rao Bahadur. Yogavasistha and Bhagawadgita. By P.C. Divanji. Broach, [India] 16 p.

339. Haldipur, A.V. Significance of vocatives in Bhagwatgita. Sholapur,

[India, 1936]. 12 p.

340. _____. Touch of humor in Bhagwat Gita. Sholapur, [India, 1936]. 25 p.

341. Ledrus, Michel. The secret of the Gita. Calcutta: Macmillan and co, Ltd. [24 p.] (New Review, vol. 3, pp. 277-288, 379-390.)

342. The psalms of Krishna. Another ed. of item 315. Los Angeles: Suttonhouse, Ltd. 51 l., col. front.

343. Rangacharya, Malur, Rao Bahadur. The Hindu philosophy of conduct; being class-lectures on the Bhagavadgita, by the late M. Rangacharya, M.A., rao bahadur… Another ed. of item 195. Madras: G.A. Natesan & Co., 1936-1942. 3 v., 24.5 cm. Vol. 1, 3d ed., edited by M.R. Sampatkumaran, 1942. v. 2k-3 editedby M.B. Varadaraja Iyengar and M.R. Sampatkumaran, 1936-1939.

344. Shah, Ramanlal Vadilal. Message of Shrimad-Bhagvad-Gita, by R.V. Shah with a foreword by D.Y. Fell. [Ahmedabad, India: R.V. Shah, 1936.] xvi, 75 p.

345. Srinivasa Rau, K. The significance of the Faltering of Arjuna…. Gita- 1st chapter and 10 Slokas of 2nd chapter. Chittoor, [India]: The Author. Iii, 47 p.;

1937

346. Belvalkar, Shripad Krishna, Rao Bahadur. Miscarriage of the attempted stratification of the Bhagwadgita; being a detailed examination of R. Otto's latest theory. Bombay: [Bilvakunj]. (70 p.); 25 cm. (Reprinted from the Journal of the University of Bombay, vol. 5, part 6, pp. 63-133.)

347. The Bhagavad-Gita, the book of devotion….From the Sanskrit by William Q. Judge. 13th ed. of item 65. Los Angeles: The Theosophy Company. Xviii, 133 p.; 15 cm.

348. Ghose, Aurobindo. Essays on the Gita. First series. [By] Sri

Aurobindo. Calcutta: Arya Publishing House, (1937). 5 p. l., [33-380 p.; 21 cm. (See also items 232, 258 and 273)

349. Lectures on the Bhagavad Gita, with an English translation of the Gita, by D[ittakavi]. S[ubrahmanya]. Sarma. Rajahmundry, [India]; N. Subba Rau Pantulu, [1937]. Xiii, 213 p.; 19 cm

350. Ramaswami Sastri, K.S. The Gospel of the Gita. Delhi:P Dharmarajya Press. 54 p. Cover title.

351. Shri Bhagavadd Gita; revised in the light of a rare and ancient manuscript with various readings incorporated herein and edited with its gloss "Sidhi Datri" in its English rendering explaining the variants. By Rajvaidya Jivaram Kalidas Shastri, Gondal, Kathiawar, India: Published by the Rasashala Aaushadhashram (Ayurvedic Pharmaceutical Works). 5 p.l., 28, 77, 153 p., port .; 25 cm. "With this is bound Mahabharata. Bhagavadgita. Sanskrit and English. Shri Bhagavad Gita chapter: 1-2 and 3. Edited with its commentary Chandraghanta. Gondal, 1937."

352. Srimad-Bhagavata, condensed from the original and translated by T.R. Ganapathiramier. Tinnevelly, [India]; Ganapathiramier, [1937. xviii, 4, iv, 216 p.; illus.

1938

353. The Geeta; as a Chaitanyite reads it, by Tridandi Swami B.H. Bon. Bombay: Popular Book Depot, [1938]. Xxiv, 382 p.; 22cm.

354. Kirfel, Willibald. Verse index to the Bhagavadgita. Pada-Index, compiled by Dr. W. Kirfel…Leipzig: Otto Harrassowitz. 45 p.; 25 cm.

355. Macnicol, Nicol. Hindu scriptures; hymns from the Rigveda, five Upanishade, the Bhagavadgita, edited by Nicol Macnicol. London: J.M. Dent & Sons, Lts., New York: E.P. Dutton & co., Inc., [1938]. Xxiv. 293 p.; 17.5 cm. (Half-title: Everyman's library, ed. by Ernest Rhys. Theology & phisophy. [No 944]). "First published in this edition, 1938." The Upanishads are from Max Müller's translation of the Sacred books of the East.

356. The Message of the Gita, as interpreted by Sri Aurobindo; edited by Anilbaran Roy. London: G. Allen & Unwin, Ltd., [1938]. Xiv, 281 p; 25 cm. "First published in 1938." Sanskrit text and English translation. "The notes have been entirely compiled from... [Aurobindo Ghose's] Essays on the Gita." – Pref.

357. Shrimad Bhagavad-Gita. Sanskrit text with English translation. By Bawa Jivan Singh. Ranchi, [India]: B.J. Singh. V, 206 p.; 8*.

358. **Sri Krishna Prem. The Yoga of the Bhagawat Gita. London: John M. Watkins. Xxix, 220 p. illus.: 22cm.**

359. Vasudeva Row, R. The heart-doctrine of Sri Bhagavad Gita & its message (in terms of Adhividya)...By R. Vasudeva Row, assisted by T.M. Janardanam, and published by him for Suddha Dharma Mandalam Association. Madras, S. India: The Suddha Dharma Office. (Suddha Dharma Tracts, no.3) xiii, [3], 144, [1] p., pl.; 18.5 cm. "Includes excerpts from the Bhagavadgita, with transliteration, translation and commentary."

1939

360. Barborka, Geoffrey A. Gods and heroes of the Bhagavad-gita: a brief description of the mythology of ancient India as contained in the Bhagavad-gita, including technical terms and explanations in the light of theosophy. Point Loma, California: Theosophical University Press, xii. 134, 10 p.; 15.5 cm.

361. Belvalkar, Shripad Krishna, Rao Bahadur. The so-called Kashmir recension of the Bhagavad-Gita. Bombay. [21 p.] (New Indian antiquary, vol. 2, pp. 211-231.)

362. The Bhagavad-gita...Another imprint of item 281.

363. The Bhagavad-gita, the book of devotion; dialogue between Krishna, Lord of devotion, and Arjuna, prince of India. Verbatim reprint of W.Q. Judge's 6th edition. Point Loma, California: Theosophical University Press. xii, 133 p., pl." 16 cm. (See item 89)

364. The last message of Sri Krishna. Text, with English translation and

notes, by Swami Madhavananda. Mayavati, Almora, Himalayas: Advaita Ashram. vi p., 1 l., 380 p.; 18.5 cm. Text in Sanskrit and English. " New edition – 1939." "First published with the title 'Sri Krishna and Udhava' and corresponds to chapters six to twenty-nine of the Eleventh Skandha of the Bhagavata."

365. Lectures on the Bhagavad gita, with an English translation of the gita and the original Sanskrit text....3d ed. of item 349. [1939]. 3p.l., cvii, 233 p.; 18.5 cm.

366. Maitra, S.K. "The Cosmic Significance of Karma in the Bhagavad-Gita". Calcutta. Prabuddha-Bharata, v. 44, pp. 60-71.

367. Narasimham, P. The Gita: a critique. Madras: Huxley Press. 270 p.;

368. Obhrai, Diwan Chand, Rai Bhadur. The Bhagavad-Gita Philosophy of war. Being a commentary on the first six discourses of Bhagavadd-Gita reprinted from the "Song of the Sour" or the "Sacred Science of Self". Lahore, [Pakistan]: Civil and Military Gazette. ii, 151, xi p.;

369. ____. Song of the Soul or the Sacred Science of Self. Comprising an analytical and critical exposition of the soul-wisdom of the Upanishads and the teaching of Bhagavad Gita. Lahore, [Pakistan]: Civil and Military Gazette. xvi, 478 p.;

370. **The original Gita, the song of the supreme exalted one; with copious comments and notes by Rudolf Otto...translated and edited by J.B. Turner...London: G. Allen and Unwin Ltd., [1939]. 3p. l., [9-309], [1] p.; 22 cm. "The German originals, Des sang des heher-erhabenen, Die urgestalt der Bhagavad-gita, Die lehrtraktate der Bhagavad-gita, were published in Stuttgart in 1933, 1934 and 1935. First published in English in 1939."**

371. Ramaswami Sastri, K.S., Dewan Bhadur. Problems of the Bhagavadgita. Madras, [1939]. 68 p.

372. The song celestial; or, Bhagavad-Gita...Another ed. of item 45. Philadelphia: D. McKay Co., [1939]. xii, 111 p.; 15 cm. (The pocket classics).

1940

373. Belvalkar, Shripad Krishna. The Bhagavadgita "riddle" unriddled. [S.l.:S.n. c194-?] p. [335-348.; 24 cm. Caption title. "Reprint from the Annals of the Bhandarkar Oriental Research Institute, vol. 19, part 4, 1939." Includes bibliographical references.

374. The Bhagavad-gita; with Sanskrit text...and revised ed. of item 133. Adyar, Madras, India: The Theosophical Publishing House. 472 p.; 19 cm.

375. Gems of Bhagavat Gita; choicest one hundred and eight slokas by Murli Dhar. [1st ed.] New Delhi: Amrit Books, [1940]. iii, 180 p., pl., port.; 19 cm. In Sanskrit, with translation and commentary in English.

376. Gode, Parshuram Krishna. The Bhagavadgita in the pre-Samkara-carya Jain sources. By P.K. Gode. [Poona. 8p.]

377. Porizka, Vincenc. The Bhagavadgita and the new Testament; some notes on the presumed parallelism. Prag. [Prauge]. [42 p.] (Archiv Orientalni, vol. 11, no. 2-3, pp. 210-241.)

378. Sarma, Dittakavi Subrahmanya. Krishna and his song. Bombay: International Book House. vii, 98 p.; 19 cm. "Appeared in the form of articles in the Aryan Path from January to September 1940."

379. Srimad-Bhagavad-gita; with text, word-for-word translation...6th ed. of item 166. Mayavati, Almora, Himalayas: Advaita Ashrama. xiv, 439 p.; 18 cm.

380. Vasudeva Row, R. An introduction to the study of Srimad Bhagavad Gita. Mylapore, [India]: Suddha Dharma Office. iv. 128 p. (Suddha Dharma tract, no.5)

1941

381. Barborka, Geoffry A. Gods and heroes of the Bhagavad-gita... Another imprint of item 360. 16 cm.

382. The Bhagavadgita, authorized version. Edited with index of quarter-lines by Shripad Krishna Belvalkar. Poona, [India]: Bilvakũnj Publishing House. 20, 151 p. Text and added t.p. in Sanskrit; pref. in English.

383. Bhagavad-gitarthaprakasika of Sri Upanaisad-brahma-yogin, with the text [of the Bhagavad Gita]. Edited by the Pandits of the Adyar Library. Adyar, [India]: Adyar Library. Xxxiv, 457 p.; 22cm. Added t.p. in Sanskrit. Text in Sanskrit; introd. In English. [Adyar Lirary series. 25]

384. Jnanadeva, [Dnyaneshwari fl. 1290. Gita explained by Dnyanesh-war Maharaj, translated into English by Manu Subedar.... 2d ed. of item 309. Bandra, [India]: Manu Subedar. 336 p.; 25 cm. "References to Dῆyaneshwar Maharaj and the 'Gita explained', or Dῆyaneshwari," typewritten list, p. [2] of cover.

385. Munshi, Kanaiyalal Maneklal. Bhagavadgita: an approach. Bombay: Bharatiya Vidya Bhavan, [19411. 22 p.

386. Rajagopalachari, K. The Bagavath gita. Tirupapuliyur. v, x, 174 p., illus.

387. Rele, Vasant Gangaram. Bhagavad-gita, an exposition ... 2d rev. ed. of item 276 [1941?l xxxii, 198 p., illus., pl., diagr. ; 15.5 cm. Bibliography: p. 197-198.

388. ___13d ed.] xxxiii, 200 p., illus, table; 20 cm. Bibliography: p. 199-200.

389. Roy, Satis Chandra. The Bhagavad-Gita and the modem scholarship. By S.C. Roy.... London: Luzac & Co. xviii, 270 p.; 22 cm. (At head of title: Interpretation of the Bhagavad Gita. Book I.) Preface by Betty Heimann. (See item 390

390. ____. Interpretations of the Bhagavad-Gita.... by S.C. Roy. London: Luzac & Co., 1941-. 1 v.; 22.5 cm. Book I: (See item 389). "[Book I] Part I ... was published in several installments during the year 1935, in the Indian Messenger, v. 1, p. xiii."

391. Shri Bhagavad gita (745 shlokas, Bhojpatra ms.). Edited by Rajvaidya

Jivaram Kalidas Shastri. 1st ed. Gondal, India: Rasashala Aushadhashram. 24, 91, 98 p. Added title page in English with editor's autograph.

392. Srimad-Bhagavad-gita; with the Jŋakarmasamuccaya commentary of Ananda Vardhana. Edited from an unique Sarada ms... by Shripad Krishna Belvalkar, with an introduction discussing the problem of the Kashmir recension and two appendices. Poona, [India!: Bilvakunja Publishing House. 26, 387 p. Text and added t.p. in Sanskrit; introd. in English.

393. Srimad-bhagavadgita: The song celestial. Edited with Telugu commentary and English translation by K. Saccidanandamurti. Sangam Jaganlamudi (Guntur), [India]: Anandasram. xxvi, 454, 56 p.; 21 cm. [Text in Telugu script]

1942

394. The Bhagavad-gita or, The Lord's song, with the text in Devanagari and an English translation by Annie Besant. 13th ed. of item 148. vii, 264 p.; 13 cm.

395. The Bhagavad-Gita, the book of devotion...14th ed. of item 65. Los Angeles, California: Theosophy Co. xviii, 133 p.; 14 cm.

396. The Geeta; the gospel of the Lord Shri Krishna, ... Reprint of item 329.[1942] 2 p. l., 7-95 p.; 22.5 cm. "First published in July MCMXXXV ... Reprinted September MCMXLII."

397. Judge, William Quan. Notes on the Bhagavadgita.,.. 2d ed, of item 213. Los Angeles, California; Bombay: The Theosophy Company. (See also item 275)

398. Mehta, Sushila. Some linguistic peculiarities of the Bhagavata. Bombay. [11 p.] (Bharatiya Vidya, vol. 4, pp. 30-40.)

399. Rangacharya, Malur. The Hindu philosophy of conduct; being class-lectures on the Bhagavadgita. Another ed. of item 195. Bangalore,

[India]; Kannada Sahita Parishat Press, 1942-. 3 v.; 25cm. Vol. 1

400. Srimad-Bhagawad-gita; or, The Blessed Lord's Song; translated from the original Sanskrit text by Swami Paramananda. Reprinted in The Wisdom of China and India. Edited by Lin Yutang. New York: Random House. pp. 54-114. (See item 187)

1943

401. The Bhagavad Gita. With commentaries by Rishi Singh Grewal. An exposition of the inner teaching of the yoga of the Gita. [Santa Barbara, California, 1943.] l v. (various paging); 29 cm.

402. The Bhagavadgita. With the commentary called Sarvatobhadra by Rajanaka Ramakantha. Edited by Pandit Madhusudan Kaul Shastri. Bombay: Printed at the Nirnaya Sagar Press. Ll, 420 p.; 23 cm. (Kashmir, Research Dept. Kashmir series of texts and studies, no. 64) Added t.p. and text in Sanskrit; preface and introduction in English.

403. The Bhagavadgita; an English translation with an introduction critically expounding the argument of the poem, and index of proper names by Shripad Krishna Belvalkar. Poona: Bilvakuñja Publishing House. xcv, 123 p.; 19 cm.

404. The Bhagavadgita; or the song divine. [With Sanskrit text and an English translation.] Gorakhpur, India; Gita Press. 369, [1], 33, [1] p.l., illus. col. pl.; 12x9 cm. (See items 177 and 323)

405. Macnicol, Nicol. Hindu scriptures: hymns from....Another ed. of item 355.

1944

406. The Bhagavadgita; or, The song divine....2d ed. of tiem 404. "An introduction by Syt. Jayadayal Goyandka and a synopsis of the Gita have been prefixed...and an article by the same author hearing on the Gita has been appended."—p. 4. "First edition....1943. Second

edition....1944."

407. **Bhagavad-gita, the song of God. Translated by Swami Prabhavananda and Christopher Isherwood, with an introduction by Aldous Huxley. Hollywood: The Marcel Rodd Co. 4 p.l., 187 p.; 17.5 cm.**

408. **The Bhagavad-gita; translated and interpreted by Franklin Edgerton Cambridge, Mass.: Harvard University Press; London: H. Milford, Oxford University Press. 2 v.: 26 cm. (Added t.p.: Harvard Oriental series, ed. by W.E. Clark. V. 38-39.) Sanskrit transliteration and English translation on opposite pages of v.l. "The second volume contains a careful revision of... [the editor's] 'interpretation'...(The Bhagavad gita or Song of the blessed one, Chicago: Open Court, 1925),"-v.l, p. v-xi. (See item 248)**

409. **The Bhagavad-gita, translated by Swami Nikhilananda. New York: Ramakrishna-Vivekananda Center. Xxix, 226 p.; 15.5 cm.**

410. **The Bhagavad-gita, translated from the Sanskrit, with notem, comments, and introduction by Swami Nikhilananda. New York: Ramakrishna-Vivekananda Center. xvii, 386 p., 20.5 cm.**

411. Ghokale, Ladshman Raghunath. Bhagavadgita-laghukosha: A concise dictionary of the Bhagavadgita. Poona. 14, 2, 60, 382, 19 p. "Part one contains a complete text of the Bhagavadgita and parsing of each verse and part two is arranged in dictionary form giving meanings of Sanskrit words in English, Hindi and Marathi."

412. Roy, Satia Chandra. The Bhagavad-gita and its bacckgroaund Calcutta: Satis Chandra Seal, 1944-, v. (Interpretations of the Bhagavadd-gita, vol. 2.) (See item 390)

413. ____. Interpretations of the Bhagavad-gita, by S.C. Roy. 24 ed. of item 390. Calcutta: Bharati Mahavidyalaya, 1944-, v.; 22 cm. (Bharati Mahavidyalaya publications. Religious series, no. 5)

414. Sircar, Mahendranath. Mysitcism in the Bhagavad-gita, Calcutta; S.C. Seal, Bharati Mahavidyalaya. Xix, 229 p.; 19 cm. (Religion series, 4)

415. The song celestial; or, Bhagavad-gita.....Another ed. of item 46. Allahabad: Kitabistan, [1944]. xii, 108 p.; 18 cm. "First published in India 1939 ... Third impression, 1944."

416. The song of God: Bhagavad-gita. Another ed. of item 407. New York: New American Library. 143 p.; 18 cm. (Mentor Religious Classic)

417. Shrimad Bhagawad-Gita. With a commentary explaining the object of human life by Shripad Damodar Satwalekar. Translated by Vaman Narayan Godbole. Aundh, Dist. Satara, [India]: Swadhyaya Mandal, 1941—54. 4 v. Sanskrit and English text; commentary in English. Chapter 4-13 translated by Raghunath Ramakrishna Deshpande. Chapter 14-18 translated by Ramakrishna Vithal Matkari.

418. Srimadbhagavadgita; the holy Gita. Text, with an English translation and notes by J.J. Pandya. Rajkot, [India]: Kitabghar. xxvi, 246 p., col. front.; 28 cm.

419. Srimad-Bhagavad-gita; with text, word for word translation 7th ed. of item 166. xiv,439 p.

420. The Upasana Gita; eighteen verses from the Bhagavad Gita for meditation, with text, transliteration, translation and commentary, by D.S. Sarma. Madras: M.L.J. Press. 21 p.;17 cm.

1945

421. The Bhagavad Gita: an immortal song; an interpretation sacred epic, by Wesley La Violette. [First edition] Los Angeles: De Vorss & Co., [1945]. 5 p. l., 13-209 p.; 19.5 cm

422. Bhagavad-Gita: The song of God.... Another ed. of item 407. Madras: Sri Ramakrishna Math. 260 p.; 13 cm.

423. The Bhagavad Gita or, The Lord's song 15th ed. item 148. vii, [13], 264 p.; 12 cm. (Natesan's national classics)

424. The Bhagavadgita; being a reprint of relevant parts of Bhismaparvan from Bhandarkar Oriental Research Institute's ed. of the Mahabharata, for the first time critically edited by Shripad Krishna Belvalkar. Poona, [India]: Bhandarkar Oriental Research Institute, xxxii, 108 p. mounted col. plates, facsim.; 28 cm. Added title page in Sanskrit. 'This reprint contains pp. 114-188 of Fasc. 15 (Bismaparvan, pt. 1) and parts of the Introduction, Appendices, etc. froFasc. 16 (Bhismaparvan, pt. 2)."

425. Jῆandeva. Gita explained, by Dnyaveshwar Maharaj. Translated into English, by Manu Subedar. 3d ed. of item 309- Bombay. 318 p.; 25 cm. "Translated from the modern Marathi version of Pandit G.R. Moghe." (See also item 381)

426. Sarma, Dittakavi Subrahmanya. Lectures and essays on the Bhagavadgita 4th ed. of item 349. Madras: M.L.J. Press.145 p.; 18 cm.

427. Steiner, Rudolf. The Bhagavad gita and the Epistles of St. Paul. Five lectures. Cologne, 28th Dec, 1912-lst Jan., 1913. [London]: R. Steiner; New York: Anthroposophic Press, [c1945]-128 p., illus.; 19 cm. (See item 253)

1946

428. Lanasaktiyogal The Gospel of selfless action or the Gita according to Gandhi. Translation of the Gujarati original, with an additional introduction and commentary by Mahadeva Desai. Ahmeddabad, [India]: Navajivan Publishing House, [1946]. vi, 392 p- Port, (index); 22 cm. "The introduction comprises pp. 1-134."

429. The Bhagavad-Gita, the book of devotion Another ed. of item 65. Covina, [California]: Theosophical U. P. 133 p. "Preface signed: William Q. Judge, New York, October, 1890." [Translated by William Q. Judge.]

430. The Bhagavad gita; translated and interpreted by Franklin Edgerton... . Another imprint of item 408.

431. Divanji, Prahlad Chandrashekhar, Rao Bahadur. SrimadbhagaVadgita-Vivecanatmakasabdakosah: Critical word-index to the Bhagavadgita ... foreword by Dr. S.M. Katre Bombay Distributor: New Book Co. 12, xviii, 366, [4] p.; 25 cm. "List of publications of Rao Bahadur P.C. Divanji: [4] p. at end." [It gives an alphabetical listing of all the words and their meanings. Also treats the Vulgate and Kashmir recensions separately with a comparative table of variant readings.]

432. _____. "Probable sources of the Bhagavadgita". All India Oriental conference. Proceedings and Transactions. Nagpur 25 cm. {no.} 13, [pt. 23 pp. 299-309. "Bibliographical footnotes."

433. **Gandhi, Mohandas Karamchand. Gita the mother, by M.K. Gandhi edited by Jag Parvesh Chander. 4th ed. Lahore, [Pakistan]; Indian Printing Works, 1946-47.**

434. Gems of Bhagvat Gita....2d ed. of item 375. iii, 174 p.

435. A Layman's Bhagavad Gita. [Translated and edited] By Aiylam]. Subramanier Panchapakesa. Ayyar. Mylapore, [India]: Alliance Co.

436. The message of the Gita...Another ed. of item 356. xix, 311 p.; 26 cm. Append. Gloss, index. Added t.p. in Sanskrit.

437. The song of celestial; verses from sri Bhagavd-Gita, selected and reset by Ramana Maharshi. [Tiruvannamalai, India: Sri Ramanasramam, 1946.] 27 p.; 19 cm. Cover title. Title also in Sanskrit; text in Sanskrit and English.

438. Srimad Bhagavadgita. [Gorakhpur, India: Gita Press, 1946-48.} 5 v. in 1 col. illus. (Kalyana Kalpataru, v. 12, no. 1; v. 13, no. 1; v. 14, no. 1. Gitatativa no. 1-3) Caption title. With commentary in English by Jayadayal Goyandka.

1947

439. The Bhagavad-Gita; with commentary of Sri Sankaracharya....4th ed. of item 97. Madras: V. Ramamswamy Sastrulu & Sons. Xii, 522

p.; 18 cm. Text in Sanskrit and English.

440. The Bhagavad-gita, the book of devotion… 15th ed. of item 65. Los Angeles; Theosophy Co. xviii, 133p.

441. Bhagavad-gita, the song of God. Another ed. of item 407. London: Phoenix House. 185 p.

442. **The Bhagavadgita. With an introductory essay, Sanskrit text, English translation and notes by Sarvepalli Radhakrishnan. London: George allen & Unwin. 388 p.; 19.5 cm.**

443. Divanji,k Prahlad Chandrashekhar, Rao Bahadur. "Probable sources of the Bhagavadgita". (See item 432) Ganganatha Jha Research Institute. Journal. Allahabad. May-August, 1947. pp. 279-294.

444. Gandhi, Mohandas Karamchand. Gita the mother…Another imprint of item 433. 8, 157 p.

445. Gita: Sreemad-Bhagabat gita rendered in English. [Translated by Bejoy Kumar Banerrjee] Calcutta: Aparajita Press Depository, [1947], 125 p. (Oriental religious series, 2)

446. Munshi, Kanaiyalal Maneklal. Bhagavad Gita and modern life, Bombay: Bharatiya Vidya Bhavan. Vii, 224 p.; 23 cm. (Bharatiya Vidya Studies,6)

447. The song of God: Bhagavad-gita…Another imprint of item 422. (See items 407 & 416) [3] l., 185 p.; 15 cm.

448. Sreemad-Bhagabat Gita. Translated into English by B.K. Banerjee. See item 445. Calcutta: Probathan. 125 p.;

449. The Upasana Gita…3d ed. of item 420. 32 p.

1948

450. Avinasananda, Swami. Gita letters. Bombay: Hind Kitaba, [[1948]. Viii, 199, [20] p.; 19 cm. Includes index.

451. The Bhagavadd Gita. (With English translation) By D.S. Sarma, 5th ed. Mylapore, Madras: Madras Law Journal Office. 200 p.; 17 cm. Sanskrit and English.

452. Bhagavadgita. [Compiled from Sri Aurobindo's "Essays on the Gita".] Edited by Anilbaran Roy. Text, translation and notes. London: Allen & Unwin. 311 p.;. (See items 232, 258 & 273)

453. The Bhagavaddgita, with an introductory essay, Sanskrit text [transliterated]...Another ed. of item 442. new York, Harperr, [1948]. 388 p.' 23 cm. Bibliography: p. [384.]

454. ___. Another imprint. [London: G. Allen and Unwin.] New York: Harper, [1948]. 388, [21] p.; 22.5 cm. Bibliography: p. [384.]

455. ____Another imprint of item 442. [I948] 21 cm.

456. Buddhi yoga of the Gita; or the basic science of the Soul. [Edited and translated by] Magdal Ramchandra. Bangalore: Magdal Ramchandra. viii, 62, 21*8, 56 p., CI] fold, leaf of plates, chart; 19 cm.

457. The Geeta: the gospel of the Lord Shri Krishna.... Another ed. of item 329. (See also item 396)

458. The Gospel of selfless action; or, The Gita according to Gandhi. Another ed. of item 428. [1948] vi, 390 p. , port.; 22 cm. "The Sanskrit text is accompanied by English translation and commentary. In part, a translation of Gandhi's Anasaktiyoga."

459. Macnicol, Nicol. Hindu scriptures. ... Another ed. of item 355. [With a foreword by Rabindranath Tagore.] London: Dent; New York: Dutton,

460. The Message of the Gita.... Another ed. of item 356.

461. Rele, Vasant Gangaram. Bhagavad-Gita; an exposition..3d ed. of item 276. [1948] xxxii, 200 p., illus.; 18 cm. (See also items 266 and 387)

462. The song of God: Bhagavad-gita.... Another ed. of item 447. (See also items 407, 416 and 422)

463. The song of the Lord: The Bhagavadgita. ..Another imprint of item 304.

464. Sri Krishna Prem. The Yoga of the Bhagavat Gita. [2d ed.] (See item 358) vii-xxxix, 224 p.; 22 cm.

465. Srimad Bhagavad-gita. Edited and translated by Tridand Gosvami Enl. and rev. 3d ed. Calcutta: Gaudiya Mission, xxxii, 626, [I], 57 P-; 19 cm. "Text in Sanskrit with translation and commentary in English."

466. Srimad-Bhagavad-gita. Text, translation of the text and of the gloss of Sridhara Swami, by Swami Vireswarananda. [1st ed.] Madras: Sri Ramakrishna Math, [1948]. vi, 536 p.; 19cm.

467. Srimad-Bhagavadgita. 8th ed. of item 166. Mayavati, Almora [India]: Advaita Ashram.

1949

468. Bhagavad-gita; abridged and explained, ... [5th ed.] (See item 336) 143, 5 p.; 19 cm. "Index of slokas quoted": p. [11-5].

469. The Bhagavadgita; ... Another imprint of item 442. (See also item 453)

470. The Bhagavadgita; or, The Song divine ... [Uth ed.] (See items 404 and 406) [1949] 403 p., col. pi.; 12 cm.

471. Ghose, Aurobindo. Essays on the Gita. 2d series. 4th ed. of item 273. (iii), H18 p. (See items 232 and 258)

472. ---- . 5th ed. of item 273- (See items 232, 258 and 471)

473. Kosambi, D.D. "The Avatara syncretism and possible sources of the Bhagavad-Gita". Royal Asiatic Society. Bombay Branch. Journal. Bombay. 1948-49, v. 2U-25, pp. 121-148.

474. A Layman's Bhagavad Gita. [With English translation and commentary] By A.S.P. Ayyar. 2d rev. and enl. ed. of item 435. Mylapore, Madras: Madras Law Journal Press. Vol. 1. xcv, 259 p.; 19 cm. "Text in Sanskrit."

475. Munshi, Kanaiyalal Maneklal. Bhagavad gita and Modern life. [1st ed.] Delhi: Rajkamal Publications, [1949]. 224 p.; 23 cm. Loc.:

476. Sri Krishna Prem. The yoga of the Bhagavat gita. Another ed. of item 358. New York: Harper, [1949]. xxix, 224 p.; 22 cm.

477. **Srimad Bhagavad Gita; text, meaning, notes and commentary by Sri Swami Sivananda. Rev. and enl. 4th ed. Rishikesh, [India]: The Divine Life Society, The Yoga-Vedanta Forest University, ix, 910 p., illus.; 19 cm. (The "Gita" series, no. I)**

478. **Srimad-Bhagavad-gita, the revelation of the supreme self; translated from the Sanskrit. With original parallel interpretive spiritual text, by Swami Premananda. Boston:Christopher Pub. House, [1949]. 231 p., port.; 21 cm. "At head of title: Salvation is the birthright of everyman."**

479. Teachings from the Bhagavadgita, ... Rev. 2d ed. of item 332. London: S. Sadin. 96 p.; 19 cm.

1950

480. Baba, Bengali. Few crucial points from the Shreemad Bhagava Gita . Poona, [India!: Annaji Deorao Inamdar, [cl950]. 29 p.; 18 cm.

481. The Bhagavad-Gita, with the commentary of Sri Sankaracharya. 2d rev. ed . of item 299- 308 p.; 18 cm. Sanskrit title at head of t.p. (Poona Oriental series, no. 1)

482. Bhagavad-gita; or, the Lord's song. Translated by Annie Besant and Bhagawan Das. 4th ed. Adyar, [India]; Theosophical Publishing House. 516 p.

483. The Bhagavadgita; with an introductory essay, Sanskrit text.... [2d ed.l New York: Harper, 195-. (See items 442 and 453)

484. Ghose, Aurobindo. Essays on the Gita. Another ed. of item 232. (See also items 258, 273, 471 & 472) New York: E.P. Dutton, [c1950]. 580 p.; 22 cm. (Sri Aurobindo Library) "Part 2 also published under title: Essays on the Gita. Second series."

485. Khanna, B. N. Lights of Bhagawad gita. 3d ed. New Delhi: Chand.

486. Krishnam, John R. "Bhagavadgita and the Fourth Gospel". Ph.D. Dissertation, Boston University. 176 p.

487. Rangachari, M.V.V.K. The twilight song; aspects of humanism in the Bhagavad Gita. (dialectical studies in modern thought) [Kakinada, India: Author, 1950] iv, 81* p.; 18 cm.

488. Shrimad Bhagavad Gita; the solution of life-problems, annotated by Bengali Baba. 2d ed.... [Poona city, India: Ramchandra Ambadas Joshi.] 95, 437 p.; 19 cm. Text in Sanskrit and English; with commentary in English. "Few crucial points from the Shreemad Bhagavad Gita by Bengali Baba ... [Poona city: A.D. Inamdar, 19503." 29 p. inserted. (See item 480)

1951

492. Bhagavadgita; or the Lord's song. Another ed. of item 132 (See also items 224 and 269) Boston: Beacon Press, vi, 211 p., illus.; 16 cm.

493. Chandy, Malieckel G. "Visvarupa Darsana, a study of the vision of God in the Bhagavadgita".PH.D.Dissertation. The Hartford Seminary Foundation.

494. Divati, Sir Harsidbhai Vajubhai. The art of life in the Bhagavad-Gita. With a foreword by B.G. Kher. Bombay: Bharatiya Vidya Bhavan. xv, 179 p.; 19 cm. (Bhavan's Book University, 2)

495. Diwan Chand. Short studies in the Bhagavadgita. [Sholapur, India: S.R. Sharma.1 il, 68 p.; 19 cm. (Sain Das Foundation Publication, no. 2)

496. The Gospel of selfless action; or, the Gita according to Gandhi Another ed. of item 428. (See also item 458)

497. Panse, Muralidhara Gajanana. Linguistic Peculiarities of Jnanesvari Poona: CS.M. Katre for the Deccan College Post-graduate & Research Institute! 1951-53. (Bulletin of the Deccan College Research Institute. Vol. 10, nos. 2-4)

498. The song celestial; verses from Sri Bhagavad-gita. 4th ed. of item 437. 31 p.

499. The song of God, Bhagavad-gita. Another ed. of item 407. Hollywood, California: Vedanta Press, [1951]. 191 p. (See also items 416, 422, 447 and 462)

500. ---- . Another ed. New York: Harper, [1951]- 191 p.; 15 cm.

501. ......Another ed. of item 416. [c1951-l (A Mentor religious classic, MD - 103) "First ed. published in 1944 under title: Bhagavad-gita, the song of God." (See item 407)

502. . Another imprint of item 501.(Mentor religious classic, MT 711)

503. Shri Krishna Prem. The Yoga of the Bhagavat Gita Another ed. of item 358. (See also item 476)

504. Sreemad Bhagavat Geeta ... [by! K.S. Ramakrishna Iyer. Palghat. [India]: Printed by Pioneer Electric Printers, [1951]-85 p.; 19 cm.

1952

505. The Bhagavad gita.... Another imprint of item 410.

506. ___. Another ed. of item 409-

507. The Bhagavad-Gita; a book of Hindu scriptures in the form of a dialogue between Prince Arjuna and the God Krishna. With decorations by Ruth McCrea. Mount Vernon, N.Y.: The Peter Pauper Press, [c19to52]. 114 p., 1 I., col. illus.; 23 cm. "The text of the present edition is an entirely new version. It owes a heavy debt to Radhakrishnan, Paramananda, Barnett, and other translators."

508. The Bhagavad-Gita.... Another ed. of item 408. Part 1: Text and translation, part 2: Interpretation and Arnold's translation. (See item 248)

509. Mirchandani, Lakshmi. Gita for the young. Sivanandanagar Yoga-Vedanta Forest University. 44 p. (Gita series no. 2)

510. A synthesis of the Bhagavad-Gita.... [2d ed.l of item 267. Fintry, [Scotland!: Shrine of Wisdom, [19521. 72 p.; 22 cm.

511. Venkatesananda, Swami. Bhagavad Gita for Students [With plates including a portrait.! Rishikesh Yoga Veda - a Forest University, xv, 66 p.;

1953

512. The Bhagavad Gita; or, The Lord's song. 3d Adyar ed. Madras: Theosophical Publishing House. 254 p.; 15 cm. "Imprint on label mounted on t.p.: Wheaton, 111., sold by the Theosophical Press." (See items 86 and 188)

513. Bhagavad-gita, the song of God….another ed. of item 447.

514. The Bhagavadgita. 2d [abridged] ed. of item 271. Madras, New York, Indian Branch: Oxford University Prss. 234 p.; 19 cm.

515. The Bhagavad-Gita.... Another ed. of item 408. Part 1: Text and translation, part 2: Interpretation and Arnold The Bhagavadgita, with an introductory essay.... Another ed. item 442. (See also items 453-455 and 469) 21 cm.

516. Blanchard, William M. "An Examination of the Relation of the New Testament to the Bhagavad Gita". Ph.D. Dissertation. Northern Baptist Theological Seminary, Lombard, Illinois.

517. Parashuram. Bhagwat-gita and Hindu-dharma. Poona, [India], iii, 4ll, vi p.

518. Divatia, Sir Harsidbai Vajubhai. The art of life in the Bhagavad-Gita___[2d ed.] of item 494. 164 p.

519. Ghose, Aurobindo. Essays on the Gita. Another imprint of

item 484. (See also items 258, 273, 471 and 472) [1953, c1950.1 23 cm.

520. Jinarajadasa, Curuppumullage. Discourses on the Bhagavad Gita, given at Bangalore, 1946. Edited by Elithe Nisewanger. Adyar, India: Theosophical Pub. House, viii, 115 p.; 19 cm. Author's first name is also spelled as: Kuruppumullage.

521. Jnanadeva, fl. 1290. (Also known as Dnyanadeva.) Bhavartha-Dipika, otherwise known as Dnyaneshwari; being an illuminating commentary in Marathi on Bhagwad-Gita by the celebrated poet-saint, Shri Dnyandev. Rendered into English by R.K. Bhagwat. Revised by S.V. Pandit. Poona, India]: Published by B.R. Bhagwat for Dnyaneshwari English Rendering Publishing Association, 1953-54. 2 v. illus.; 25cm. Vol. 2 revised by V.V. Dixit.

522. Munshi, Kanaiyalal Maneklal. Bhagavad gita and modern life. Another ed. of item 446. [1953] 224 p.; 22 cm. Bibliographical references included in "Notes": p. 193-224.

523. Nagaraja Rao, P. The Bhagavad Gita and the changing world. Ahmedabad, [India] : Sri Ramakrishna Seva Samiti. Distributor; The New Order Book Co., [1953]. T, 160 p.; 19 cm. ncludes bibliography.

524. Panse, Muralidhara Gajanana. Linguistic Peculiarities of Jfianesvari . Poona, [India]: Deccan College Post-graduate & Research Institute, xiii, 655 P- (Deccan College dissertation series, 13) "First ed. 250 copies." Bibliography p.: 151-180. (See item 497)

525. Ramanuja, founder of sect. Ramanuja on the Bhagavadgita; condensed rendering of his Gitabhasya with copious notes and an introduction, door Johannes Adrianus Bernardus van Buitenen. S-Gravenhage: H.L. Smits, [1953]. xiii, 187 p.; 24 cm. The editor's Proefschrift-Utrecht. Bibliographical references included in "list of abbreviations."

526. Shankarananda, Swami, ed. Basic Materials of Gita. [Colombo, 1953]

527. ----- Another ed. Poona, [India!: Deluxe Printers. 16p.; 22 cm.

528. Shri-Bhagavad-Gita, with complete 745 verses (incorporatinoriginal shlokas and elaborate English introduction) by Rajvaidya J.K. Shastri. 5th ed. of item 391- Gondal, Kathiawar, [India!: Rasashala Aushadhashram. 68, ll4 p. (Shri Bhuvaneshwari Granthmala series, no. 113)

529. Sivananda, Swami. Gita meditations. [2d enl. ed.l Ananda Kutir, Rishikesh, [India!: Yoga-Vedanta Forest University, Divine Life Society, xviii, 62 p., port.; 19 cm.[His Gita series, no. 6.] "Selections from the Bhagavadgita in Sanskrit and English"

1954

530. The Bhagavad gita. Translated with notes by John Davies. [4th ed.l Calcutta: Susil Gupta, [1954]. 152 p.; 22 cm. (See item 39)

531. Bhagavad-gita; Gita Essence for Children. By Dr. Lakshami Mirchandani. Rishikesh, [India]: Yoga-Vedanta Forest University. 59 p.; (Gita series, no. 10)

532. The Bhagavad-gita, the book of devotion ... [W.Q. Judge recesion]. Pasadena, California: Theosophical University Press, [1954]. xii, 133 p.; 16 cm. (See items 65 and 347)

533. The Bhagavad Gita explained. With a literal translation from the original Sanskrit by Ernest Wood. Los Angeles: The New Century Book Shop, 232 p., illus. ; 22 cm.

534. The Gita, with text, translation and notes compiled from Sri Aurobindo 's Essasys [sic! on the Gita, edited by Anilbaran Roy. Pondlcherry: Sri Aurobindo Ashram. Sanskrit text and English translation. "First impression 1946, Second impression ... 1954." Earlier editions issued under title: The message of the Gita, as interpreted by Sri Aurobindo. (See items 356 & 436)

535. The Gita in pictures. [Title in Sanskrit] [Originated, produced and published by Parmanand Sugarmal Mehra. Bombay, 1954.] 1 v. (unpaged), col. illus. ports.; 36 cm.

536. Mascaro, Juan. A star from the East: an appreciation of the Bhagavad Gita. An address given at the Royal Castle of Het Oude Loo in Holland on Saturday, 28th August, 1954; with a foreword by Hugh Anson Funsset. [Cambridge: W. Heffer, 1954?] 201 p.; 19 cm.

537. Mishra, Umesha. A critical study of the Bhagavadgita. Allahabad, [India]: Tirabhubti Publications, v, 65 p.; 25 cm.

538. Ramchandra, Magdal. Shashvata dharma in Srimad Bhagavad Gita; or The Lord's science of eternal religion. [With a foreword by P.V. Rajamannar}. Bangalore, [1954], x, 223 p.; 19 cm.

539. Roy, Satis Chandra. The Bhagavadd-gita and its background 2d ed. of item 412. (Interpretations of the Bhagavad-gita, vol.2) (See item 540) [Calcutta]: Suryamani and Lalita.

540. _____Interpretations of the Bhagavad-gita. 2d ed. of item 390. (See also items 389 & 413) [Calcutta]: Suryamani-Laita, 1954. v. Vol. 2. The Bhagavad-gita and its background. (See item 539)

541. The song of God: Bhagavad-gita....Another ed. of item 416. (See items 407, 447, 462 & 500) [1954, c1951]. (N. A. L. Mentor Books, M 106). "First ed. published in 1944 under title: Bhagavad-gita, the song of God."

542. The world-song: the scientific translation of Srimad Bhagavad-gita [by] M.V.V.K. Rangachari. Kakinana, [India, 1954]. 103 p.

1955

543. Bhagavad-Gita, abridged and explained setting forth the Hindu creed, discipline and ideals. Edited by Chakravarti Rajagopalachari. [6th ed.] (See item 3360 New Delhi: The Hindustan Times, Ltd., [1955]. 177 p.

544. The Bhagavadgita; a fresh approach, with special reference to Sankaracarya's Bhasya. Text with Sankara Bhasya, and an introduction and notes by P.M. Modi. With a foreword by K.M.

Munshi, and with a pref. by F. Otto Schrader. [Baroda, India: P.M. Modi, 1955]. L v. (various pagings); 22 cm.

545. The Gita in pictures....2d ed. of item 535. Bombay: Parmanand publications. 25 cm. Text of the Gita in Sanskrit and English; commentary in English. Includes bibliography.

546. Lean, Phyllis Scarnell. A short introduction to the Bhagavad Gita... Pictermaritzburg, [South Africa]: Natal Witness, [1955]. 51p.;

547. Munshi, Kanaiyalal Maneklal. Bhagavad Gita and Modern Life. [4th ed., rev. & enl.] Bombay: Published for Hindustan Cellulose & Paper Co. by Bharatiya Vidya Bhavan. Xviii, 274 p.; 19 cm. (Bhavan's Book University, 33) (See item 446)

548. The new Gita; an interpretation of the Bhagavad gita [by] Wesley La Violette. [10th anniversary ed.] Los Angeles: De Vorse, [1955]. 202 p.; 24 cm. (See item 421)

549. Sarma, Dittakavai Subrahamanya. Introduction to the Bhagavadd Gita. 2d ed. of item 251. Bombay: International Book House, [1955]. [vii], 69 p.

550. The song celestial; or, Bhagavad-Gita....Anotherr ed. of item 45. London: Routledge & K. Paul. Xii, 111 p.; 15 cm.

1956

551. The Bhagavadgita; with an introductory essay....2d ed. of item 442. 388 p.; 20 cm. "India Edition." Bibliography: p. 384.

552. The gospel of selfless action...Another ed. of item 428. [1956] (See also item 433) "First published 1946."

553. Shrima-Bhagavad-Gita...Another ed. of item 166. (See also items 217 &260) Calcutta: Advaita Ashrama, [1956]. Xiv, 436 p.; 19 cm.

554. Sivananda, Swami. Bhagavad Gita. One act play. [With portraits] Rishikesh, [India]: Yoga-Vedanta Forest University. 8*. (Yoga-

Vedanta Forest University Weekly, vol. 8, no. 8)

555. The song of God: Bhagavad-gita...Another ed. of item 447. (See also items 407, 416, 422, 462, 513 and 541) 187 p.; 14 cm. "Fifth impression 1956 (revised)."

556. Song sublime or "Geeta". [Verse translation] By Prafulla Kumar Lahiri. Calcutta: The Translator. 148 p.

557. Srimad Bhagavad gita; text, transliteration, and translation by Jagadguru Sri Swami Sivanand. Ananda Kutir, Rishikesh, [India]: The Yoga-Vedanta Forest University. 237 p., front. 18 cm.

558. Stephen, Dorothea Jane. The Gita in life. [Madras]: Christian Literature Society, C1956]. 98 p.; 21 cm.

1957

559. The Bhagavad Gita; ov the Lord's song. 4th Adyar ed. of item 188. Madras: Theosophical Pub. House 231 p.; 15 cm. (See also item 148)

560. Geeta; text with English translation, introduction and appendice by N.V. Gunaji. [1st ed. Bombay]: Phoenix,[1957]. 368 p.; 17 cm.

561. Rangacharya, Malur. The Hindu philosophy of conduct, ...Another ed. of item 195- (See also item 343) Madras: Educational Pub. Co., [1957-66]. 3 v.; 24-26 cm. v. 1: 4th ed., vols. 2-3 ed. by M.B. Varadaraja Iyenger and M.R. Sampatkumaran v.3, 1st ed. Includes text of the Bhagavat Gita in Sanskrit.

562. Sivananda, Swami. Ethics of the Bhagavad Gita. [With portraits] Rishhikesh, [India]: Yoga-Vedanta Forest University, 296 p.;

563. The song celestial; or, Bhagavad-gita....Another ed. of item 45. Bombay: Jaico Publishing House, [1957]- 92 p.; 17 cm. (Jaico Books)

564. Sunderlal. The Gita and the Quran, rendered into English by Syed Asadullah. Hyderabad, India: Institute of Indo-Middle East

Cultural Studies, [19571- viii, 145, iii p.; 25 cm. (Indo-Middle East Cultural Studies, v. l)

1958

565. The Bhagavadgita, with an introductory essay... [2d ed.l of item 442. [1958] "Second edition ... 1949 ... Fifth impression1958." (See items 453 and 469) Sanskrit text in transliteration.

566. Bhave, Vinoba. Talka on the Gita. [1st ed.] Kashi, [U.P., India]: Akhil Bharat Sarva Seva Sangh Prakashan. 283 p.; 18 cm. (Written originally in 1932)

567. Gaiichhwal, Balbir Singh. A comparative study of the ethica teachings of Kant and the Bhagavadgita. Hoshiarpur, [India]: [Vishveshvaranand Vedic Research Institute]. 28p.; 25 cm. (Punjab University, Lahore Research Bulletin, [arts], no.26)

568. "Om" Geeta, the celestial song. [1st ed.] [By] Subodh Chandra Ghose. Rishikesh. [Calcutta: S.L.M. Sinha, 1958]. 146 p.

569. Sri Krishna Prem. The Yoga of the Bhagavat gita. [Revised 2d ed.l of item 358. (See also item 476) Baltimore: Penguin Books. 224 p.; 23 cm. (Penguin metaphysical library) Includes bibliographical footnotes.

1959

570. Beerman, Hans. "Hermann Hesse and the Bhagavad-Gita".The Midwest Quarterly, 1959, v. 1 , pp. 27-40.

571. Bhagavad-gita. Adhyaya XL only. Ed. with English introduction, English and Bengali translations of the Mula English explanations and notes by SaradaraHjana Raya and Kumadarafljana Raya. 3d .ed. Devanagari and Bengali characters Calcutta. 180p 18 cm.

572. Bhagavad-gita; a book of Hindu scriptures.... Another ed. of item 507 . [1959] 61 p., col. illus.; 19 cm.

573. Bhagavad-gita, a simple paraphrase in English by S. Parthasarth Iyenger. Madras: Gnana-vigHana Trust, [19591. 138 p.;18 cm.

574. The Bhagavadgita (Sanskrit and Romanised text, word to word English running translation with a critical introduction). By Shakuntala Rao Sastri. [Edlitors: Louis Renou [and] Walter Donald Kring. [1st. ed] New York: East West Institute, xii, 448 p.; 19 cm. (East West Institute series, no. l)

575. The Bhagavadgita or the Song Divine. [English and Sanskrit] 11th ed. Gorakhpur, [India]: Gita Press. 400 p

576. The Bhagavat-Geeta (1785). Translated, with notes, by Charles Wilkins. A facsimile reproduction with introduction by George Hendrick.Gainesville, Florida: Scholars' Facsimiles & Reprints, xiv p., facsim: 156 p.; 21 cm. (Scholars facsimiles and reprints) "Reprinted from a copy in the Library of Congress." (See item l)

577. Bhave, Vinoba. Talks on the Gita. [2d ed.l of item 566 Rajghat, Kashi, India]: Akhil Bharat Sarva Seva Sangh Prakashan. 283 p.; 19 cm.

578. Ranade,Ramchandra Dattatraya. The Bhagavadgita as a philosophy of God-realisation (being a clue through the labyrinth of modern interpretations). Nagpur, [India!: M.S. Modak. (ii), xiii, 321 p., port.; 22 em.

579. The song of God: Bhagavad-Gita. Another ed. of item 447. (See also items 1*07, Ul6, 422, 462, 499, 541 and 555) 143 p.

580. Another ed. of item 4l6. (See item 407) (Mentor Books, no. MD 103)

581. The song of the Lord: Bhagavadgita, ... Another ed. of item 304. 128 p.; 20 cm. "Distributed in the U.S.A. by the Grove Press New York."

582. Srimad-Bhagavadgita; edited and translated by Shripad Krishna. Belvalkar. [Varanasi: Hindu Vishvavidyalaya Sanskrit Publications Board; sole distributor: Banaras Hindu University Press Book Depot, intro. 1959-1 vii, 236, 95 p.; 25 cm. (Hindu Vishvavidyalaya Nepal Rajya Sanskrit series, v . 1) Title also in Sanskrit; Sanskrit text with English translation. Bibliography: p. 1891-95 at end. "Corrigenda slip tipped in."

1960

583. Bhagavad Gita. [Translated by] Harish Chandra Gupta. Allahabad, Clndial: Indian Press, xxiv, 142 p.

584. The Bhagavad-gita; or The Lord's lay.... Another ed. of item 34. (See items 48-51 and 55) New York: Julian Press, xxi, 283 p.; 24 cm. Preface by Ainslie Embree.

585. The Bhagavadgita; with an introductory essay... Another ed. of item 442. (See also items 453-455 and 483) [1960].

586. Bhakti Vedanta, Swami. Essence of the Vedas: Bhagavad Gita as it is. New York: Iskcon Press. [1960] 20 p.; 23 cm.

587. Bhave, Vinoba. Talks on the Gita. Another ed. of item 566. (See also item 577) London: George Allen & Unwin. 268 p.;

588. _____. Another ed. [Translators have retained some essential Sanskrit words) Introduction by Jayaprakash Narayan. New York. Macmillan. 267 p.; 23 cm.

589. **Chinmayananda, Swami. The holy Geeta: a commentary. Bombay Central: Chinmaya Mission Trust, [1960] xxxvi, 1133 p.; 23 cm.**

590. Jhabwala, Shavakesha Hormusji. Geeta and its commentators. Bombay: Dhawale Popular. x, 160 p.

591. ____. Another ed. Bombay: Nandi Books. Ix, 160 p.; 8*.

592. Munshi, Kanaiyalal Maneklal. Bhagavad Gita and modern life. [5th ed., revised and enlarged] (See items 446, 475 and 522) xvi, 255 p.; 19 cm. (Bhavan's book university, 33)

593. Raman, D.V. Service of Truth and science. Sermadevi, India. [196-] 2 v. Vol. I: Sri Gita, science and modernity, a spiritual cum socio-political gospel. Vol. II; Gita slokas, freely rendered into English prose, with running commentary and elucidatory notes.

594. The song of God: Bhagavad-gita. Another imprint of item 501. (See also items 407, 416, 422, 447, 462 &499) 143 p.; 18 cm

1961

595. The Bhagavad Gita; a sublime bymn of dialectics, composed by the antique sage-bard Vyasa, with general and introductory essays, verse commentary, word notes, Sanskrit text and English translation by Nataraga Guru. Bombay, New York: Asia Pub. House, [1961]. Xv, 753 p.; 23 cm. Text in Sanskrit (romanized)

596. TheBhagavad-Gita. With the commentary of Sri Sankaracharya. 5th ed.of item 97; Madras: Ramaswamy Sastrulu.

597. The Bhagavad gita explained, with a literal translation from the original Sanskrit, by Ernest Wood.San Francisco, California: The American Academy of Asian Studies^ Graduate School, 1961 (See item 533)

598. Gita 40 CUO select-slokas from the different chapters of the Bhagavad-gita.1 Tiruvallur, Clndial: Students'Club. 20 p. In Sanskrit and English

599. Gita's Light in Every Home. [Translated byl Rangaswamy

Kalkunte Ramadhyani. Delhi: Atmaram & Sons, xvi,264 p.

600. Scared writings. With introductions and notes. New York: Collier, c1961, c1938 2 v. (1007 p.), illus.; 22 cm. (The Harvard Classics, v. 44-45)

601. The song celestial, or Bhagavad-gita.... Another ed. of item 45. London: Routledge & K. Paul. Ill p.; 16 cm.

1962

602. Bhagavad Geeta: song of the divine. Rendered into English blank verse from the original Sanskrit by Lalitmohan Chatterjee. Calcutta: M.C. Sarkar, vi, 117 p.; 21 cm.

603. The Bhagavad Gita; a sublime hymn of dialetics.... Another ed. of item 595. London; Madras: Asia Publishing House. Printed, 119621. xv, 763 p.; 23 c

604. ------. ... Another ed. of item 595. [1962]

605. The Bhagavad gita. Translated from the Sanskrit with an intro-duction by Juan Mascaro. Baltimore: Penguin Books, C19621. 121 p.; 18 cm. (The Penguin classics)

606. The Bhagavad-Gita. Translated by Annie Besant and Bhagawan Das. 5th ed. rev. Adyar, Madras: Theosophical Publishing House, xlix, 460 p.

607. Bonnerjee, Jitendriya. The Gita; the song supreme. Introduction by S. Radhakrishnan. Cist ed.1 Bombay: D.B. Taraporevala, C1962:. ix, 133 p.; 23 cm.

608. Chinmayananda, Swami. 101st Geeta Gyana lagna . New Delhi, March 10-31, 1962; Souvenir. [Delhi: Laxmi Press, 57 p., illus.; 24 cm.

609. Faucett, Lawrence William. Seeking Krishna in his teachings; an analytical arrangement of the Bhagavadgita.[Randor Pa.] 145 p, illus.; 29 cm. "A source book of the whole of the

Bhagavadgita and of related selections from the Ramayana the Upanishads, the Arthashastra, the edicts of Asoka with references to passages in various scriptures."

610. Malhotra, Shadi Lai. The role of the Bhagavadgita in Indian politics. Chandigarh: University of the Panjab. 16 p.; 24 cm. (Panjab University, Lahore, Research Bulletin no. 36: 4)

611. Munshi, Kanaiyalal Maneklal. Bhagavad Gita and Modern Life. [6th ed.] Chowpatty, Bombay: Bharatiya Vidya Bhavan. xvi,256 p. ; 8". (Bhavan's Book University, 33) (See items 446, 475, 522 & 592)

612. Parrinder, Edward Geoffrey. Upanishads, Gita and Bible. A comparative study of Hindu and Christian scriptures. London: Faber & Faber, C19621. 136 p.; 23 cm.

613. Sarma, Dittakavi Subrahmanya. Pearls of Wisdom. With a foreword by S. Radhakrishnan. [1st ed.] Bombay: Bharatiya Vidya Bhavan. xiv, 244 p.; 19 cm. (Bhavan's Book University, 104)

614. The sermon of the Lord, or Bhagavad-Geeta, from the Mahabharata; an interpretation in simple verse of the discourse between Lord Krishna and Arjuna, the warrior, on the battlefield of Kurukshetra. Translated from the Sanskrit text by Baburao Patel. Bombay: Girnar Publications, [1962]. 201 p., illus.; 19 cm.

615. Srimad Bhagavad Gita. Text and commentary by Sri Swami Sivananda [6th ed.l Durban: Divine Life Society of South Africa, C19621. 816 p., illus. (col.); 21 cm. (See also item 477)

616. Thus spake Sri Krishna. Compiled by Swami Suddhasatwananda. Mylapore, Madras: Sri Ramakrishna Math, xix, 102 p., illus.; 11 cm.

1963

617. The Gita, with text, translation and notes compiled from Sri Aurobindo's Essays on the Gita. Edited by Anilbaran Roy. Another ed. of item 534 . xvi, 335 p.; 18 cm.

618. Jacob, George Adolphus. [Upanisadna Kyakosah : A concordance to the principal Upanisads and the Bhagavadgita.Delhi: Motilal Banarsidas. 8, 1038 p.; 23 cm. Reprint of item 68.
At head of title: Published under the auspices of Government of India Reprinted from the 1891 edition under the "Scheme of reprinting of important out-of-print Sanskrit books" sponsored by the Ministry of Education, Govt, of India.

619. Jaya Chamaraja Wadiyar, Maharaja of Mysore. The Gita and Indian culture. Bombay: Orient Longmans, vi, 68 p.; 19 cm.

620. Macnicol, Nicol. Hindu scriptures: hymns from the Rigveda, five Upanishads, the Bhagavad gita. Another ed. of item 355

621. Parrinder, Edward Geoffrey. Upanishads, Gita and Bible..Another ed. of item 612. New York: Association Press.

622. Rajagopalachari, Chakravarti. Bhagavad-Gita, [On its teachings with selected extracts.] Rev. ed. Bombay: Bharatiya Vidya Bhavan. (Bhavan's Book University, 115)

623. Singh, Kirpal. The Divine cowherd and the divine milk-maids.1st ed. Bombay: Sindh Navavidhan Mission trust, 162p.; 19 cm. Stamped on t.p. Printed on behalf of Sindh Navavidhan Mission Trust Bombay. "An English translation-cum-commentary of certain chapters from the Bhagwat."

624. The song of God: Bhagavad-gita..Another imprint of item 422 (See also items 407, 416, 447, 462, 499-502, and 579) Mylapore, Madras: Sri Ramakrishna Math, 239 p.; 14 cm.

625. Srimad Bhagavad Gita, or the song divine; a true verse for verse translation in simple English rhyming verses by Kamakshi Dasa [pseud] With a foreword by CP. Ramaswami Aiyar. [Mylapore, Madras] 125p.

1964

626. Atharasloki Gita; with the original Sanskrit slokas. [Translated into English by] Purusottam Pandurang Gokhle. Karhad, [India]: Sulochana Gokhle. iv, 40 p.

627. The Bhagavad Gita. Translated and interpreted by Franklin Edgerton. Another imprint of item 408. New York: Harper & Row, 1964, c1944. xii, 202 p.; 21 cm. (Harper torchbooks. The Cloister library, TB 115) Includes index. Reprinted with revisions and omissions, of two-volume work published in 1944 by Harvard University Press.

628. ------. Another imprint. New York: Harper Torchbooks. 202 p.

629. —--. Translated from the Sanskrit with notes, comments, and introduction by Swami Nikhilananda. Another imprint of item 410. New York: Ramakrlshna-Vivekananda Center, 1952 [i.e. 1964]. 21 cm. (See also items 409, 505, and 506)

630. ---------.Version consisting of 745 verses edited from a birch-bark manuscript by Charanatirtha Maharaja of Gondal, with English introduction by the editor. 7th ed. of item 391. Gondal, [Surashtra, India]: Shri Bhuvaneshwari Pith. 84 p.; 21.5 cm

631. Bhagavad Gita; the song celestial. The Sanskrit text, translated into English verse by Sir Edwin Arnold. Another ed. of item 45. With an introduction by Sri Prakasa. Illustrated with paintings by Y. G. Srimati. Bombay: Printed for members of the Limited Editions Club [at the Commercial Printing Press], xx, 128 p., col. plates; 26 cm.

632. ----- Another ed. [New York] Printed for the members of The Limited Editions Club [in] Bombay, xx p., 2 I., 118, 118, 119-128 p, mounted col. front, mounted color plates; 27 cm. Sanskrit and English on opposite pages, numbered in duplicate from p. 2-118; pages of Sanskrit text numbered in Sanskrit characters. “Original decorated orange cloth case.”

633. The Bhagavadgita; or, the song divine. Another ed. of item 1*06. [1961*3 1*03 p.. illus., col. pi.; 12 cm. Introduction by Jayadayal Goyandka.

634. Bhave, Vinoba. Talks on the Gita. 3d ed. of item 566.

Varanasi, [India]: Sarva Seva Sangh Prakashan,. 307p [Translators have retained some essential Sanskrit words.] (See also item 577)

635. The Gita in pictures. l*th ed. of item 535. [By P.S. Mehra. Bombay: Mehra Printers, 1961.] 25 cm. "Parmanand publications." Cover title: Shrimad Bhagavadgita in pictures. Captions and summaries in English. Text in Hindi and English. Includes bibliography.

636. Shri Bhagavad gita Bhojpatri with complete 745 verses (incorporating original shlokas and elaborate English translation.) by Acharya Shri Charanatirth Maharaj. 7th ed. of item 391. (Another imprint of item 630) 72, 84 p.

637. The song of God: Bhagavad-gita.... Another imprint of 501. [1964, c1951] (See also it ems 407, 416, 422, 447, 462 & 499 502)

638. Srimad-Bhagavad-gita; text, translation of the text and of the gloss of Sridhara Swami, by Swami Vireswarananda. 2d ed. of item 466. [1964] Text in Sanskrit, with translation and commentary in English.

1965

639. The Bhagavad gita. Original stanzas, split up reading, transliteration, word for word translation, a lucid English rendering and commentary, by Swami Chidbhavananda. Tirupparait-turai, [India: Tapovanam Publishing House. iv, 1007 P>, col. illus.; 23 cm. (Tapovanam series, 80) Added title in Sanskrit. "Tamil version of this book first published in 1951.

640. -------. Transcreated by P. Lai. [Delhi]: Hind Pocket Books, [1965]. 107 P-; 18 cm. "Orient Paperbacks."

641. ______. Another imprint. New Delhi: Orient Paperbacks.

642. -------. Translated and interpreted by Franklin Edgerton. Another imprint of item 627. (See also item 408)

643. ____; a new translation by P. Lai. [Calcutta: Writers Workshop, c1963. 71 p.; 23 cm. "Writers Workshop Saffronbird book." Paperback edition.

644. The Bhagavad Gita; or the Lord's song. 5th Adyar ed. of item 188. Madras: Theosophical Pub. House. 231 p.; 15 cm. (See item 559) On label mounted on t.p.: Sold by the Theosophical Press, Wheaton, 111.

645. The Bhagavad-Gita, the book of devotion. Another ed. of item 65. (See also items 66, 347, 363, 440, and 532) Bombay: Theosophy Co. xx, 133 p., illus.

646. Bhagavad Gita; the song celestial. Another ed. of item 631. (See also items 1*5 and 632) New York: Heritage Press, [1965]-Sanskrit and English

647. Bhagavadgita, the songs of the Master; ... Another ed. of item 153. (See also item 152) London: John M. Watkins. 132 p.; 20 cm. "First published by the Quarterly Book Department, New York, 1908. Reprinted in new format 1965."

648. The Bhagavadgita; with the Sanatsugatiya and the Anugita. Reprint of item 40. Delhi: Motilal Banarsidas, [1965]. 446 p 23 cm. (The Sacred books of the East, v. 8) Reprint of the 1882 ed. (See also item 155)

649. Gandhi, Mohandas Karamchand. Gita, my mother, by M.K. Gandhi. Ed. and published by Anand T. Hingorani. Another ed. of item 433- Bombay: Bharatiya Vidya Bhavan. viii, 208 p.; 20 cm. Bibliography: p. 203. (See also item 444)

650. The Geeta, the gospel of the Lord Shri Krishna..Another ed of item 329. (See also item 396) 95 p.; 20 cm

651. Krishnamoorty, P. Sree Krishnarjuneeyam; a drama on Gita. Foreword by Swamy Rajeswarnanda. [Secunderabad, 1965] v, 30 p.; 19 cm. Cover title. Added t.p. in Telugu.

652. Ranade, Ramchandra Dattatraya. The Bhagavadgita as a philosophy of God-realization; being a clue through the labyrinth of modern interpretations 2d ed. of item 578. Bombay: Bharatiy Vidya Bhavan. xii, 287 p.; 19 cm.

653. The song of God: Bhagavad-gita. 3d ed. of item 499. [1965] 191 p" ; 15 cm. (See also items 407, 416, 422, 447, 462, 500 502, 579, and 624)

654. Tilak, Bal Gangadhar. The Hindu philosophy of life, ethics, and religion.... 2d ed. of item 333. Poona, [India: Tilak Bros.], Saka year 1887, 1965. lvi, 1220 p. col. illus.; 22 cm. Cover title: Gita rahasya. Bibliography in "abbreviations": p. liii-lvi.

655. Wadsworth, Cleome Carroll. Bhagavad Gita; a psychological recension. [1st ed. New York]: Pageant Press, [1965]. xxii, 95 p.; 21 cm. Interpretive commentary on an English translation of the text. Bibliography: p. 93-95.

1966

656. The Bhagavadgita. An English translation and commentary by W. Douglas P. Hill. Reprint of item 51U (See item 271) [2d abridged ed. Madras, New York]: Oxford University Press, [1966]. [10], 23U p.; 22 cm. Bibliographical references included in "abbreviations": p. [10]

657. Bhave, Vinoba. Steadfast Wisdom.[Translator Lila Ray] 1st ed., Varanasil: Sarva Seva Sangh Prakashan 136 p.; 22 cm.

658. Mehta, Rohit. From mind to super-mind: a commentary on the Bhagavad Gita. Bombay: Manaktalas, [1966]. viii, 202 p.; 23 cm.

659. The message of the Gita; a new translation & summarization in simple and easy-to-understand English, [by] Keshob Kanto. [Gauhatil: Bholanath Borooah Educational Trust. xxxvi, 288 p. port.; 23 cm. English and Sanskrit [romanizedl.

660. Ramdas, Swami. Gita Sandesh: message of the Gita. Bombay:published for Anandashram by Bharatiya Vidya Bhavan. x, 124 p., port.; 19 cm. (Bhavan's Book University, 139)

661. Rao, K. L. Seshagiri. "The Concept of Sraddha (in the Brahmanas the Upanishads and the Gita)". Ph.D. Thesis, Harvard University, viii, 300 p.; 28

662. Shankar, Bhavani. The doctrine of the Bhagavad Gita
. Bombay: Popular Prakashan. xi, 148 p.; 19 c

663. Srinivasachari, P. N. The ethical Philosophy of the Gita. [3d ed.] Mylapore, Madras: Sri Ramakrishna Math, xi, 163 p.; 19 cm.

664. Vaswani, Thanwardas Lilaram. Gita: a bible of humanity. Issued on the occasion of Sri T.L. Vaswani's 87th birthday by Mira. Poona, [India, 1966]. 172 p., illus. (Fruit gatherings, 7) "Supplement to Mira (Nov.-Dec 1966)." Cover title.

1967

665. Bhagavad-Gita. By Cihakravarti Rajagopalachari. 3d ed. Chowpathy, Bombay: Bharatiya Vidya Bhavan cl967. 128 p.; 19 cm. (Bhavan's Book University)

666. Bhagavad-Gita, a new translation and commentary with Sanskrit text, by Maharishi Mahesh Yogi. [London, Los Angeles] International SRM publications, [1967] v. plates. 25 cm. With concordance prepared by Charles Donahue and Donna Seibert (87 p.)

667- ------- Another ed. Chapters 1 to 6. Livingston Manor, New York: MIU Press. 371p.,illus.; 25 cm.

668. The Bhagavad-gita; the Lord's song. 11th Adyar ed. of item 86. Madras: Theosophical Pub. House, xv, 260 p.; 13 cm. English and Sanskrit

669. The Bhagavadgita, with an introductory essay.... 2d ed. of item 442

670. Bhagavat Geeta. [Translated by] Swami Vividishananda. Puri, [India]: Ramakrishna Asram, [19671. xx, 228 p.

671. Bharati, Shuddhananda. Sri Krishna and his gospel. Madras: Shluddhananda Library, Yoga Samaj, [1967] viii, 107 p.; 18 cm. Includes selections from the Bhagavadgita.

672. Chinmayananda, Swami. The Sreemad-Bhagawad-Geeta: the art of right action, text in Sanskrit, each verse followed by Roman

transliteration, word for word meaning, translation, and exhaustive commentary. C3d ed.l Bombay Central: Chinmaya Mission Trust, [1967]. 4 v.; 23 cm. Cover title: The Bhagawad Geeta.

673. Faucett, Lawrence William. Seeking Krishna in his teachings; a comparison of teachings of Krishna and Christ. 2d ed. rev. (See item 609) [San Marcos, California, 1967, c1962.1 vi, 62 p., illus.; 28 cm. Student's ed. "Selections from the Bhagavad Gita and the Bible, an analytical arrangement in twenty categories of moral and spiritual concepts of great worth."

674. Gauchhwal, Balbir Singh. The concept of perfection in the teachings of Kant and the Gita. Cist ed.l Delhi: M. Banarsidass, C1967 - xi, 184 p.; 23 cm. Based on the author's Ph.D. thesis, Punjab University. Bibliographic footnotes. Author's last name is also spelled as Gochhwal.

675. Jnanadeva, fl. 1290. Jnaneshvari (Bhavarthadipika); translated from the Marathi by V . Cithall. Ganesh Pradhan, edited and with an introduction by Hester Marjorie. Lambert. London: G. Allen & Unwin, I967-69. 2 v.; 24 cm. (UNESCO collection of representative works: Indian series)

676. Kalelkar, Dattatraya Balkrishna. The Geeta as Jeevan-Yoga. By Kakasaheb Kalelkar. Cist ed.l Bombay: Bharatiya Vidya Bhavan. xi, 38 p.; 19 cm. (Bhavan's Book University)

677. Mishra, Umesh. The Bhagavadgita; a critical study. [Revised 2d ed. Allahabad, [Indial: Tirabhukti Publications, [19671. viii, ll6 p.; 25 cm. Bibliographical footnote

678. Shrimad-Bhagavad-Gita. Another ed. of item 553- (See also items 166, 217, 260 and 321)

679. Shrimat Bhagwat Gita. Rohri, [Pakistani: Hari Shewa Satsang, [1967] xiii, 185 p., col. illus., port.; 18 cm.

1968

680. **Barborka, Geoffrey A. The Pearl of the Orient: the message of the Bhagavad-Gita for the Western World. Wheaton,**

111.: Theosophical Pub. House, iv, 191 p.; 21 cm. (A Quest book)

681. The Bhagavad Gita. Translated, with introd. and critical essays,by Eliot Deutsh. [1st ed.l New York: Holt, Rinehart and Winston, xi, 192 p.; 22 cm . Bibliography: p. 191-192.

682. The Bhagaval Gita; or, the Lord's song. 6th Adyar ed. of item 188. 231 p.; 15 cm.

683. **The Bhagaval Gita as it is. With introd., translation, and authorized purport by A.C. Bhaktivedanta Swami.London: Collier-Macmillan, [1968]. 318 p.; 21 cm. (Collier Books)**

684. ------. Another imprint. New York: Macmillan, [1968]

685. ------- Another ed. New York: Bhaktivedanta Book Trust, [1968]. xxxvii, 331 p.; 21 cm.

686. Davis, Roy Eugene. The Bhagavad-Gita: God's revealing word, a liberal restatement of the Bhagavad-Gita, with an introductory essay and definitive commentary. Lakemont, Ga.: CSA Press. 149 p.; 21 cm.

687. Gita darsan as bhakti yoga as a Chaitanyite reads it. Madras: Sree Gaudiya Math; [copies can be had of Sri Chaitanya Math, Sree Mayapur, Dt. NadiaJ. 123 p., illus. (part col.), port.; 25 cm.

688. Indian miniatures; the song celestial or Bhagavad-Gita. [Text translated by E. Arnold. Paris: Editions Du Sud, 1968. 48 p., col. illus.; 31 cm.

689. 0 thou Arjuna; a fresh flash photo of Shri Bhagavad-geetaa. [Translated by] Govind Vaman Apte. C Satara: Vikram Govind Apte and Alhad Govind Apte, 1968.1 vii, 26, 87 p.; 23 cm.

690. Parrinder, Edward Geoffrey. The significance of the Bhagavad- Gita for Christian theology. London: Dr. William's Trust. [2], 2k p.;22 cm. (Friends of Dr. William's library. Lecture, no. 22, 1968) Bibliographical footnotes.

691. Ramanuja, founder of sect. Ramanuja on the Bhagavagita. 2ded. of item 525. Delhi: Motilal Banarsidass. xiii, 187 p.; 25 cm

. Previously published in 1953 as the editor's proef-schrift, Utrecht Rijksuniversiteit. Bibliographical footnotes..

694. Srimat Bhagavat Gita. With an introduction, Sanskrit text, translation, syntax, word for word translation and substance of each sloka in English. English rendering by Bani Basu and Kajal Sen Gupta from original Bengali of Yatindra Ramanujacharyya. [1st ed.] Khardah, 2l+ parganas, [India]: Sree Balaram Dharm Dharmasopan; [distributor: Firma K.L. Mukhopadhyaya, Calcutta, I968]. xv, 175 p. 23 cm. Cover title: Srimat Bhagabat Gita.

695. Steiner, Rudolf. The Occult significance of the Bhagavad Gita; nine lectures, Helsingfors, May 28-June 5, 1913. [Translated by George and Mary Adams] New York: Anthroposophic Press, [1968]. v, ll+2 p.; 22 cm. Translation of Die Okkulten Grundlagen der Bhagavad Gita.

696. Vaswani, Thanwardas Lilaram. The heart of the Gita, by T.L.Vaswani. Poona, [India]: Gita Pub. House, [1968]. 92 p.; 22 cm. (East and West Series, nos. 135-136)

1969

697. Abhedananda, Swami. Bhagavad Gita = The Divine message. Calcutta: Ramakrishna Vedanta Math. 2 v. (viii, 1012, vii p.,[4] leaves of plates), ill. ; 22 cm. Includes bibliographical references.

698. Tlhe Bhagavad Gita. Text, word-to-word meaning, translation, and commentary by Swami Sivananda. [7th ed.] Sivanandanagar, [India]: Divine Life Society, vlviii, 630 p., col. illus.,facsim., port.; 23 cm. English and Sanskrit; introductory natter and commentary in English. (See also items 477 and 515)

699. The Bhagavad Gita as it is, ... Another imprint of item 683. "First Collier books edition 1968."[Second printing 1969]

700. The Bhagavad Gita; translated from the Sanskrit with an introduction by Juan Mascaro. Another ed. of item 605. [Middlesex]:

Penguine Books, [1961]

701. **The Bhagavad-Gita, with a commentary based on the original sources, by R.C. Zaehner. Oxford: Clarendon Press, xi, 480 p.; 23 cm. Includes transliteration of original Sanskrit. Bibliographical footnotes**

702. Bhagavad-gita; recension by William Quan Judge, combined with his essay on the Gita. Pasadena, Calif.: Theosophical University Press, [1969]. ix, 220 p., illus.; 21 cm.

703. The Bhagvat-Geeta (1785). Translated with notes, by Charles Wilkins. A facsimile reproduction.... Another imprint of item 576.

704. Chinmayananda, Swami. Sreemad Bhagawad Geeta; text with word for word meaning, translation, and commentary. [Madras: Chinmaya Publications Trust, 1969-71, v. 1, 1971.1 [103 v. in 3; 23 cm. Cover title: The Bhagawad Geeta; caption title: Geeta. English and Sanskrit commentary, introduction, gloss and summary of the Mahabharata in English. (See also item 672)

705. Gokhale, Sadashiv Dhondo. The message of the song celestial Shrimad-Bhagavadgita, as revealed by Shri Dhyandeo, by S.D. Gokhale. [Inchgeri, India, 1969.I ‘ 14, 269, 66 p.; 22 cm. Includes quotations from the Bhagavad-gita in Marathi.

706. Khair, Gajanan Shripat. Quest for the original Gita. Bombay Somaiya Publications, [19693. xiv, 248 p.; 23 cm. With the text of the Trikala Gita in Sanskrit. Bibliography: p. [242]-244.

707. Mahesh Yogi, Maharishi. Maharishi Mahesh Yogi on the Bhagavad gita: a new translation and commentary with Sanskrit text. Chapters 1 to 6. Another ed. of item 667. (See also item 666) Harmondsworth: Penguin 494 p.,illus,; 18cm.

708. Mainkar, Trimbak Govind. A Comparative study of the commentaries on the Bhagavadgita. [2nd ed.] Delhi: Motilal Banarsidass, vil, 65, ii p., tables; 24 cm.

709. Ramanuja, founder of sect. The Gitabhashya of Ramanuja. Translated into English by M.R. Sampatkumaran. 1st ed.Madras:

Prof. M. Rangacharya Memorial Trust;.xxxi, 585 p; 23 cm Includes complete Sanskrit text of the Bhagavadgita. "The Gitartha-sangtaha of Shri Yamunacharya": p. [535-545 (See also item 525)

710. The song of God: Bhagavad-Gita. 3d ed. (5th printing of item 499) . (See also items 407, 416, 422, 447, 462,500-502, 624, and 653)

711. Sri Krishna Prem. The Yoga of the Bhagavad Gita. Another ed. of item 358. (See items 476 & 503) London: Stuart & Watkins.

712. Srimad Bhagavadgita; with Sanskrit text and English translation. Translated into English by the editorial staff of the Kalyana-Kalpataru. Edited by Jayadayal Goyandka. [1st ed.l Gorakhpur, [India]: Gita Press, E19691. 25, 6, 803, p. col. illus. ; 25 cm.

1970

713. Betai, Ramesh S. Gita and Gandhiji. Foreword by P.M.Modi.[1sted.] Ahmedabad, India Gujarat Vidyapith,[1970]. xii, 293 p.;25 cm. Includes bibliographical references. (Gujarat Vidyapith. Samshodhan Shreni, 3)

714. The Bhagavad Gita. Another ed. of item 605 London: Rider, [1970]. 127 p.

715. The Bhagavad Gita; a new verse translation [by Ann Stanford. [1st ed. New York]: Herder and Herder, [19701. xxvii, 145 p.; 2.1 cm. (An Azimuth book)

716. ——. Another ed. New York: The Seabury Press. (A Continuum book)

717. The Bhagavad gita; or, The Wisdom of Krishna. Translated by Archie J. Bahm. Bombay: Somaiya Publications, [1970]. 178 p. 23 cm. "Originally published as Srimad bhagavadgita."

718. Bhagavad-gita. By Chakravarti Rajagopalachari. 4th ed (See item 665) Edited by Kanaiyalal Maneklal Munshi and Ranganath

Ramchandra Divakar. Bombay: Bharatiya Vidya Bhavan. 128 p.; 18 cm. (Bhavan's Book University, 115)

719. The Bhagavadgita. Original stanzas, split up reading, transliteration, word for word translation, a lucid English renderingand commentary, by Swami Chidbhavananda. Another Imprint of item 639.

720. The Bhagavadgita: The song of life. English translation andexplanatory notes by Tlhanwardas1. Lilaram. Vaswani. Edited by J.P. Vaswani. Poona, [India!: Gita Publishing House, [19703. 2 v. in 1., 246 p.; 21 cm. Vol. 1: "issued on the occasion of Sri T.L. Vaswani's 90th birthday [25-11-693-Vol. 2: on the occasion of his Maha yagna [17-170]" (See item 112)

721. ...... Another imprint. Edited by J.P. Vaswani. 246 p;22 cm.

722. The Bhagavadgita: With an introductory essay.... Another ed. of item 442. (See also items 453-455, 483 and 585)
Bombay, India: Blackie & Sons (India). 388 p.; 21 cm.

723. The Bhagavadgita; with the Sanatsugatiya and the Anugita. Another imprint of item 648. (See items 40 and 155]

724. Bhave, Vinoha. Talks on the Gita. 4th ed. of item 566. (See also item 577) Varanasi, India: Sarva Seva Sangh Prakashan. xii, 254p

725. Gitamamthi ounti Kadhela 108 sloks. [English and Gujarati translation of the textl Bombay: J.D. Lakhami, [1970]. 208 p.

726. The gospel of selfless action; or, The Gita according to Gandhi. Translation of the original Gujarati, with additional introduction and commentary, by Mahadev Desai.... Another imprint of item 428. (See also items 458 and 552)

727. Krsnasvami Ayyar, Panaiyur R. Gleanings fvom the Gita. Madras: P.K. Venkataraghavan. iv, 91 p.; 18.5 cm.

728. Lai, Rajendra Behari. The Gita in the light of modern science. Bombay: Somaiya Publications, xvi, 315 p.; 22.5 cm. Bibliography: p. [3071-309. Foreword by R.R. Diwakar.

729. Misra, Bairagi Charan. ISamaja Samskaraka Bairagi Misra Gyanthabali. Title in Oriya. Oriya and English. Includes an Oriya translation of the Bhagavadgita with notes. [1970] 24, 1250 p., port.; 23 c

730. The song celestial; or, Bhagavad-gita. Another ed. of item 312.(See item 45) 111 p.

731. ----- Another ed. First Quest book miniature edition. Wheaton, 111.: Theosophical Publishing House. 154 p.; 15 cm. A Quest book miniature. "Published under a grant from the Kern Foundation

732. -----. Another ed. Madras: Theosophical Publishing House. xii, 154 p.

734. Studies in the Gita. Edited by Moreshivarl. Dinkar.Firadka-. Bombay: Popular Prakashan, [19703. xxxiv, 410 p.; 22 cm. Includes quotations from the Gita in Sanskrit. "The compilation of these articles was done by the Gita Mandai of Ratnagiri...."

735. Timple, Eugene F. "Hesse's Siddhartha and the Bhagavad Gita". Comparative Literature, 1970, v. 2, pp. 346-357-

1971

736. Betai, Ramesh S. Gita and Gandhiji. Another imprint of item 713.

737. The Bhagavad gita. Translated from the Sanskrit with an introduction by Juan Mascaro. Another ed. of item 605- (See also items 700 and 714)

738. The Bhagavad-gita; the book of devotion.... Another ed. of item 65. (See also items 66, 347, 440, 532 and 645). Los Angeles: The Theosophy Co. (Bombay, India) 133 p.; 14 cm.

739. Bhagavadgita: a new translation by Purushottama. Lai. Another ed. of item 641. Calcutta: P. Lai

740. ---- Another ed. Delhi: Hind Pocket Books. 107 P; 17cm

741. The Bhagavadgita, translated from Sanskrit by Shakuntala Rao Sastri. Another ed. of item 574. Bombay: Bharatiya Vidya Bhavan. viii, 448 p.; 19 cm.

742. Bhagavadgita translated from Sanskrit by Sarvepalli Radhakrishanan. 2d ed. of item 442. (See also items 453-455, 483, 585 and 722) Bombay: George Allen and Unwin.

744. The Bhagivadgita explained [by Swami Sivananda]. 2d ed. [India]: Divine Life Society. 160 p., plates 14 cm. (See also items 477, 615 and 698)

746. Gandhi, Mohandas Karamchand. The teaching of the Gita. Ed. by Anand T. Hingorani. 2d ed. Bombay: Bharatiya Vidya Bhavan. x, 103 p.; 16 cm. (Pocket Gandhi Series, 5)

747. Gita Samiksa. Edited by E.R. Sreekrishna Sarma. Tirupati: Sri Venkateswara University. Ciiil, v, 174 p.; 25 cm. "Papers presented to the Seminar of the Gita held in March, 1970." (Sri Venkateswara University. Sanskrit Department. Symposium, no. 5)

748. Jacob, George Adolphus. A concordance to the principal Upanishads and Bhagavadgita. Reprint of item 618. (See item 68)

749. Kaveeshwar, Gajanan Wasudeo. The ethics of the Gita. With a foreword by S. Radhakrishnan. Cist ed.l Delhi: Motilal Banarsidass, [1971]. xiv, 316 p.; 22.5 cm. A revision of the author's original Marathi work entitled: Gitatattva darsana. Includes bibliographical references.

750. Mutturaman,M.Gita and Kurul. With a foreword by T.M.P. Mahadevan. Madras: The author. CAvailable at Higginbo-thams1 63 p.; 22 cm. Includes bibliographical references.

751. Ramanujachariar, V.K. Gitavtha Sangraha of Yamunarya (Alavandar) . With Sanskrit text and English Commentary. [Madras: Sri Ranganatha Padukal. 71 p.: 22 cm.

752. Rao, K. L. Seshaglri. The concept of Sraddha (in the Brahmanas, the Upanisads, and the Gita). Patiala: Roy Publishers, C197H- xii, 197 p.; 23 cm. Bibliography: p. C1943-197- A revision of the author's thesis, Harvard University. (See item 661)

753. Steiner, Rudolf. The Bhagavad Gita and the Epistles of Paul; five lectures. Cologne, December 28, 1912- January 1, 1913-New York: Anthroposophic Press, [19711. 102 p.: 22 cm. (See items 253 and 427) "Translated from shorthand reports unrevised by the lecturer ... with the title: Die Bhagavad Gita und die Paulusbriefe."

754. Tolani, Pribhdas Sakhavaum. Gita-my guide; pearls from the fathomless ocean. [1st ed.l Bombay: Bharatiya Vidya Bhavan. xii, 102 p.; 19 cm.

755. Upadhyaya, Kashi Nath. Early Buddhism and the Bhagavadgita. [1st ed.l Delhi: Motilal Banarsidass. xix, 567 p.; 22 cm. A revision of the author's thesis, University of Ceylon, 1964.

756. Venkateswaran, C. S. The Vedas, Upanisads and the Bhagavadgita: the path of action-Karma Yoga. Madras: University of Madras, [1971?] 24 p.; 26 cm. Includes quotations in Sanskrit. (Prof. L. Venkataratnam Endowment Lectures, 1971/72)

757. Warty, Kashinath G. The Geeta way of life. With a foreword by Swami Hiranmayananda. [1st ed.l Bombay: Bharatiya Vidya Bhavan. xiii, 241 p.,pl.; 19 cm. (Bhavan's Book University, no. 169

1972

758. The Bhagavad Gita. Translated and interpreted by FranklinEdgerton. Another ed. of item 408 (See also items 508 and 627) Cambridge, Mass.: Harvard University Press, xv, 202 p.; 21 cm. "Originally published as volumes 38 and 39 of the Harvard Oriental series The Sanskrit text and Sir Edwin Arnold's translation have been omitted

in this edition." Includes bibliographical references.

759. -----• Another ed. 20 cm. (A Harvard paperback, 34)

760. The Bhagavad Gita; or, The Lord's song. 7th Adyar ed. of item 188. (See also items 559, 644 and 682) 231 p.; 15 cm.

761. The Bhagavad-Gita. With the commentary of Sri Sankaracharya. 6th ed. of item 97- Madras: Ramaswamy Sastrulu. xii, 522 p.; 19 cm. Parallel texts in Sanskrit and English. Commentary in English.

762. Bhagavad-Gita, the song of God. Another imprint of item 407. (See also items 416, 422, 447, 462, 499-502, 624, 653 and 710) Hollywood: Vedanta Press, [1972, c19441. 191 p.; 15 cm.

763. The Bhagavad-gita, with a commentary based on the original sources by R.C. Zaehner. Reprint of item 701.

764. Bhagavad-gita as it is [by] A.C. Bhaktivedanta Swami Prabhupada Complete ed., with original Sanskrit text, Roman transliteration English equivalents, translation and elaborate purports. New York: Macmillan, xiii, 981 p. illus.; 25 cm. (See also items 683 and 699)

765. ------• Abridged ed. of item 764. New York: Bhaktivedanta Book Trust, c1972. xxxvii, 330 p., C271 leaves of plates, illus.; 24 cm. Includes bibliographical references and index.

766. The Bhagvat-Geeta (1785). Translated, with notes by Charles Wilkins. Another imprint of item 576.[Delmar, New York] Scholars Facsimiles and Reprints,

767. The Bhagvat-Geeta (1785); or Dialogues of Kreeshna and Arjoon; in eighteen lectures, with notes. Translated by CharlesWilkins. London, printed for Nourse, 1785. [Franklin,N.H.: Hillsdale Press, 19721. xvi, 56 p.front.; 6 cm. "This edition limited to 250 numbered copies"

769. Ghose, Aurobindo. The Gita. Compiled by Vijay from the writings of Sri Aurobindo and the Mother.Pondicherry:Sri Aurobindo Society. 31 p.; 18 cm. (Sri Aurobindo and the Mother, v. 38)

770. Gitananda, Swami. Gita inspivation; a collection of short talks, written articles, insights, and inspirations. Pondicherry: Ananda Ashrama, [1972]. 93 p.; 18 cm.

771. Jnanadeva, fl. 1290. Gita the mother. Commentary by Dnyaneshwar Maharaj. Translated in English by Manu Subedar. Universal goodwill ed. New Delhi: Kalyani Publishers. 318 p.; 24 cm. Translation of Jnanesvari

772. Jnanesvari. The monumental Marathi commentary on Shrimad Bhagavadgita, chapter V, theory and practice of the science of God-realization/ [Dhyaneshwar]; Dhyaneshwari in English garb by S.D. Gokhale. 11, 51 P-, 121 leaves of plates, illus.; 22 cm Includes original text of chapter 5 of the Bhagavadgita in .Sanskrit (See also item 675)

773. Josh , N.V. The Three founiainheads of Indian philosophy. Bombay: Somaiya Publications, c1972. x, 146p.; 23 cm. Bibliography: p. [147]

774. Makkcla gita. Comp. and translated by B. Sridhara. Bangalore: Daipana. vi, 168 p.; 19 cm. Selection of some slokas with Kannada and English translations. Slokas in Devanagari script.

775. Parrinder, Edward Geoffrey. Upanishads, Gita and Bible. Another ed. of item 612. New York: Harper & Row, [1972, C1962]. 21 cm. (Harper Torchbooks, TB 1660) Includes bibliographical references.

776. Ranada, Ramchandra Dattatraya. Dr. R.D. Ranade's Dhyana Gita. Elucidated and translated by MCanoharl. SCriniwasl. Deshpande. Cist ed.l Bombay: Bharatiya Vidya Bhavan. xxii, 130 p.; 19 cm. (Bhavan's Book University, no. 187)

777. Satya Nand, D. Dynamic psychology of the Gita of Hinduism. Abridged ed. New Delhi: Oxford and I.B.H. Pub. Co., c1972. iii, xvii, 150 p.; 22 cm. Bibliography: p. C1491-150.

778. Shrimad-Bhagavad-Gita. . . . 11th rev. ed. of item 166. Calcutta: Advaita Ashram, xiv, 430 p.; 19 cm.

779. The song celestial; or, Bhagavad-gita.... Another ed. of item 312 . (See item 45)

780. Srimad-Bhagavad-gita...3d ed.of item 466.(See also item 638) Madras: Sri Ramakrishna Math. [Label: distributed by Vivekananda Vedanta Society, Chicago], viii, 536 p.; 19 cm.

781. Venkatesananda, Swami. The song of God. Rev. enl. 3d ed. Cape Province, South Africa: Children Yoga Trust, cl972. xii, 392 p., col. illus., ports, (part col.); 23 cm.

1973

782. Bhagavad Gita. Translated from Sanskrit by Purushottami Lai. Another ed. of item 643. (See also items 739 and 74o) Thompson, Connecticut: Interculture Associates. 71 p.

783. The Bhagavad Gita. Translated from Sanskrit by Arthur Osborne and G.V. Kulkarni. Tiruvannamalai, [India]: Sri Ramanasramam. viii, 127 p.; 18 cm.

784. The Bhagavad Gita; a translation and critical commentary, by A.L. Herman. Springfield, 111.: C.C. Thomas, [cl9731. xii, 188 p., illus.; 24 cm. Bibliography: p. 172-174.

785. The Bhagavad Gita: a sublime hymn of dialectics..2d ed. of item 603 . (See also item 595) London: Asia Publishing House. Includes indexes.

786. -------. Another ed. New Delhi: R & K Publishing House. Text in Sanskrit (romanized). Includes indexes.

787. The Bhagavad gita. Translated from the Sanskrit ... Another imprint of item 605. [Harmondsworth!: Penguin Books, [1973, c1962].

788. The Bhagavad-Gita; the Lord's song.... 13th Adyar reprint of item 188. xv, 260 p. (See item 86)

789. The Bhagavad-Gita, with a commentary based on the original sources by R.C. Zaehner. Another ed. of item 701. London, New York: Oxford University Press, [1973, c 1969] ix, 480 p.

790. The Bhagavad-gita, ... Another ed. London: Oxford University Press. 23 cm.

791. The Bhagavadgita: or, The song divine; with Sanskrit text and an English translation. 21st ed. of item 177- Gorakhpur, [India!: Gita Press. 403 p. ; 13 cm. Introduction by Jayadayal Goyandka. (See item 406)

792. The Bhagavadgita; with an introductory essay.... Another imprint of item 442. (See also items 453-455, 483, 585, 722 and 742) 20 cm.

793. -------. Another imprint. [1st Harper torchbook ed.1 (Harper Torchbooks, TB 1759)

794. Bhagavadgita Sar, with English and Hindi translation. Comp. by Sand'iyalal Sarma. Una, [India!: The compiler, [19731. xii, 156 p.; 18 cm.

795. Bhave, Vinoba. Steadfast Wisdom, translated from Hindi by Lila Ray. 2d ed. of item 657. 168 p.; 22 cm. Originally published in Marathi as ' Sthitaprajtla darsan'. Hindi Title: Sthita-prajha darsan.

796. Chinmoy. Commentary on the Bhagavad Gita; the song of transcendental soul. Blauvelt, N.Y.: R. Steiner Publications, [1973]. xviii, 164 p.,illus.; 18 cm. (Steinerbooks 1731)

797. Joshi, N.V. The Three fountainheads of Indian philosophy. Another ed. of item 773. Tunbridge Wells, Kent: Abacus Press, xi, 147 p.; 22 cm. Bibliography: p.[14] Printed in Bombay.

798. Mahdi Imam, Sayyid. The drama of Prince Arjuna; being a revaluation of the central theme of the Bhagavad Gita. Delhi: Motilal Banarsidass. xx, 118 p.; 22 cm.

799. Mahesh Yogi, Maharishi. Concordance for the Bhagavad-Gita to be used with the new translation and commentary, Chapters 1-6, prepared by Charles Donahue and Donna Seibert. [Los Angeles: MIU

Press, 1973] 87 p.; 18 cm

800. The New Gita..Another ed. of item 548. Los Angeles, CA: DeVorss
. Illustrated.

801. Science of human development: Bhagavad Gita, compiled and edited by T.S. Avinashilingam. -[2d ed.] Sri Ramakrishna Mission Vidyalaya. ix, 134 p.; 17 cm. In English and Sanskrit, text in Devangari and Roman script; introductory matter in English.

1974

802. The Bhagavad Gita; translated by H. Saraydarian. Agoura, California: Aquarian Educational Group, [1974?3 95 P- ; 27 cm.

803. The Bhagavad Gita: a revelation. [Translated by Dilip Kumar Roy.] New Delhi: Indian Book Co., [1974]. 189 p.; 22 cm. "Introduction: Thoughts on the Gita": p. 11-81. Includes glossary.

804. The Bhagavad Gita; a verse translation [from the Sanskrit] [by] Geoffrey Parrinder- London: Sheldon Press, xi, 115 p.; 21 cm.

806. The Bhagavad Gita and the Bible: Proceedings of the seminar under the auspices of the Christian Retreat and Study Center, Rajpur, Dehradun, May 5 to 9, 1972. Editor: B.R. Kulkarni. Delhi: Unity Books, xiii, 203 p.; 19 cm.

807. The Bhagavad Gita or the Lord's song. Translated by Annie Besant. 8th Adyar ed. of item 188. (See item 86) 231 p.; 14 cm.

808. The Bhagavad gita: a new translation by P. Lai. 3d rev. ed. of item 643. (See items 739 and 740) [Calcutta: Writers Workshop, 1974]. 79 p.; 23 cm. "Writers Workshop saffronbird book."

811. Bhagavadgeeta, [translated from the Sanskrit by] Satramdas K. Bhagwanani. Poona, [India]: The Translator, xx, 167 p.; 111.

812. The Bhagavadgita; with an introductory essay.... Another ed. of item 722 [1974]. (See also items 442, 453-455, 483, 551, 743 and 792)

813. Feuerstein, George A. Introduction to the Bhagavad-gita; its philosophy and cultural setting. London: Rider & Co. 3-191 p., ill.; 23 cm. Bibliography; Includes index.

814. Ghose, Aurobindo.The Gita. Compiled by Vijay Another ed. of item 769.

815. The Gita. [with text, translation and Sri Aurobindo's comments] rev. ed. of item 617. (See also items 356 and 534) Edited by Shyam Sunder Jhunjhunwala. [Pondicherry]: Auro Publications, [1974]. xiii, 1 I., 270 p.; 23 cm. Includes Sanskrit text.

816. Pandit Madhav Pundalik, ed. Gems from the Gita. [Madras]: Ganesh & Co. 128 p.

817. Rajagopalachari, Chakravarti. Bhagavad-Gita.... 4th ed. of item 622. 128 p.; 19 cm. Includes index.

818. Ramanuja, founder of sect. Ramanuja on the Bhagavadgita.... Reprint of item 691. [1974] (See also item 525) Bibliographical footnotes.

819. Srimad Bhagavadgita, translated by Swami Vireswarananda.... Another ed. of item 466. (See also items 638 and 780) Hollywood, California: Distributed by Vedanta Press. xii, 369 p.

1975

820. Bazaz, Prem Nath. The Role of Bhagavad Gita in Indian History. 1st ed. New Delhi: Sterling Publishers, xii, 747 p.; 23 cm. Bibliography: p. [704-710. Includes index.

821. Bhagavad Geeta [by] S.K. Bhagwanani. Poona, [India].

822. The Bhagavad Gita; a verse translation [from the Sanskrit by] Geoffrey Parrinder. Another imprint of item 805. (See also item 804) x, 115 p.; 21 cm.

823. ----. Another ed. (A Dutton paperback; D 390)

824. Bhagavad-Gita: chapters 1-6; a new translation and commentary with Sanskrit text.... Another imprint of item 667. (See also item 666)

825. The Bhagavad-gita: a sublime hymn of dealeatics.... Another ed.of item 595- (See also items 603 and 785) London: Asia Publishing House, xv, 763 p.

826. The Bhagavadgita: with an introductory essay.... Another ed. of item 722. (See also items 442, 453-455, 483, 551, 585, 743, 792, and 812) Includes index

827. The Bhagavadgita; with the Sanatsugatiya and the Anugita.... Another imprint of item 648. (See item 40. See also item 155)

828. Das, Kalicharan. Concept of personality in Samkhya-yoga and the Gita. 1st ed. [Gauhatil: Department of Publications, Gauhati University. Civ], viii, 220 p.; 25 cm. Bibliography: p. C2171-220. Originally presented as the author's thesis, University of Gauhati.

829. Easwaran Eknath. The Bhagavad Gita for daily living: commentary, translation and Sanskrit text. Berkeley, Calif.: Blue Mountain Center for Meditation, 1975- v.; 24 cm. Includes indexes. Vol. 1. Chapters 1 through 6.

830. Gita in Sankara's own words: chapters one to three. [Translated] by V. Panoll; foreword by B.D. Jatti. Calicut, CIndial: S. Paramasivan. xx, 200 p., port.; 22 cm. Commentary on Bhagavad gita with both text and commentary in Sanskrit and English.

831. Bhagawad Gita. Translation in English by B.L. Uppal. New Delhi: Uppal, [1975?] iil, 102 p.; 18 cm.

832. Hoon, Vishwa Nath. The symphony of the Bhagavad-Gita. 1st ed. Bombay: Bharatiya Vidya Bhavan. xii, 139 p.; 23 cm.

Bibliography: p. C1251. Includes index.

833. Parrinder, Geoffrey. Upanishads, Gita and Bible. 2d ed. of item 612. (See items 621 and 775) London: Sheldon Press. 136 p.

1976

834. Athavale, Pandurang Vaijnath. Glimpses of life of Lord Krishna: from the discourses of Rev. His Holiness Shastri Shri Pandurang V. Athavale 1976 (Bombay: Associated Advertisers and Printers) xx, 315 p, C2] leaves of plates, ill.; 23 cm. Life and teachings of a Hindu deity in the context of the Bhagavadgita, Hindu scripture.Includes scattered Sanskrit names mainly from the Bhagavadgita.]

835. The Bhagavad-Gita and Hymn to llarayena: two classic texts edited for students of literature by Kenneth Walter Cameron. Hartford: Transcendental Books, cl976. leaves, 156 p. on 79 leaves, ill.; 29 cm. Issued with Sanborn, F.B. Sixty years of Concord. Hartford, cl976. Reprint of the 1785 ed. of the Bhagvat Geeta .. translated by Charles Wilkins and printed for C. Nourse, London (See item l); with a hymn to Narayena (from the Rigveda) translated by Sir William Jones and reprinted from the 1799 ed. of his works, published by G.G. and J. Robinson, London.

836. The Bhagavadgita; with an introductory essay -- Another ed. of item 722. New Delhi: Blackie & Sons (India). (See also items 453-455, 483, 551, 585, 743, 812, and 826)

838. De Nicolas, Antonio T. Avatara, the humanization of philosophy through the Bhagavad Gita; a philosophical journey through Greek philosophy, contemporary philosophy, and the Bhagavad Gita on Ortegay Gasset's intercultural theme, Man and circumstance; including a new translation with critical notes of the Bhagavad Gita. With prologue by Raimundo Panikkar. New York: N. Hayes, xv, 465 p., ill.; 24 cm. Includes bibliographical references and index

839. Ghose, Aurobindo. Essays on the Gita. By Sri Aurobindo; abridgement Cby Sisir Kumar Ghosel. Calcutta: Sri Aurobindo

Pathmandir. xi, 254 p.; 14 cm. (See items 258, 273, 471-472, 484, and 519)

840. ---. 10th ed. Pondicherry: Sri Aurobindo Ashram; Pomona, Calif.: distributed in N. America by Auromere, 1976, cl972. 588 p.; 23 cm. Distributor from label on verso of t.p. First published in the monthly journal 'Arya' from August 1916 to July 1920. "Reproduced in reduced facsimile from the Sri Aurobindo Birth Centenary Library." Includes index. (See items 258, 273, 471-472, 484, and 519)

841. Krsnamacarya, Ekkirala. The Mandra Scripture: Explanatory Rendering of the Bhagavadgit Visakhapatnam, India: Mithila Publishing House. 116 p.; 23cm.

842. The Song of God, Bhagavad-gita; translated from the Sanskrit .Another ed. of item 407. (See also items 416, 422, 447, 462, 499-501, 624, 653, 710, and 762) London: Dent, 1975 Ci.e. 1976]. Co], 187 p.; 19 cm. (Everyman's library) First ed. published in 1944 under title: Bhagavad-gita, The Song of God.

843. Srimad Bhagabadgita. Translated from Sanskrit by P.D. Ghauekar. Pune, Indial: Datta Laxmi Trust. 140 p.

1977

844. The Bhagavad Gita: A new verse translation [by] Ann Stanford. Another ed. of item 716. (See item 715) New York: Continuum Books. 176 p.

845. The Bhagavad Gita: the gospel of the Lord Shri Krishna. Translated by Shri Purohit Swami; photography by Curt Bruce. 1st ed. London: Faber & Faber. 170 p., illus.; 29 cm. (See also item 329)

846. ------. Another ed. Translated by Shri Purohit Swami; photographs by Curt Bruce. 1st ed. New York: Knopf,

847. Another ed. Translation by Shri Purohit Swami;

photographs by Curt Bruce. 1st ed. New York: Vintage Books 28 cm. English and Sanskrit.

848. The Bhagavad Gita, with the commentary of Sri Sankaracharya; translated from the original Sanskrit into English by Alladi Mahadeva Sastry. 7th ed. of item 97. (See item 761) Madras: Samata Books, xii, 522 p.; 19 cm. Parallel text in Sanskrit and English. First published in 1897

.

850. Bhagavadgita Illustrated: Sanskrit Slokas, complete and unabridged, with English translations [by] N.V. Vyas. New Delhi: Navrang Publications. 200 p., 36 color plates;

852. Deshpande, Manohar Sriniwas. Sri Gita Sara - Essence of the Gita; by M.S. Deshpande. 3d ed. Bombay: Bharatiya Vidya Bhavan. xv, 77 p., [1] leaf of plates, port.; 20 cm. (Bhavan':'. Book University, 218) Includes selections from the Bhagavadgita with English translations.

854. Jñanadeva, fl. 1290. Dnyaneshwari. Rendered into English in poetic form by S.M. Upalekar. 1st ed. (See also items 309, 521, 675 and 771)

855. Joshi, N.V. The Three Fountainheads of Indian Philosophy- Another ed. of item 773. (See also item 797)

856. Madhusudana Sarasvati, disciple of Visvesvara. Madhusudana Sarasvati on the Bhagavad Gita: being an English translation of his commentary Gudhartha Dipika; by Sisir Kumar Gupta. 1st ed. Delhi: Motilal Banarsidas. xvi, 343 p.; 25 cm. Contains text of the Bhagavadgita in Sanskrit and English translations of both the text and Madhusudana Sarasvati's commentary. Includes index to the verses of the text.

|

857. The Message of the Gita: with text, translation and notes, as interpreted by Sri Aurobindo; edited by Anilbaran Roy. Another ed. of item 356. Pondicherry: Sri Aurobindo Ashram, xix, 311 p.; 23 cm. Label on verso of title page reads: Distributed in N. America by Auromere, Pomona, Calif. Sanskrit text and English translation.

859. Sharan, Mahesh Kumar. The Bhagavad-gita and Hindu Sociology. Delhi: Bharat Bharati Bhandar. xxx, 144 p.; 22 cm. Bibliography: p. 83-84. Includes index. Includes the Sanskrit text of the Bhagavadgita portion of the Mahabharata: p. 1971-144

860. Singh, Iudu Prakash. The Gita: a workshop on the expansion of self. Bombay: Somaiya Publications, xii, 15'(p.; 22 cm.

861. Sircar, Mahendra Nath. Mysticism in the Bhagavad-Gita. New Delhi: Classical Publications, xiii, 229 p.; 19 cm. Reprint of 1929 ed. published by Longmans, Green, Calcutta. Includes bibliographical references

862. Virajeshver. Science of Bhagavadgita: a study of ancient wisdom through modern science. Delhi: Spiritual India Publishing House, viii, U78 p., ill leaf of plates, ill.; 23 cm. Includes English translation and Sanskrit text with roman transliteration of the Bhagavad gita.

1978

863. Bajpai, Buddhi Prakash. Secret Doctrine of the Gita. A collection of the verses from the Gita and the Gita-Rahasya of Navrang Swami; translation and comments by B.P. Bajpai. 1st ed. New Delhi: Shri Prannath Mission,

864. Bhagavad Gita in the light of Sri Aurobindo. Ed. by Maheshwar. Pondicherry, India: Sri Aurobindo Ashram Press, xii, 270 p.; 23 cm.

865. The Bhagavad Gita, or The Lord's song. Translated by Annie Besant. 9th Adyar printing of item 188. (See item 86) Madras: Theosophical Publishing House. 231 p.; 14 cm. Includes index.

866. The Bhagavad-gita: the gospel of the Lord Shri Krishna Another ed. of item 845. (See also item 329) viii, 174 p., ill., ports.; 29 cm. Parallel Sanskrit text and English translation. This translation originally published in 1935

867. The Bhagavadgita [Exegesis, with the English translation] by Mahatama Mohandas Karamchand Gandhi. [1978] 30 p.; 19 cm.

868. Chandra, J.N. This is Gita of earth man is fragrance: one man, one world. Allahabad, CIndial: Bliss & Light Publications. Cxviiil, 342, xiii, ix, 2 p.; 21 cm.

869. The song celestial: Shrimad Bhagavad gita; ... Another ed. of item 45. New Delhi: Interprint. 151 p.; 26 cm.

870. (Sreemad) Bhagavadgeeta: The way for happiness and success; with a critical and comparative commentary titled 'Sriranga', by M.C. Ramalingeswara Rao. Meerut, [India].

871. Subba Row, Tiruvalum. Notes on the Bhagavad-Gita. 2d ed. Pasadena, Calif.: Theosophical University Press.

872. Sunder Rajan, Sellakrishnan. The Esoteric gospel of Gita. By Susrava [pseud.] i.e. S. Sunder Rajan New Delhi: Affiliated East-West Press. ix, 216 p.; 19 cm.

1979

873. Avadhoota Gita, with English translation by Shree Purohit Swami and edited by Dr. Shankar Mokashi Punekar. New Delhi. 280 p.

875. **The Bhagavad Gita; an interlinear translation from the Sanskrit, with word-for-word transliteration and translation, and complete grammatical commentary, as well as a readable prose translation and page-by-page vocabularies by Winthrop Sargeant. Garden City, N.Y.: Doubleday. ix, 751 p.; 24 cm.**

876. The Bhagavad Gita; with the commentary of Sri Sankaracharya ... Another imprint of item 848. Corrected and reprinted. 1979, c 1977. xiv, 534 p.; 19 cm. In English and Sanskrit. First published in 1897- (See items 97 and 761)

877. **The Bhagavadgita: a new translation. By Kees W. Bolle. Berkeley, Calif.: University of California Press. 318 p.; 24 cm. Sanskrit transliteration and English translation on opposite pages. Bibliography: p. 259-260. Includes index.**

878. **The Bhagavadgita in the Mahabharata: the text and translation by J.A.B. Van Buitenen. Chicago: University of Chicago Press. Includes bibliographical references**

879. The Bhagwad Gita. CTranslated by N.S. Subramanian. Sahibabad, Meerut, CIndial: Vikas Pub. House. 79 p.

880. Davis, Roy Eugene. The Bhagavad-Gita: God's revealing words Another imprint of item 686.

881. Easwaran, Eknath. The Bhagavad Gita for daily living: commentary, translation and Sanskrit text.... (See item 829) Petaluma, Calif.: Nilgiri Press, 1979- v.; 24 cm. Includes indexes. Vol. I: The end of sorrow. Vol. II: Like a thousand suns.

882. Jaya Chamaraja Wadiyar, Maharaja of Mysore. Gita and Indian culture. Another ed. of item 619. New Delhi: J.K. Publications. 74 p; 21 cm.

883. Jnanadeva, fl. 1290. Sri Jnanadeva's Bhavartha Dipika: Otherwise known as Jnaneshwari. Sanskrit text of the Gita with English translation by Shripad. KXrishnal. Belvalkar followed by Jnaneshwari translated from original Marathi into English by Ramachandra Keshav Bhagwat. Madras: Samata. xxxi, 689 p., ill.; 23 cm. (See also item 675)

884. Kriyananda, Swami. Keys to the Bhagavad Gita. Nevada City, Calif.: Ananda Publications. 48 p.

885. Pandey, Ram Kewal. The concept of avataras: with special reference to Gita. Delhi: B.R. Pub. Corp.; New Delhi: Distributed by K.K. Publishers' Distributor. 92 p.; 23 cm. Includes quotations in Sanskrit (romanlzed). A revision of the author's thesis, Lucknow University, 1961. Includes bibliographical references and index.

886. (Shrimad) Bhagavad Gita or Song Celestial. Translated by Sir Edwin Arnold.... Reprint of item 45. New Delhi.

887. Sinha, Himmat Singh. Communism and Gita: a philosophicoethical study. Delhi: Concept Publications Co., 1979, cl978. viii, 288 p.; 22 cm. Bibliography: p. 12711-284. Includes index.

888. The Bhagavad Gita. Translated by Goswami Kriyananda; Temple of Kriya Yoga [1979]; 137 pages

1984

889. Bhagavad Gita: with commentary of Sankaracharya; translated by Swami Ghambhirananda; Advaita Ashram [Calcutta]; 647 pages

890. The Doctrine of the Bhagavad Gita by Bhavani Shankar; Concord Grove Press; 131 pages;

891. Srimad Bhagavad Gita. The Scripture of Mankind. Translation by Swami Tapasyananda. Sri Ramakrishan Math (India); 517 pages; xvi;

1985

892. Perennial psychology of the Bhagavad Gita by Swami Rama; Honesdale PA [Himalayan Institute] 443 pages

893. The Bhagavad Gita with the Uttara Gita. Edited by Raghavan Iyer; Concord Grove Press; 408 pages

894. The Bhagavad Gita. Translated from the Sanskrit with Introduction and Notes by S. Srinivasa Murthy; Long Beach Publications; 146 pages;

1987

895. New Essays in Bhagavad-Gita. Compiled by Arvind Sharma; [c 1987 by Dept. of Religious Studies, University of Sydney (Au)]; 204 pages;

1988

896. **Prasad, Ramananda. The Bhagavad Gita. American Gita Society 1988. xxii, 345 pages. With glossary and index.**

1991

897. The Bhagavad Gita. A scripture for the future. Translation and commentary by Sachindra K. Majumdar; Asian Humanities Press [Berkeley]; 261 pages.

1992

898. Sri Ramanuja Gita Bhasya. Translated by Swami Adidevananda; Vedanta Press; 620 pages

1994

899. Sargeant, Winthrop. The Bhagavad Gita. Foreward by Christopher Chapple. State University of New York Press, 1994. xxi, 739 pages. [refer item 675]

1995

900. Bhagavad and its message:Sri Aurobindo. Lotus Light Publications [WI]; 306 pages; xix; refer item 348.

901. **Realization of the Supreme Self. The Bhagavad Gita Yogas. By Trevor Leggett; Kegan Paul International [1995]; 234 pages; x;**

902. The Bhagavad Gita. Bhashya and Tatparyanirnaya of Sri Madhva. Translated by Nagesh D. Sonde; Published by Vasantik Prakashan (India); 420 pages;

903. Bhagavad Gita. A New Perspective. A Universal Message for the for the Modern Society. Ila Ahuja and M. Raj Ahuja; Vikas Publishing House (India); 270 pages;

1998

904. Tat Tvam Asi. The Universal Message of the Bhagaadgita, Translation and commentary by PV Nath. 435 pages; xli.

1999

905. Bhagavad Gita. India's Ancient Book of Wisdom. Fully Illustrated. By Jean Griesser. Jain Publishing Company; 205 pages.

906. Third revised edition of Prasad; item 896;

2000

907. Gajjar, Irina N. The Gita. A New Translation of the Hindu Sacred Scripture.Axios Press 2000. xvii, 315 pages. Sanskrit illuminations by Navin J. Gajjar.

908. **Bhagavad Gita A New Translation by Stephen Mitchell; a literary version; Harmony Books (Random House); 224 pages**

2001

909. The Bhagavad Gita. A Walkthrough for Westerners, Jack Hawley; New World Library; 194 pages; xxvi;

2002

910. Abhinavagupta's Commentary on the Bhagavad Gita Translated from Sanskrit with introduction and notes by Boris Marjanovic Indica Books (2nd ed in 2004);

2004

911. Paths to God: Living the Bhagavad Gita by Ram Das; Harmony Books; 352 pages.

2007

912. Schweig, Graham M. Bhagavad Gita. The Beloved Lord's Secret Love Song. Harper One (imprint of Harper Collins) 2007. 360 pages;

With introduction and index.

913. Reprint of item 906.

2011

914. The Bhagavad Gita. A new translation by Georg Feurstein, with Sanskrit text, romanized transliteration, extensive notes and supporting essays; Shamballa Publication; 509 pages; xvi; s elect bibliography, glossary and index.

2012

915. Yogesvari Srimad Bhagavad Gita. Yogic Commentary by Shailendra Sharma; Independent Publishing; 418 pages.

2013

916. Bhagavad Gita In the Light of Kashmir Shaivism by Swami Lakshmanjoo; Lakshmanjoo Academy [2013, 2015] 683 pages; Introduction and index

2017

917. Study Guide to the Bhagavad Gita: with practical concordance. Les Morgan; Independent Publishing; 404 pages

2021

918. Bhagavad Gita: Essentials. By Praramhansa Vishwananda; Independent Publishing; 397 pages;

2022

919. The Gita and the Battle for Selfhood; by C.R. Lundley; 87 pages.

Books by Rudra Shivananda

Chakra selfHealing by the Power of Om

Yoga of Purification and Transformation

Surya Yoga - Healing by Solar Power

Breathe Like Your Life Depends On It

In Light of Kriya Yoga

Healing Postures of the 18 Siddhas

Insight and Guidance for Spiritual Seekers

Practical Mantra Yoga

Breathe Better Live Longer

Nada: The Yoga of Inner Sound

Living A Spiritual Life In A Material World

Transformed by the Presence

website: www.rudrashivananda.com
blog: www.sanatanamitra.com
www.youtube.com/user/KriyaNathYogi

About Rudra Shivananda

Rudra Shivananda, a disciple of the Himalayan GrandMaster Yogiraj Gurunath Siddhanath, is dedicated to the service of humanity through the furthering of human awareness and spiritual evolution. He teaches that the only lasting way to bring happiness into one's life is by a consistent practice of awareness and transformation. He has developed healing programs utilizing the energy centers [Chakras] and Prana Energy techniques through breath.

Rudra Shivananda is committed to spreading the message of his Master: "Earth Peace through Self Peace". He teaches this message of World and Individual Peace through the practice of Kriya Yoga. As a student and teacher of yoga for more than 50 years, he is trained as an Acharya or Spiritual Preceptor in the Indian Nath Tradition, closely associated with the Siddha tradition. He lives in the San Francisco Bay area, and has given initiations and workshops in USA, Ireland, England, Japan, Spain, Brazil, Russia, Singapore, Malaysia, Hong Kong, India, Australia, Canada and Estonia.

This book is the result of his love and devotion over several decades to the message and teachings in the Bhagavad Gita.

www.ingramcontent.com/pod-product-compliance
Lightning Source LLC
Chambersburg PA
CBHW060316100426
42812CB00003B/798
9781931833585